DESIGN ENGINE ARCHITECTS
BUILDING STORIES
Martin Pearce

We believe the best projects are born from strong working relationships, and we would like to thank all our clients and fellow consultants with whom we have worked since 2000. The projects illustrated in the book are the results of that successful collaboration and couldn't have been achieved without you.

— DESIGN ENGINE ARCHITECTS, 2017

Contents

06 **Introduction**

08 **Place**
Place and Space
The Phenomena of Place
Site and Place
Bounded Place
Shared Places
Place and Topography
Gathering Place
In-Between Places
The Identity of Places

28 **People**
The Stories People Tell
People and Patterns
Building Shared Ideas
Architecture, People and Polis
Architecture and the Digital Age
People Being Heard
People and Community

50 **Craft**
Architecture: Art and Craft
Craft and the Reform of Society
The Art of Making
Craft and Form
Arrière-Garde and Avant-Garde
Iteration and Refinement

68 **Sequence**
Spatial Sequence
The Picturesque
The Hierarchy of Sequence
Processional Sequence
Sequence and Promenade

88 **Wisdom**
Past, Future and Present
Past and Future
Universal and Particular
Vernacular Wisdom
Technical Wisdom
Old and New
Restoring Wisdom
Layers of Wisdom

112 **Surface**
The Free Facade and the Problem of Surface
Surface Follows Function
Surface Scale
The Origin of Surface
Meaning in Surface
Surface Projection
Surface and Depth
Surface Permeability

130 **Theatre**
Architecture and Theatre
Wisdom in Theatre
City as Theatre
Architecture and Event
Theatre and Flexibility
The Symbolism of Theatre

150 **Composition**
The Idea of Order
The Language of Composition
Layered Facade
Inflection and Juxtaposition
Asymmetrical Balance
Interlocking Composition
Solid and Void

168 **Colour**
Colour in Architecture
The Colour of Illumination
Colour in Heart and Mind
Le Corbusier: The Concept of Colour
Luis Barragán: The Colour of the Mind

186 **Endnotes**

187 **Credits**

188 **Project Timeline**

190 **Acknowledgements**

OPPOSITE
Main entrance to the British Embassy
Sana'a, Yemen.

Introduction
By Martin Pearce

Buildings tell stories in many ways. They are the stories of those whose lives they touch, of the hands that crafted them, of those that conceived them and the ideas from which they were shaped. This book is the story of the architectural practice Design Engine.

For Design Engine, architecture is the art of these stories, of making beautiful objects, buildings and places. Its work is characterised by the poetic possibilities of exquisitely crafted structures that are delivered with conviction, whilst embodying both lyrical and narrative depth.

The story of the making of this book is in itself a product of Design Engine's unique approach to architecture, with the structure and content of the book mirroring the emphasis it places on design as a process of dialogue and vice versa. The pages which follow began with a series of such dialogues between the author and the practice directors about the body of work created since Richard Rose-Casemore, Rodney Graham and Richard Jobson founded Design Engine in 2000. In addition, the wider team were invited to provide their own interpretation of the work in the form of written prose, photography, drawing, sketching or other imagery.

The dialogues were revealing as, rather than discussing the travails of each project, team members talked about architectural ideas that persisted across the range of projects and were concerned with how each project formed part of an ongoing narrative. In effect, the dialogues with the author were not only the story of each individual project but moreover how each formed part of a larger story that was the collected body of work. The images and texts provided were remarkable in that, whilst often being highly personal, they reflected the collective endeavour and common beliefs based on the creativity and joy in the making of both a beautiful architecture and a shared language.

For Design Engine this shared architectural language is constantly apparent and in many respects this book is a chronicle of the vital discourse that takes place each day in its studio. As with Design Engine's previous publications, *Design Engine 3, 6 and 9*—each written to mark the years since the practice's inception—this book is perhaps a moment to consolidate and reflect on all that has been achieved, and the many stories that have been told throughout the work.

The initial stage of this book was in itself a process of rediscovery, and reflected the in-depth research that Design Engine undertakes when embarking on an architectural project. It laid the ground and was a process of uncovering from which this particular 'project' could begin. During the research stage of this book a series of key themes emerged which are the architectural ideas that recur throughout the work, and these themes form the guiding structure through which the story of the practice is told. It is hoped that the focus on ideas, their implementation and manifestation will reveal to the reader that, for Design Engine, architecture is a creative pursuit built on the foundations of profound, poetic and enduring ideas.

Each theme is described from the perspective of the author's many years of experience teaching the history and theory of design at the University of Portsmouth School of Architecture. The main text describing these ideas intentionally does not refer directly to the projects illustrated, but rather sets the context, which informs the architecture. Each theme is linked to the projects through an accompanying text that explains how the practice's buildings are informed by the guiding concept. The drawings, photographs and other images illustrating the work each have text captions to guide the reader through the projects, each of which is chosen to illustrate the theme.

Buildings are inherently complex and multifaceted artefacts and this multiplicity of meaning and over-layered ideas is characteristic of Design Engine's work. Any single project invariably incorporates multiple ideas and it is this which makes the work deep in meaning and open to rich interpretation. To achieve clarity for the reader the author focuses on one aspect of a selected project in order to illustrate an important underlying architectural idea. As a consequence of Design Engine's complex and multifaceted approach some projects recur throughout the book and aspects of their design are described in the context of the idea which they illustrate.

Each architectural idea, or theme, takes the form of a chapter. Those on "Colour", "Surface" and "Craft" address the methods through which buildings are realised along with the tactile and visual delight of fine materials brought masterfully together in the passing of light and time. The chapters on "Sequence" and "Composition" illustrate the formal language of architecture as the meticulously orchestrated pattern of volumes and forms that are the space of human experience. The concerns of clients and users and the need for architecture to both serve and delight those for whom it is made are addressed through "People" and "Theatre". The profound importance of an architecture which responds to unique qualities of site and environment are covered through detailed analysis of "Place" and the importance of pragmatic "Wisdom" that informs a sustainable approach, and underpins all of Design Engine's work.

Beautiful buildings only come about from beautiful ideas, but too often forgotten is the beauty of the process. Architectural design finds a parallel with advanced mathematics in that design solutions often derive from common premises; however, the path from problem to solution can take many routes as mathematicians talk of the search for the elegant solution. Design Engine's work is in its essence also the search for the elegant solution—the sequence of design decisions that not only arrive at well-founded buildings, but achieve this resolution only through a refined and well-designed process. So this book is concerned not only with the art of the design project, but also with the art of the design process.

The celebrated eighteenth-century philosopher Immanuel Kant stated that "theory without practice is empty but practice without theory is blind". Kant's dictum is a powerful reminder that architecture is an art and so a product of the human intellect. As an outcome from the complexities of the human mind it must exceed the banality of simple pragmatics and at its best aspires to be the bearer of higher values, beliefs and dreams of those who conceive it and for those whom it serves. Architecture is therefore significant, not least in the way it will affect the lives and memories that it touches. For this the ideas and theories which guide the narrative of the design must have depth and weight and above all endure. This book shows how enduring ideas have shaped the work of Design Engine. It is a book of beautiful buildings, whose stories we hope will both delight and inspire.

Place

Place and Space

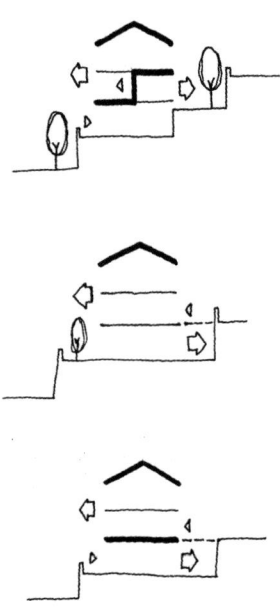

ABOVE, RIGHT & OPPOSITE
Roseville Housing is set into a granite hillside overlooking the sea; this scheme of 37 new housing units and community buildings is arranged on existing natural contours. Efficient landscaped car parking courts for the whole site are designed on two levels at the foot of the site: one below ground and one at grade.

In abstract terms architecture might be considered the manipulation of space. However, the immaterial quantities of volume and dimension cannot accommodate the specifics of location, material and cultural significance that give rise to meaningful places. Prioritising the unique characteristics of 'place' above the rational idea of 'space' gives rise to an architectural approach where building and landscape enter into a more expressive dialogue in pursuit of a meaningful architecture that can only be found in a deep understanding of the unique qualities and particularities of place.

The greatest appeal and ultimate failure of the Modern movement in architecture was the belief in a universal grammar of building. The International Style coined by Philip Johnson and Henry-Russell Hitchcock was based on an idea that architecture, driven by primarily programmatic concerns, was something akin to a science which, through the discovery and application of absolute rules or laws, transcended matters of time, place and culture.[1] This appeal to the rational mind gave rise to buildings of extreme rigour and functional clarity; the so called 'white-walled' modernism of the early part of the twentieth century was characterised by Le Corbusier's famous dictum that a house was no more than "a machine for living in". However, houses and our built environment are so much more than crude mechanisms, as they are the embodiment of our personal and cultural values, the places of memory which affect our lives in ways that any set of scientific, deterministic laws can never fully capture. This contrary view gave rise to a new way of thinking about architecture which drew on the philosophical tradition of phenomenology.

BUILDING STORIES | 08

The Phenomena of Place

ABOVE
Roseville Housing is fundamentally concerned with placemaking. Using the topography, local materials and a rich palette of textures, the buildings create a unique spirit of place.

Phenomenology draws on the ideas of the philosophers Edmund Husserl and Martin Heidegger, and in its essence rejects abstract concepts in favour of the particular nature of the individual's lived experiences.[2] For these thinkers, scientific universal laws, whilst having an important role to play, were one step removed from the nature of our human existence that took place against the background of a world made up of tangible experiences, memories and beliefs.

This was a world they described as the "concrete" contents of mental activity and so was deeply rooted in human psychology and the nature of experience. Above all, phenomenology focused on this world as being context dependent, in that things only really made sense when viewed as part of an articulated relationship of events that took place in particular and unique environments, through the flow of time and within which a human life takes place.

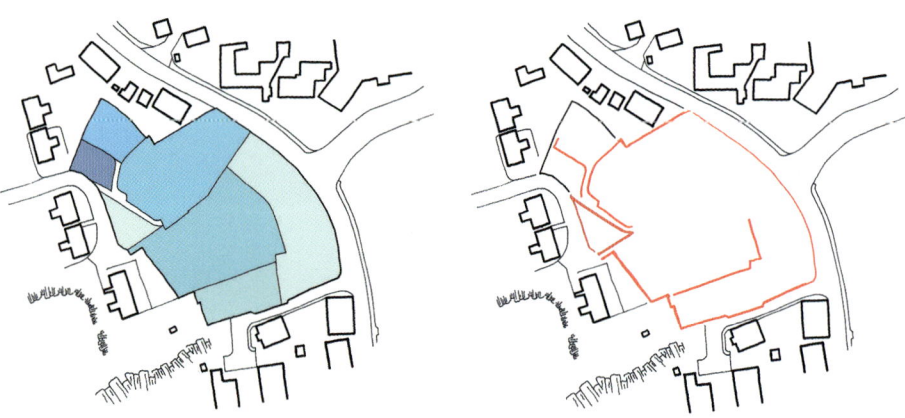

ROSEVILLE HOUSING, GUERNSEY

For Design Engine buildings are deeply rooted in place and feel naturally a part of the land. However, they do not seek to imitate their surroundings and this strategy is not in any way a pastiche of local vernacular. Rather, their approach reveals the unique nature of the site through the juxtaposition of crisp white rendered volumes contrasting with the detailed texture of traditional stone work. At Roseville Housing, the corner windows speak of the views to the sea whilst the stepped echelon arrangement of the houses brings the topography to the fore, revealing the qualities of the site. Architecture of this sort might be considered, as with any work of art, to bring to our attention aspects and qualities of the world that we might otherwise overlook. In this way the site is segmented by the buildings and discloses its unique nature as a result of that which is built there.

The making of meaningful places begins with reading the site. Reading the site is different from the abstract site analysis, which focuses on quantifiable phenomena such as orientation, site area, points of access and a host of other neutral observations. With the Roseville Housing project the practice set out to identify the unique character of the location and initiated a process of analysis, which sought to prioritise a qualitative understanding of place. The reading of this steeply sloping site revealed the historic field boundaries and stone walls that characterise the Channel Island of Guernsey. This understanding provided the key that unlocked a design approach deeply rooted in the unique character of the environment and that integrates a series of retaining walls that form parterres enabling the houses to step up the site, with a network of narrow paths again drawn from the surrounding context to connect levels of parking and housing in a manner that responds to the site and indigenous patterns of the landscape.

BUILDING STORIES | 10

Site and Place

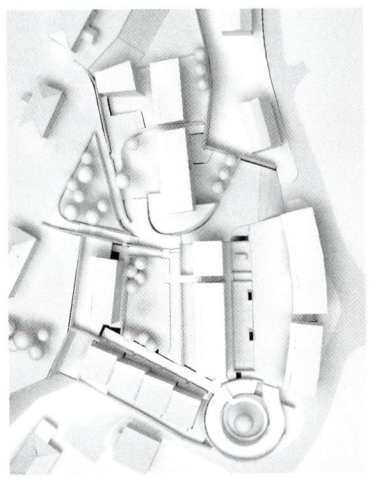

ABOVE
Initial massing model of the development.

OPPOSITE & RIGHT
Pedestrian routes through the site weave between residential buildings via existing pathways, steps and ramps between semi-public courtyards. Each house or apartment benefits from a small dedicated garden or balcony to complete the hierarchy of public, semi-public and private realms.

The Norwegian architect, theorist and author Christian Norberg-Schulz in his seminal book *Genius Loci: Towards a Phenomenology of Architecture*, 1980, emphasised the importance of site and place. He made the case for buildings to be considered not in abstract terms of space and volume but rather as the conduit that gives meaning to, and articulates the experiences of, life.[3] Architecture in this way became something more than fulfilling a set of particular uses, and in contrast was fundamentally concerned with the creation of identifiable places of memory. He drew on the ancient Roman idea of 'genius loci', or protective spirit of place, and set out the challenge of making places that somehow created a unique aura. Norberg-Schulz saw the key aspect of successful 'place making' as being heavily reliant on interpreting or reading the existent environment where a building was to be made and responding to this in a manner that reinforced its unique character.[4] This was an approach which fundamentally opposed the Modern movement position that the site was to be levelled to a tabula rasa upon which buildings were imposed. In what became termed a phenomenological design method, materials and their sensory qualities were used to evoke particular affective experiences and drew on a historic vernacular tradition of using locally sourced constituents put together in ways that responded to the specific climate, leading to buildings that were naturally empathetic to the given context. In the ideas following Norberg-Schulz, buildings become deeply rooted in the nature of each unique place and often resonate with the indigenous cultural traditions.

Bounded Place

ABOVE
The site before being built, demonstrating place from placelessness, and the completed British Embassy set within the new landscape.

BELOW
Traditional woven Islamic carpet, demonstrating four quarters of the Paradise Garden.

To make a place invariably requires some aspect of framing through establishing boundaries and limits. These frames focus attention on a particular environment captured through the lens of architecture. The framed or bounded site highlights the unique characteristics of a place and creates an internalised world. The ideal of a captured and perfected microcosm of architecture and landscape has a long and varied architectural history in mankind's many attempts to build an earthly paradise.

The term paradise originates from the Persian-Assyrian word *pardesu* or 'domain' and the Garden of Paradise of the Abrahamic faiths refers to a utopian human condition prior to man's fall from grace. The term 'utopia' was first coined by Sir Thomas More in his 1516 book of the same name, and architectural history is marked with projects across the ages that have sought to recapture this once ideal state. However, the idea of paradise finds its built origins in the arid desert environments of Persia where the barren natural landscape contrasted with the verdant captured landscape of the enclosed garden, from which the courtyards of the great mosques derive. This type of enclosure extended to the cloisters and quadrangles of the medieval Gothic monasteries and like their Islamic counterparts these held a unique cosmological importance. In both cases the gardens were clearly bounded in a rectangular frame and symmetrically subdivided to focus on a central crossing point that formed a *quadrifurcus*, and through further subdivision the garden took the form of a grid iron plan. Often oriented to the cardinal directions, this type of pattern is familiar the world over as one of the principal organising devices of city planning. For the Romans the crossing was especially significant as this point was called the *mundus* (the Latin term for the world) and marked not only the founding point of a city but also a symbolic place through which the terrestrial and celestial realms were connected. In this profound and poetic context architecture might be considered as more than a simple response to the nature of an environment; rather it is a reflection on the nature of perfection and what it means to create a place which refers to a dreamed but ever elusive condition of human perfection. Joseph Rykwert poignantly observed that it is in man's nature to impose order upon the world, and this drive is born from a searching psychological need to recapture in some way the utopian state, which we believe was once ours.[5]

> *And the Lord God planted a garden in the east in Eden.... The Lord God made all kinds of trees grow out of the ground—trees that were pleasing to the eye and good for food. In the middle of the garden were the tree of life and the tree of the knowledge of good and evil.*
>
> — GEN. 2:8–14

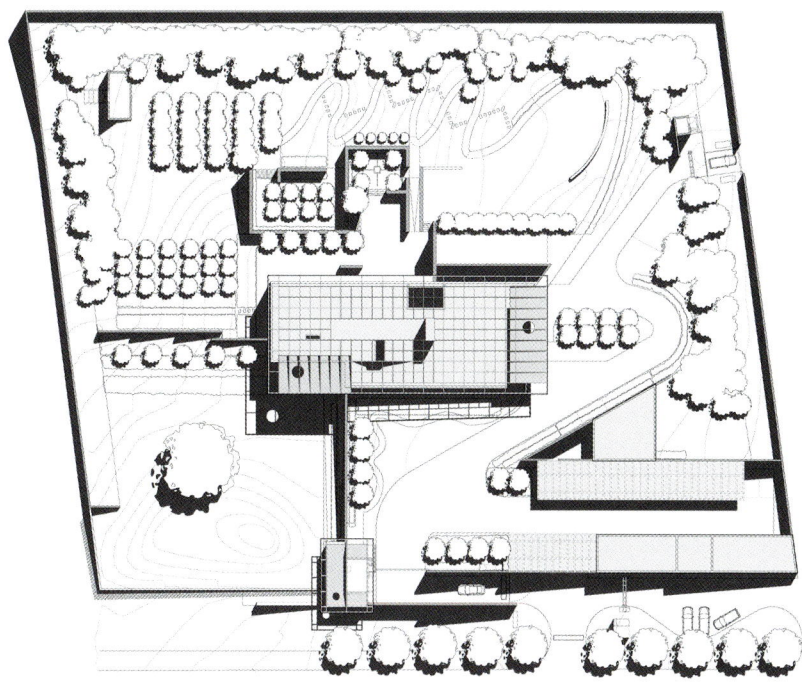

RIGHT
Site plan of the British Embassy showing the relationship of the building to the security lodge and the outer defensive boundary wall.

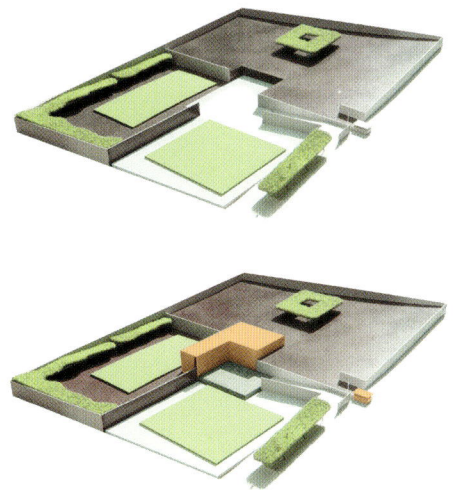

ABOVE
Development models showing the principal building components of the British Embassy.

BRITISH EMBASSY, SANA'A, YEMEN

The project for the British Embassy in Yemen is located in the historic city of Sana'a. The site is characterised by the arid desert landscape. Here Design Engine were faced with creating a place ex nihilo. Central to this was the bounding of the site and the introduction of water, which brings new life to this barren terrain and in some way seeks to build a model of paradise. Whilst the buildings and structure of the city have a unique character, the site on the urban periphery was in an open landscape of desert. Beginning with a rectilinear bounding wall, Design Engine firstly captures and defines the territory.

Secondly, the axial division of the captured landscape leads to the central focus of the embassy building, with the volume cut away to announce the pubic entrance and the site divided into four quadrants.

Thirdly, the roof frames the building, protecting it from the intense sun as a canopy frames the landscape as it oversails the volume below. The roof is punctuated with a central opening or oculus that admits a shaft of light to the centre of the plan, tracking around the interior through the passage of the day. The roof also collects water which is used to irrigate the gardens, creating an oasis of life.

PLACE | 13

BRITISH EMBASSY, SANA'A, YEMEN

The oversailing roof captures the landscape below, creating a pool of shade in the desert beneath which the embassy shelters. This great horizontal canopy projects out into the landscape and invites the visitor into an oasis of calm. In contrast to the delicate canopy which evokes the tented structure of the desert, the embassy walls are robust masses of concrete whose permanence speaks of the mountainous rocky hillsides that surround the city. In section, the horizontal constant of the roof reveals the graded topography of the site. The building changes in height around a double-height space marked by an oculus in the canopy, which admits a shaft of sunlight that tracks the passage of time as it traverses the space below.

The building adopts some of the timeless qualities of the Pantheon in Rome, and this central intangible moving focus of light alludes to the cosmological connection as this new place upon the earth is created and given meaning both in time and space. In this once barren wilderness these powerful architectural devices are employed to create a place of human inhabitation. A world is made ex nihilo, and in creating place as it were from nothing the project has a particularly utopian resonance.

TOP
Concept sketch of the British Embassy demonstrating the large overhanging roof at the main entrance.

RIGHT
Main entrance to the British Embassy with large oversailing roof providing shade throughout the day.

BUILDING STORIES | 14

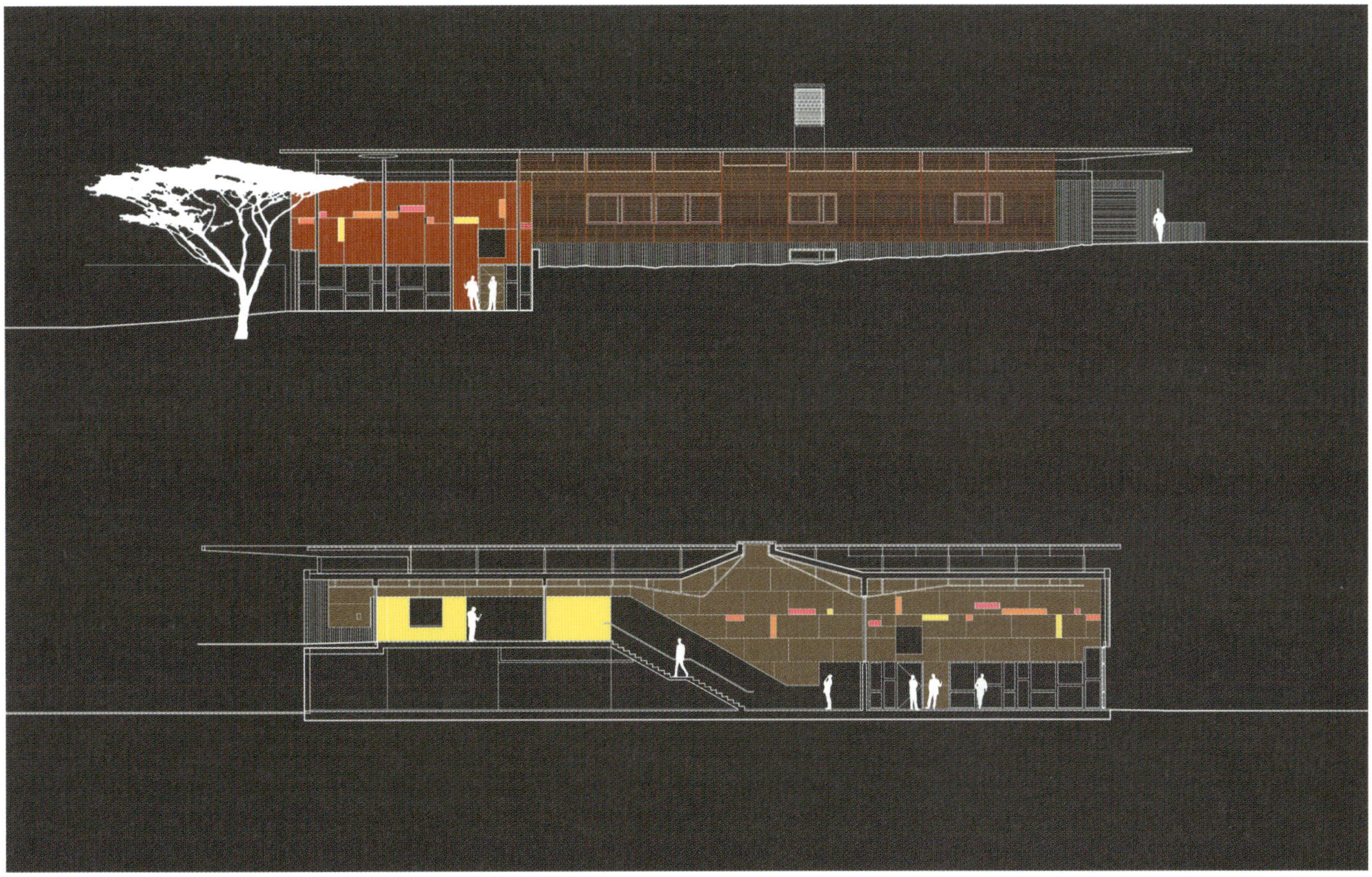

TOP
Main elevation of the long section of the British Embassy.

RIGHT
Central atrium at the British Embassy showing the specially commissioned artwork by Jenny West, illuminated by the roof light above.

Shared Places

ABOVE
Historic hilltop towns of Urbino, Northern Italy.

BELOW
Concept diagram of University Centre campus layout.

Architecture not only affects our individual lives but is the theatre of collective meaning and shared memory. The shared places in which people come together, the squares, piazzas and streets, both literally and metaphorically frame our lives. Gaston Bachelard's 1958 book, *The Poetics of Space*, exhorted architects to base their designs on the nature of these shared human experiences.[6] These, he felt, constituted both the individual and collective memory of a society and this, when seen over millennia, was the story of civilisation created, whose tangible civic presence is made manifest through the building of towns and cities.

Architecture is a civic art concerned with the making of places where people can come together and with which they collectively build a sense of identity. Whilst buildings create the interior world of shelter, equally important are the spaces between buildings. Jan Gehl in his book *Life Between Buildings: Using Public Space*, 2011, sets out the need for these external places to be considered with the same level of design attention as the interior spaces.[7] In this view he follows the great Renaissance architect Leon Battista Alberti, who set out the case for the city to be considered as analogous to a large house and the house in turn as a small city.[8] From this perspective external spaces are conceived as rooms within the city and each of these chambers requires a sense of enclosure and scale. As with a room inside a building, external spaces have walls in the form of the elevations that surround and frame the space. These walls each have a different character and enter into a dialogue with each other, each with a particular scale, orientation and material presence. Thresholds occurring at the points of entry to external space require particular attention, as it is here that the flooring materials that define the space, giving a sense of identifiable surface, become most prominent. Lastly, within these external rooms, objects are placed and topographies developed to subdivide the space, providing a variety of shared places in which people can gather.

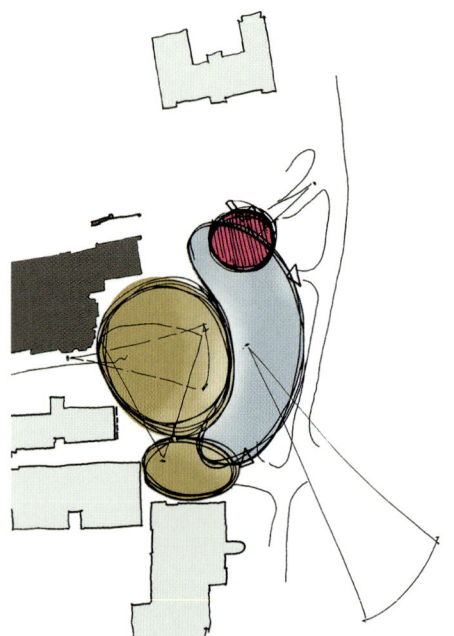

UNIVERSITY CENTRE, UNIVERSITY OF WINCHESTER

The University Centre for the University of Winchester is conceived as part of an ensemble of buildings that form the heart of the campus. Set on a steeply sloping site the centre provides a public face and entrance to the university and accommodation of cafes, nightclub and student services are set on different levels as the building steps down the site. An undulating roof hovers above, forming a constant datum across the site. Most importantly the building is not considered in isolation but rather enters into a dialogue with the earlier Design Engine John Stripe Lecture Theatre located at the bottom of the site, whose 'living' sedum roof is conceived as a fifth elevation and onto which the University Centre looks. The final part of the assembly is the later St Alphege Learning and Teaching Building, whose elevation takes the form of an artwork completing a public square.

The concept diagram is an important design tool for Design Engine. The initial diagram (left) for the University Centre shows the entrance threshold to the university in pink, whilst the body of the building in blue forms a protective shell which embraces two public squares set at different levels across the steeply sloping site, here indicated by the yellow elliptical shapes.

BUILDING STORIES | 16

ABOVE
Western view of University Centre at University of Winchester.

01. St Alphege Building
02. John Stripe Lecture Theatre
03. Public piazzas
04. Student Centre

The shared public spaces at the University of Winchester (shown in diagram) are inspired by the compact historic hilltop towns of Northern Italy (opposite top), built into the site so that architecture and landscape work seamlessly together. The Italian architect Giancarlo De Carlo believed that as an act of building the site and the city were considered to be the manifestation of the forces that operate in a given context—forces including the human, physical, cultural and historical. Here the external and internal spaces are considered simultaneously such that the public piazza and streets can be considered as rooms within the city.

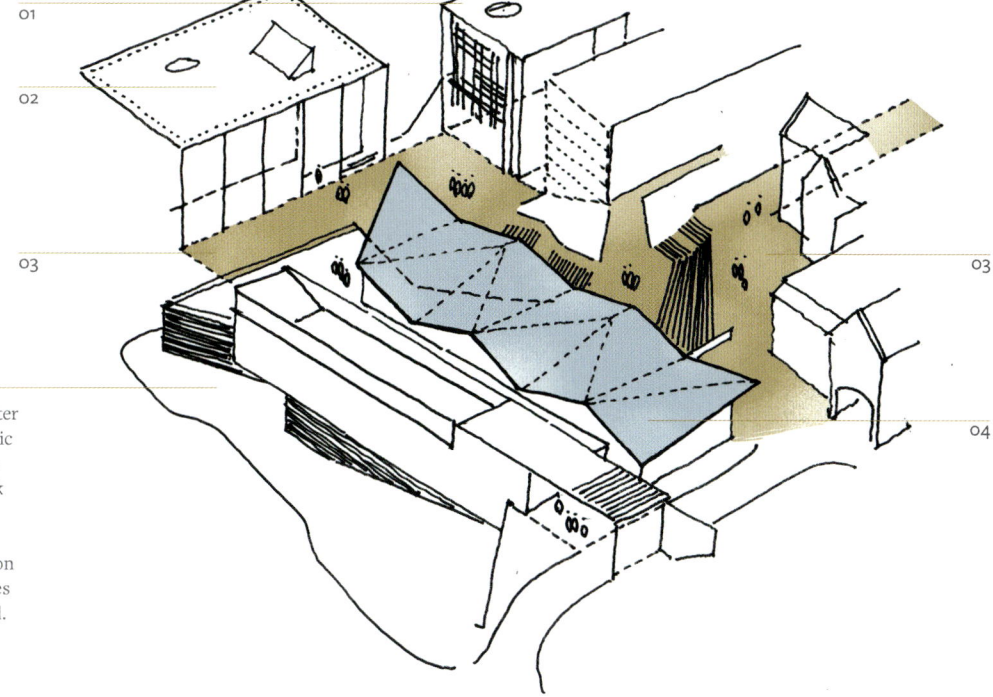

PLACE | 17

Place and Topography

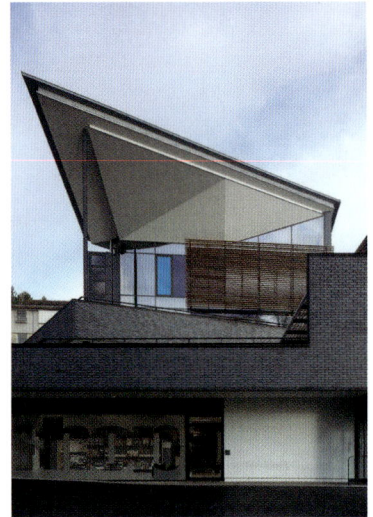

ABOVE
South elevation of University Centre at University of Winchester.

No house should ever be on a hill or on anything. It should be of the hill. Belonging to it. Hill and house should live together each the happier for the other.
— FRANK LLOYD WRIGHT

The term 'topography' has its origins in the Greek 'topos', meaning place, and 'graphia', meaning to write or draw. The drawing of architecture too frequently focuses on the building, with plans, sections and elevation set adrift in a sea of white space. However, for architecture to be meaningful it has to be set against the context of the particular location for which it is intended. In this respect the drawing and model are as much about describing this context in which the building sits as they are about depicting the detail of that which is proposed.

To draw the context is to capture the atmosphere and character of the surroundings. Here materials, foliage and the surrounding life of human activity give the drawing a vitality that discloses the way in which a building will not only relate to, but more importantly contribute to and augment, its setting. The plan and section have a unique ability to represent these surroundings as the proposed building becomes immersed in the context.

Topography in cartographic terms relates to the relative elevation though the use of contour lines and spot levels, with the form of the land providing a complex three-dimensional background. In occupying difficult sites with changing levels and irregular topographies, all of the architect's three-dimensional skills are required to create buildings on multiple levels and complex vertical circulation patterns. Yet these challenges can provide unique opportunities to exploit the potential of views and spatial separation along with the vertical interlocking of spaces that the sloped site affords. Indeed, the hillside provides greater scope for architectural dexterity than does the flat site. Building into the site provides the possibility of appealing to the primitive human need for the protection of the cave or the commanding vantage point of projecting platforms and roofs floating out into the landscape.

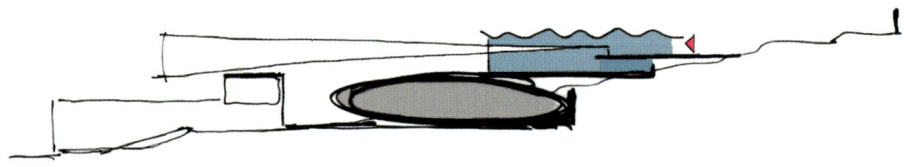

UNIVERSITY CENTRE, UNIVERSITY OF WINCHESTER

The concept diagram drawn as a section through the site (above) shows the entrance in pink and the main public space in blue, covered by an undulating roof which hovers above the site and forms a datum against which the building steps down the site. The area shown in grey is the nightclub, which is built into the hillside and has connotations of a subterranean cave.

The section also reveals the consideration of views from the higher level of the Student Centre such that the building simultaneously addresses the local needs for spatial enclosure, giving a new heart to the university, and looks to the horizon and the rolling landscape of the downs which characterises the regional context outside of the university.

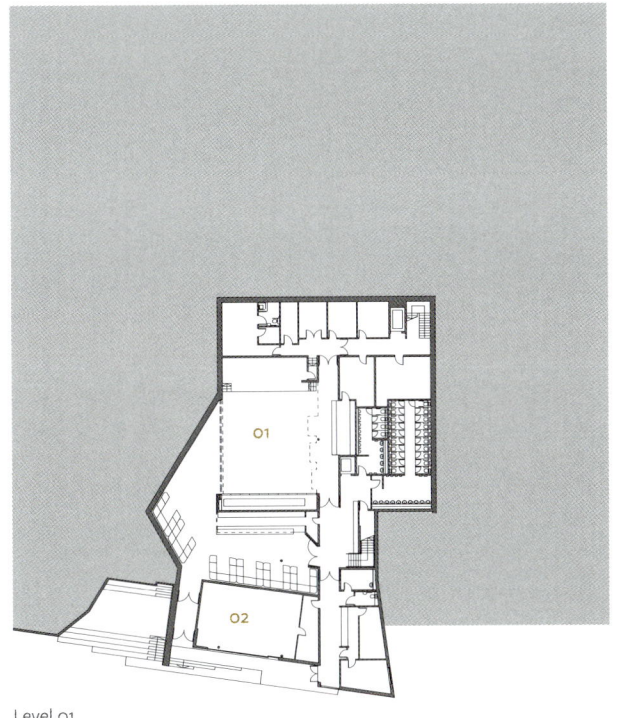

Level 01

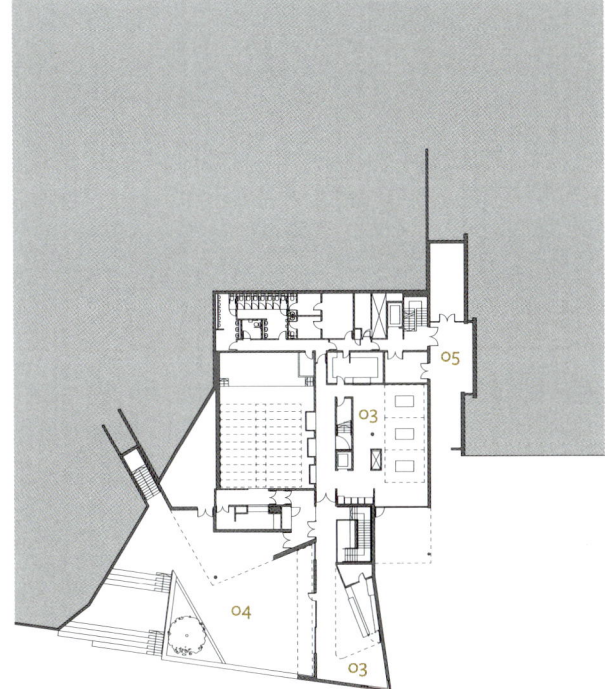

Level 02

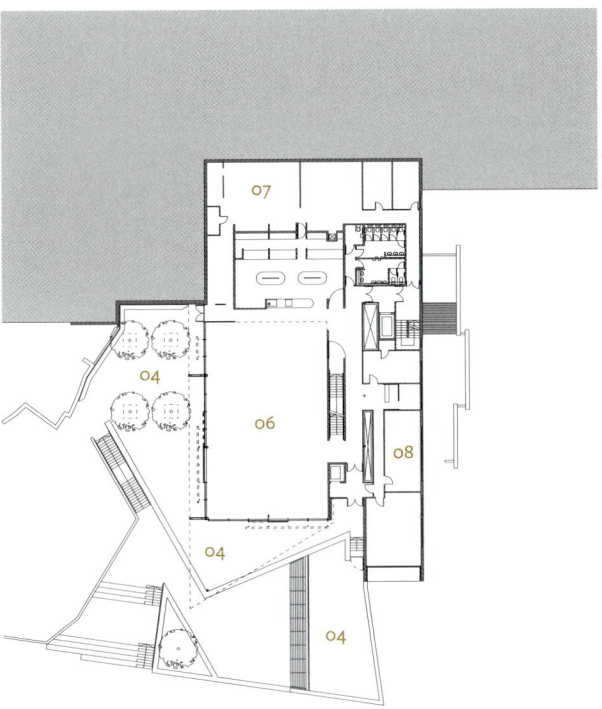

Level 03

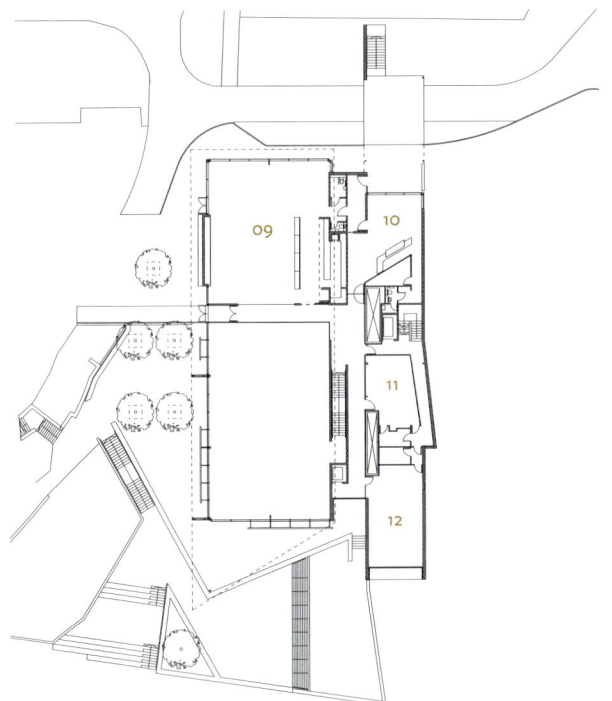

Level 04

01. Student Union nightclub
02. Shop
03. Student Union bars
04. Terrace
05. Deliveries
06. Food Hall
07. Kitchen
08. Offices
09. Learning Cafe
10. Reception
11. Book shop
12. Boardroom

Gathering Place

ABOVE & BELOW RIGHT
The St Alphege Building artwork makes reference to the idea of divinity through its allusions to the Christian faith that underpins the activities of the university. Saint Alphege (c 953–1012) was the Bishop of Winchester, later Archbishop of Canterbury.

OPPOSITE
University Centre at University of Winchester. The folded roof plane extends out beyond the building to frame the sky and landscape beyond. The building as a student centre has the function of bringing people together and marks an important stage as young people pass from adolescence into adulthood.

Architecture is the most public of all the arts, and buildings shape our lives, becoming part of our collective memories and affecting the way in which we understand and interact with other people. Buildings then have a significant obligation to the individual and society as a whole, as they are the background and markers of the events in our lives that, when seen together, form the story which is both our personal narrative and collective existence. Architecture in this way is concerned with the gathering of lives and the shaping of our individual and shared life narratives.

The way in which architecture shapes us parallels the ideas set out by Martin Heidegger whose philosophy sought to address the relationship of the interior mental world of the individual and the manner in which the consciousness of many individuals comes together in the form of a society. Heidegger looked carefully at the way in which buildings make up each person's experiences and enable gathering to take place. In his article "Building Dwelling Thinking", 1951, he frames a fourfold relationship of our coming together as being upon the earth, beneath the sky, as mortals and before the divinities.[9] Heidegger talks of the way in which these fourfold matters of existence are gathered through the act of building, which in turn reveals the underlying nature of our existence as a clearing in which these fundamental constituents of being are brought to appearance. As individuals come together they do so around meaningful places and these, he felt, were the vehicles that gave insight into the nature of what it means to be human.

In-Between Places

ABOVE
Christchurch Bridge, Reading mast.

The bridge has often been considered in terms of pure engineering, providing a pragmatic and efficient solution to connect disparate locations. However, bridges are also poetic structures and the bearers of symbolic meaning.[10] Their construction and destruction has come to symbolise the state of the relationship both physically between opposing banks and metaphorically between the people and cultures which they connect. Bridges are frequently erected to mark significant events and moments in time, just as the many pedestrian footbridges that accompanied the dawn of the second millennium were intended to signify the new era and make tangible a shared hope for the future. Thus bridges are both physically and psychologically liminal places, occupying the uniquely ambiguous territory of the in-between.

As the old disciplinary silos of engineering and architecture become ever more blurred, a new approach to interdisciplinary collaboration has merged the poetics of architecture and pragmatics of engineering. Sophisticated engineering refinements in structure, material and detail are employed to effect this poetic response, and the bridge is thus the unity of art and science condensed into a single design moment.

To make a bridge requires a deep understanding of place. Not only do the geo-tectonics and efficiencies of traversing obstructions need to be mastered, but the bridge needs also to be considered in its wider cultural context. The bridge is in many respects the coming together of places but is also the making of a new place. The bridge makes a distinct kind of place, one that in its newness not only speaks of itself but also provides a litmus that brings into sharp focus familiar surroundings, allowing us to see that which was once familiar through fresh eyes. To do so the bridge quite literally affords a new perspective on existing places, as it enables a location to be seen from a wholly unique standpoint. The inclusion of stopping places and seats across the span celebrates this new vantage point, and here the psychological importance of the bridge is brought to mind as the act of crossing any bridge carries deep rooted human significance. To cross a bridge involves the passing from one location to another and, as with any journey, it commences with a moment of departure and the anticipation of arrival. For the medieval monastic brotherhoods this journey was a powerful analogy for our passage through life as the soul crossed the turbulent rivers of life from the mortal world to the heavenly realm. In this way, the bridge is both a celebration and affirmation of life itself.

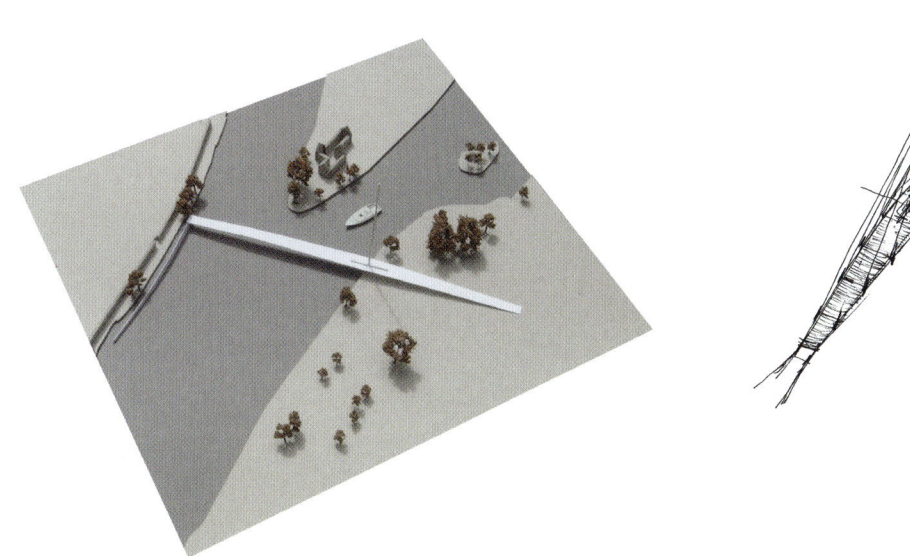

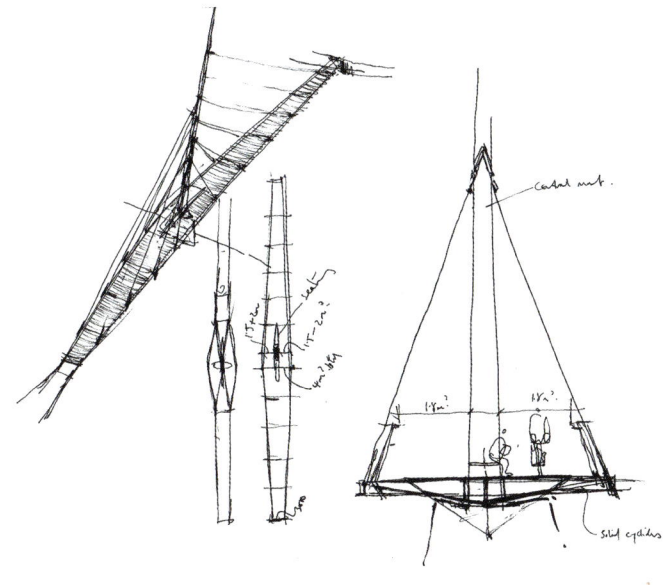

CHRISTCHURCH BRIDGE, READING

Designed in collaboration with engineers Peter Brett Associates, the new bridge provides an important new link for pedestrians and cyclists between Reading town centre, the upgraded rail station and Caversham's riverside areas. The new bridge brings together two contrasting environments: on one side is the urban setting of Reading town centre whilst on the other Christchurch Meadows comprises open riverside fields. Pedestrian and cycle paths cross the grassed areas with a route along the side of the river, forming part of National Cycle Network Route 5, and the bridge serves to connect these to the town centre.

The bridge is a single-masted cable-stayed structure, with the main upright positioned on the north bank and the land span continuing on into Christchurch Meadows to balance the river span visually and structurally. The slenderness of the mast is reinforced by continuing the two side elements of the main mast structure beyond the line of the last cable, creating a crowning or tuning fork effect, allowing the sky to be seen through the mast top. The bridge deck gently tapers from its widest point around the mast towards either end. A timber-clad bench folds out of the mast at this point, offering panoramic views of the river and the meadows beyond. A continuous handrail provides the lighting for the bridge as well as a convenient place to lean on while enjoying the new views opened up by the bridge. The bridge not only affords a place to see the river from a new perspective, but the mast, when seen from a distance, marks the location as a new focal point along the river.

TOP
View across the River Thames towards the new bridge.

ABOVE LEFT
Concept model of the bridge.

ABOVE RIGHT
Initial sketches of bridge section and deck and mast configuration.

PLACE | 23

View of bridge as it touches down in Christchurch Meadows, Reading.

The Identity of Places

ABOVE
Existing field boundary at Redbridge, Southampton.

The places in which we live and work shape our lives in powerful yet often unconscious ways. The making of place, particularly in respect of the places where people will live, requires an architecture of unique and particular environments which give a sense of belonging and a feeling of personal identity. The problem of how to provide homes for the many whilst giving a sense of individuality and personal ownership is a pressing need as societies across the globe are confronted by ever growing housing shortages. Yet these problems are not new; they originate from a time when similar questions about where people should live and how they might live together were being asked in the face of a rapidly changing world.

Sir Ebenezer Howard, the English founder of the garden city movement, published *Garden Cities of Tomorrow* in 1902, in which he described a utopian city where people lived harmoniously together with nature.[11] Howard's was a response to the Industrial Revolution in England that had led to the rapid migration of the rural poor to the industrial cities in search of better opportunities, amusement and good wages. Instead they had found urban poverty, overcrowding, poor sanitation and other terrible living conditions that led to short life expectancy. Howard asked the question "Where will the people go?" and devised a new city model that coupled the social and financial benefits of the city with the fresh air and idyll of the countryside, in which he found the essence of well-being. In a diagram showing the magnetic compulsions of the town and the country to which people were drawn, he added a third magnet, that of the 'town-country'. This third magnet grew into what we know today as the garden city, manifest in the new towns of Letchworth Garden City and Welwyn Garden City. These new suburban towns represented Howard's idea that by reforming the urban environment social reform could be achieved. Suburbs became one of the most powerful models of city growth through the twentieth century.

Whilst widely adopted, the suburb has taken on a rather pejorative meaning as, unlike Howard's clearly structured radial model, the endless, placeless sprawl of the suburb did much to consume the countryside whilst at the same time drawing the life out of urban centres. Today, however, the garden city is undergoing something of a Renaissance. Creating communities clustered around common spaces, allied with the benefits of connecting houses with countryside, has led to a reappraisal of the garden city typology. These new models employ increased housing density with fingers of greenery interlacing the residential layout. Rather than suburbia, the new garden city recaptures Howard's original ideal of community and nature working in harmony.

ABOVE
Initial masterplan of Redbridge Lane.

BELOW
Concept sketch of housing strategy community clusters.

ABOVE
Visualisation of new houses with landscape and new pedestrian focused streets.

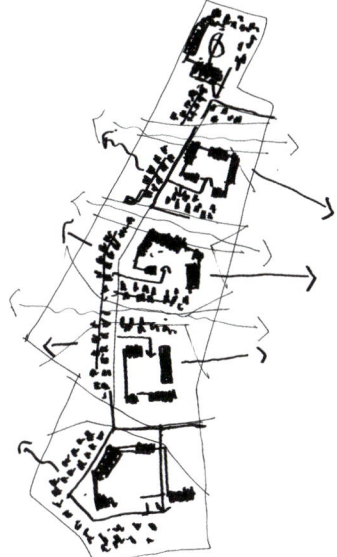

REDBRIDGE LANE MASTERPLAN, SOUTHAMPTON

The Redbridge Lane masterplan focuses on a piece of brownfield land between the urban edge of Southampton and the natural boundary of an ancient woodland called Home Covert. The ambition was to produce a dense living zone of clustered dwellings, conceived as a modern interpretation of the typology of the English farmstead. Each cluster is supplemented by a freer arrangement of innovatively designed detached and semi-detached homes to create a series of microneighbourhoods.

The composition engages with the natural landscape edges of Home Covert to the north and newly formed landscaped 'corridors' running north to south. These serve to fragment the boundary between nature and development. A new pedestrian lane is proposed to run between the clustered neighbourhoods in order to provide short, medium and longer distance connectivity across the existing and the new community. Around the clustered groups of houses and within the design of each house there is a feeling of individual identity for the owner.

Clustering buildings around open spaces whilst branching these groupings along arterial stems mirrors that observation by Richard Weston when, in describing Jørn Utzon's 1962–1965 Fredensborg Courtyard housing scheme in Denmark, he cites the influence on Utzon as coming from a lecture by Alvar Aalto. In his address the great Finnish architect proposed a branch of flowering cherry blossom as a model for housing where each flower was similar but never identical to the next, its individual pattern of growth and resulting relation to other flowers the consequence of external environmental factors that inflected each blossom through the forces of sun, wind and rain. This insightful parallel is demonstrated in much of Design Engine's work, where similar repeated elements find variety, as their relative disposition in response to the particularities of site and orientation inflect what would otherwise be a mechanically organised pattern to effect a more organic arrangement. In this way Design Engine creates uniqueness in identity and place whilst employing self-similar parts.

People
The Stories People Tell

ABOVE
Architecture is fundamentally linked to the stories we tell. For Claude Lévi-Strauss the central role of myth gave meaning and structure to human society and in turn shaped buildings and cities.

To say that architecture is about people is such an obvious truism that it is of little benefit in the complex and multifaceted task of designing a building. Certainly the architect has in mind the particularities of the functional requirements along with the physical and psychological needs of those who might experience the work. Equally there is a concern for the aspirations of the client along with the many who will be involved in the complex process of realising the building. However, in meeting all of these pragmatic concerns a building must also address the more fundamental issues of what it is to be human and live in society. In this architecture is perhaps one of the most direct representations of the values that we hold as individuals and of the societies of which we are a part.

Architecture is concerned in its most elemental sense with the interaction of people. Buildings above all provide the theatre for human engagement in all of the many and diverse forms that this entails. The history of anthropology and ethnography shows a consistency in the way in which we forge our individual identity, in the complex and often unspoken rules that govern our relationship with others. Claude Lévi-Strauss gave central importance to the role of myth—a world view based on a traditional story, and a term deriving from the ancient Greek 'mythos', that simply means story. For Lévi-Strauss the analysis of these stories revealed deep structures that symbolised the beliefs and values of society. He found the essence of myth to be based on binary oppositions such as good and evil, with each polarity strictly defined and set off against the other.[1] In these narratives the symbolic value of the story was used to govern the behaviour of the individual in society and in turn the structure of their social order and architecture. From this perspective, architecture is formed and arranged not only to serve the pragmatic needs of people, but as a direct result of the stories which bind society together.

OPPOSITE TOP
View of Les Beaucamps High School's central courtyard.

OPPOSITE BOTTOM
Conceptual diagrams illustrating the benefits of a central courtyard.

LES BEAUCAMPS HIGH SCHOOL, GUERNSEY

Les Beaucamps High School is a secondary school for 660 students, located on the island of Guernsey. Occupying a sloping site, the scheme is designed as a series of terraced floor plans linked by internal and external courtyards. The story of the design of Les Beaucamps High School is shown in the diagrams to the right. The school is formed around a courtyard which allows light to penetrate into the centre of the campus. As the shadows track around the courtyard throughout the course of the day, they give the school a temporal orientation. The courtyard forms the heart of the school protected from the external world. The idea of the protected courtyard derives from the monastic typology later adopted by early universities as the sacred quadrangle, with a focal element of captured landscape in the form of a tree. The courtyard serves the practical function of providing circulation and direct connections between the various activities of the school. Lastly, by entering the courtyard at the corner, a system of 'pinwheel' planning is established which not only serves to animate each corner of the enclosed space but also gives a sense of enhanced scale through the diagonal vista created.

BUILDING STORIES | 28

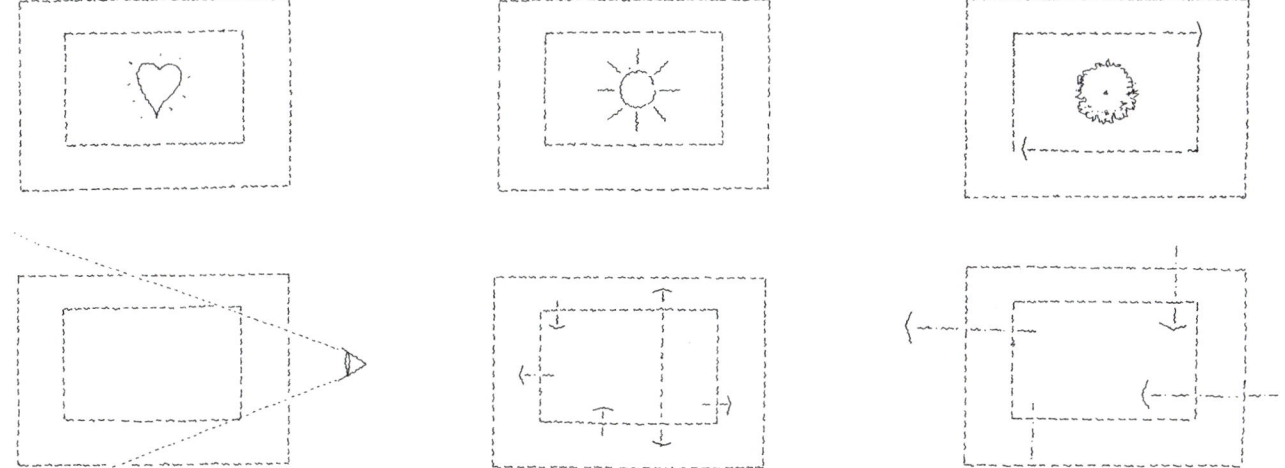

PEOPLE | 29

People and Patterns

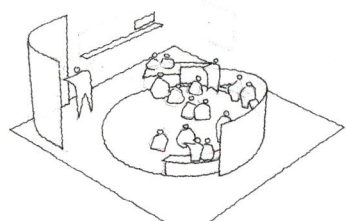

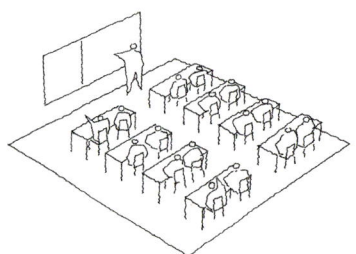

Lévi-Strauss found the same myths, albeit in different guises, to exist not only in the isolated Indigenous Bororo people of Brazil which he had studied, but also across the most developed civilisations of the present age. From his empirical observations Lévi-Strauss developed a theory that proposed that society is governed by the structure of human interaction, and accordingly he used the term 'structuralism' to describe the ordering framework or schema that govern acceptable activity within society. Across the fields of sociology, psychology and linguistics structuralism was a dominant force in late-twentieth-century thinking. With the aim of understanding the deep and often unspoken organisational systems that governed the elements of human culture, structuralism proposed that we must first look to the overarching system that makes the interrelationships between human beings meaningful. Understanding that the patterns which govern the rules of language or of social interaction were directly applicable to architecture, Christopher Alexander, in his influential book *A Pattern Language*, 1977, set out to codify what he thought were the timeless organisational systems that governed architecture and urban design.

> *The language begins with patterns that define towns and communities. These patterns can never be designed or built in one fell swoop—but patient piecemeal growth, designed in such a way that every individual act is always helping to create or generate these larger global patterns, will, slowly and surely, over the years, make a community that has these global patterns in it.*
> — CHRISTOPHER ALEXANDER, *A PATTERN LANGUAGE*

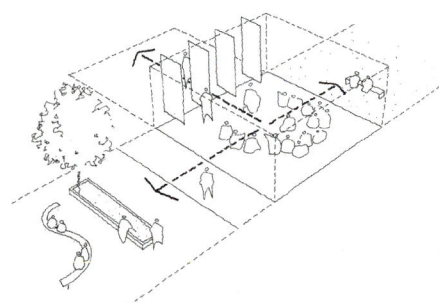

LES BEAUCAMPS HIGH SCHOOL, GUERNSEY

In designing Les Beaucamps High School in Guernsey the fundamental concern was the way in which the students would learn. The patterns of teaching and learning shown in the diagrams to the left describe formal and informal organisational patterns for the way in which a classroom might be used. The interaction between the teacher and the students along with those that take place between the students themselves are carefully considered to provide a level of flexibility that allows for different pedagogical methods to be applied. In establishing the physical arrangement of people and spaces the design parallels the structuralist ideas of Lévi-Strauss and Alexander in the need to look beyond the surface phenomena and understand the underlying relationships that enable meaningful human interaction to take place.

At a micro level, the classrooms arranged around the quadrangle have the potential to be connected together in a linear arrangement whilst each benefits from the closed view into the courtyard and open views to the landscape beyond the campus.

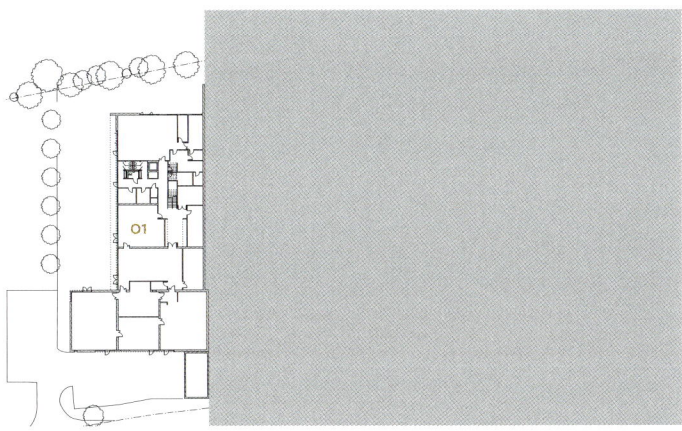

Level 01

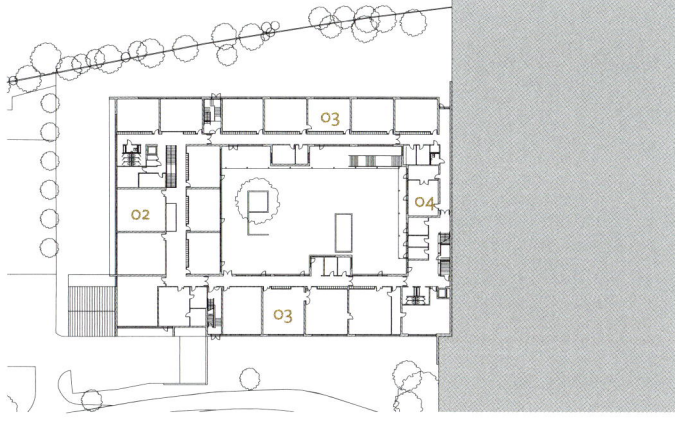

Level 02

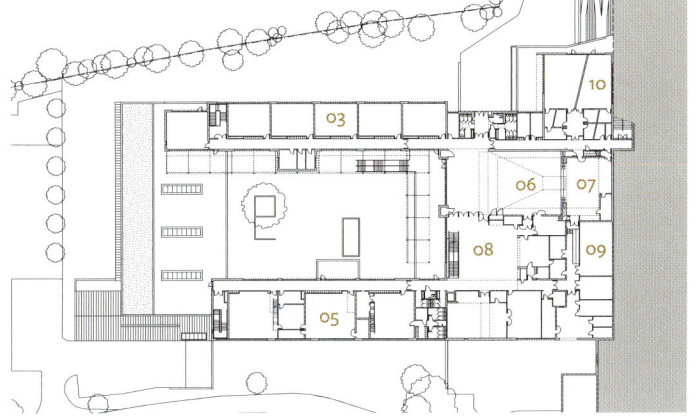

Level 03

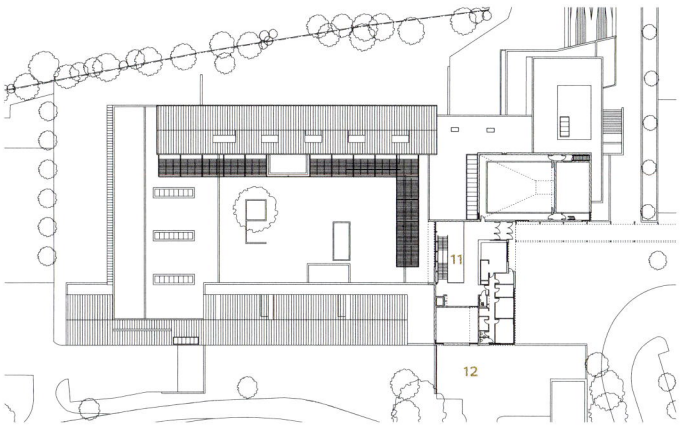

Level 04

ABOVE & RIGHT
The campus is arranged around a series of courtyards which are shown at the macro level in the site plan, with the primary enclosures around the western social court and the multi-use games area to the east framed by the sports hall and surrounding open colonnade.

01. Design Technology
02. Science classrooms
03. Teaching classrooms
04. Special Education needs
05. Art classrooms
06. Main Hall
07. Drama classrooms
08. Dining room
09. Kitchen
10. Music rooms
11. Reception
12. Administration
13. Multi-use games area
14. Sports Hall
15. Open colonnade
16. Courtyard

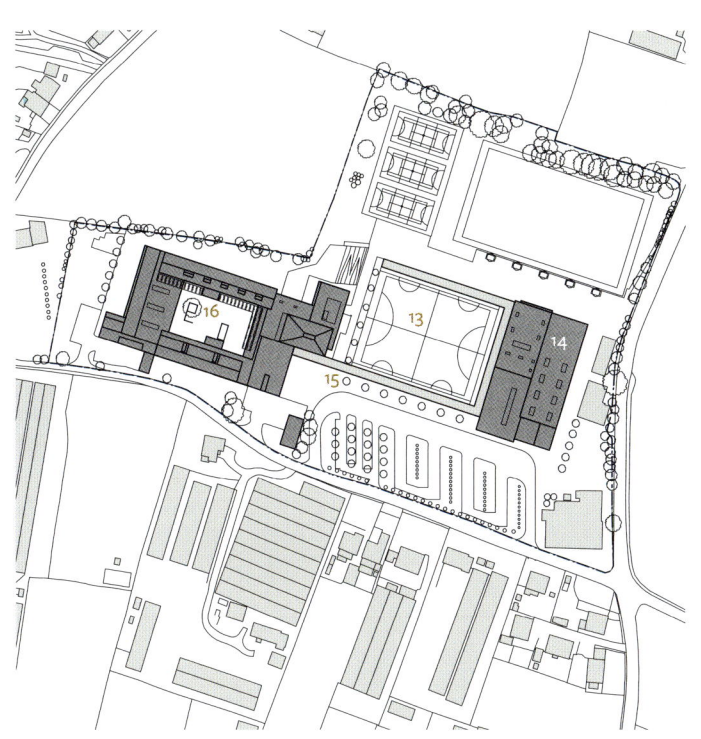

PEOPLE | 31

Building Shared Ideas

The idea of the stories and of the people for whom those stories are meaningful is at the basis of architecture. What elevates mere building to the realm of architecture is that it speaks of ideas beyond the simple pragmatics of function. This art of architecture is above all the way in which people across time have understood and given meaning to the world around them and through their buildings sought to represent the ideas, values and beliefs they held. In this architecture is the bearer of human perception, emotion and belief: a shared belief in the future importance of that which is made, how it is made and the way in which buildings become the carrier of people's memories. For those that commission buildings and for the architects themselves their work is that of entrustment to the future, and for this the relationship of trust between architect and client is more than a financial or contractual transaction. It is above all constructing a shared belief in the future, a recognition of the importance of that which is made, how it is made and the way it will over time become the bearer of the lives and memories of future generations. Great architecture must therefore have a quality of endurance. The ideas it holds and the stories it tells which in turn touch the lives of many must, like the great myths of the ancients, be of sufficient depth and weight to last.

ABOVE & OPPOSITE
Long and short sections through Les Beaucamps High School, Guernsey.

LES BEAUCAMPS HIGH SCHOOL, GUERNSEY

The section of Les Beaucamps High School, Guernsey (above), shows the space flanked by linear classroom buildings. According to orientation and function each of the buildings is slightly inflected in its arrangement. To the left the south-facing elevation to the courtyard receives a shading timber pergola, whilst on the right a mezzanine level and large north lights give a sense of space and illumination to the upper level art studios. The section drawing (right) through the school reveals the series of courtyards that step down the steeply sloping site. This change in section allows visual connection between the high level entrance across the courtyard and on to the ancillary spaces beyond. In surveying the entirety of the building from the entrance there is an immediate sense for the students of orientation and a psychological effect of feeling a part of the whole. This device engenders a sense of community and the views from the upper level entrance across to the landscape and the sea beyond also serve to connect the campus to its island location. The unique materials and vegetation of Guernsey are captured in the building through the use of brick whose shade is chosen to reflect the local stonework. Similarly the choice of colour for sections of the glazing picks up the azure of the surrounding sea and the magenta of indigenous flora in the adjacent fields. All of these devices are used to root the building in its location and give a strong psychological sense of community and identity for the people who use the building.

BUILDING STORIES | 32

RIGHT
View of first-floor art classroom.

BELOW RIGHT
Photo of indigenous red campion which influenced the colour palette.

BELOW FAR RIGHT
Photo of typical granite wall which was used to create a special brick mix for the project.

Drawing on the surrounding environment, materials and colours, the campus is very much of its place. However, in the application of materials and the detail of how they are brought together there is a strong sense of abstraction. Rather than copying the indigenous vernacular building forms that the architecture evokes, it mimics their qualities. Refined wall and roof details give a feeling of purity and volumetric precision, while the coloured glazing is reminiscent of the abstractions of De Stijl paintings.

Main enclosed courtyard with colonnade at Les Beaucamps High School, Guernsey.

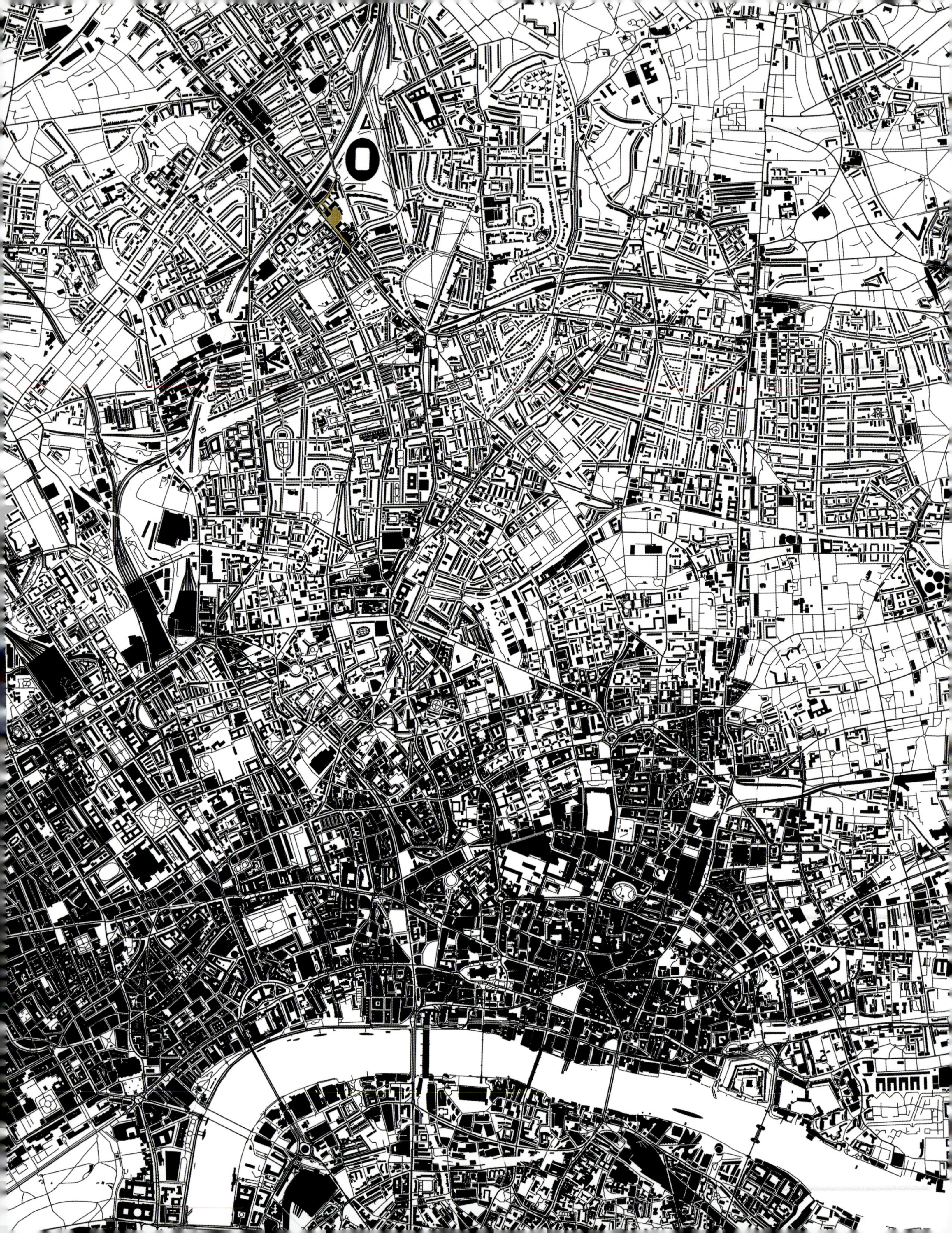

Architecture, People and Polis

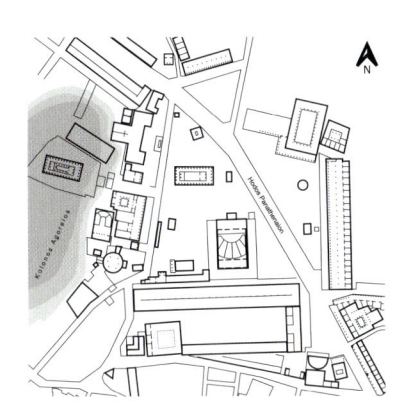

The ancient Greek word for city is 'polis', but the term also means citizenship or the collective body of citizens. In *Flesh and Stone: The Body and the City in Western Civilization*, Richard Sennett traces the relationship of the human body to public and private space. Describing the relationship of the individual to the state in the golden age of Pericles around the fifth century BCE, Sennett states:

> *Polis meant far more to an Athenian like Pericles than a place on the map; it meant the place where people achieved unity…. The Parthenon's placement in the city dramatized its collective city value.*[2]

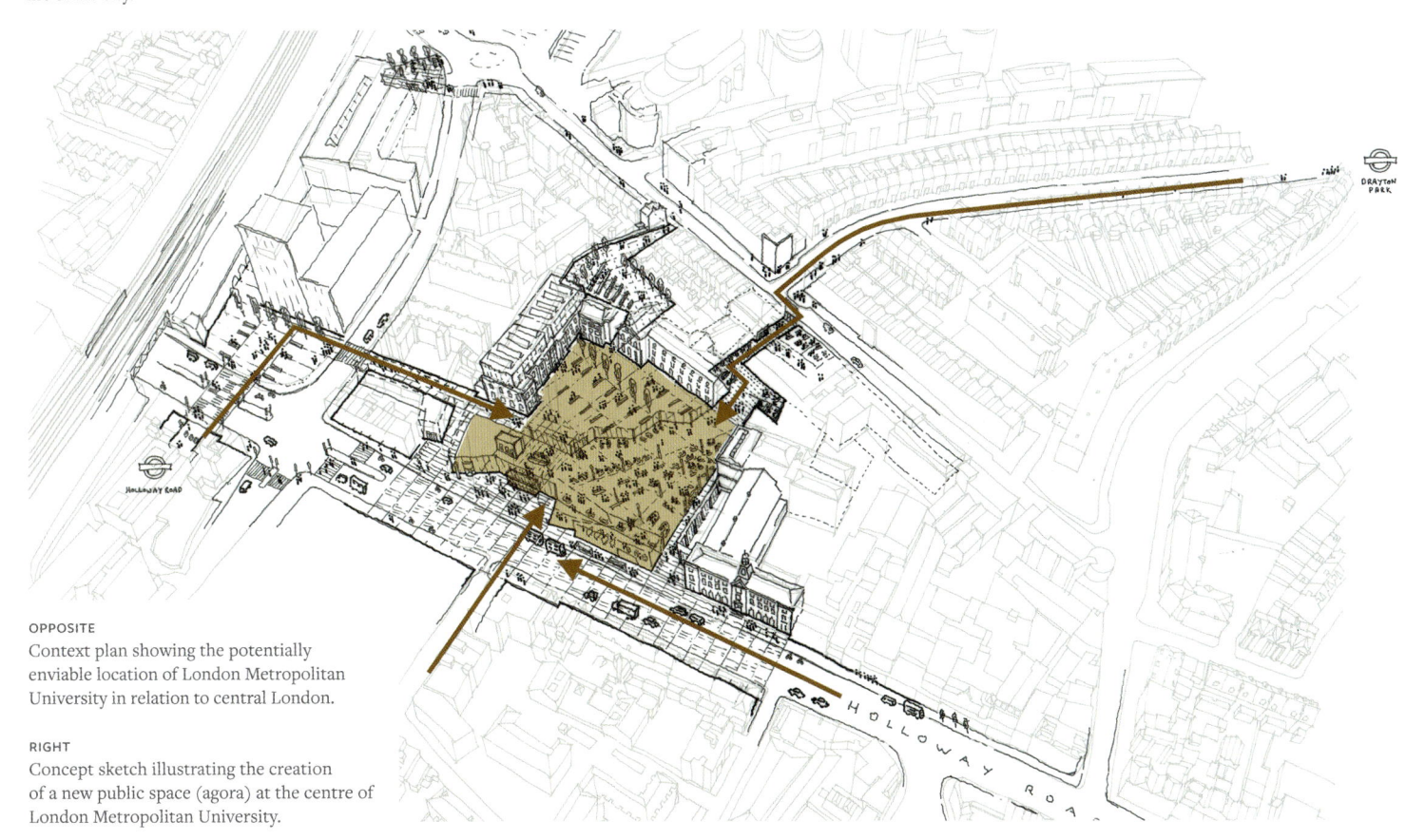

ABOVE
The Agora of Athens was the central heart of the ancient Greek city-state. The literal meaning of the word is 'gathering place' or 'assembly' and it was the focus of the economic, artistic, spiritual and political life of the city.

OPPOSITE
Context plan showing the potentially enviable location of London Metropolitan University in relation to central London.

RIGHT
Concept sketch illustrating the creation of a new public space (agora) at the centre of London Metropolitan University.

PEOPLE | 37

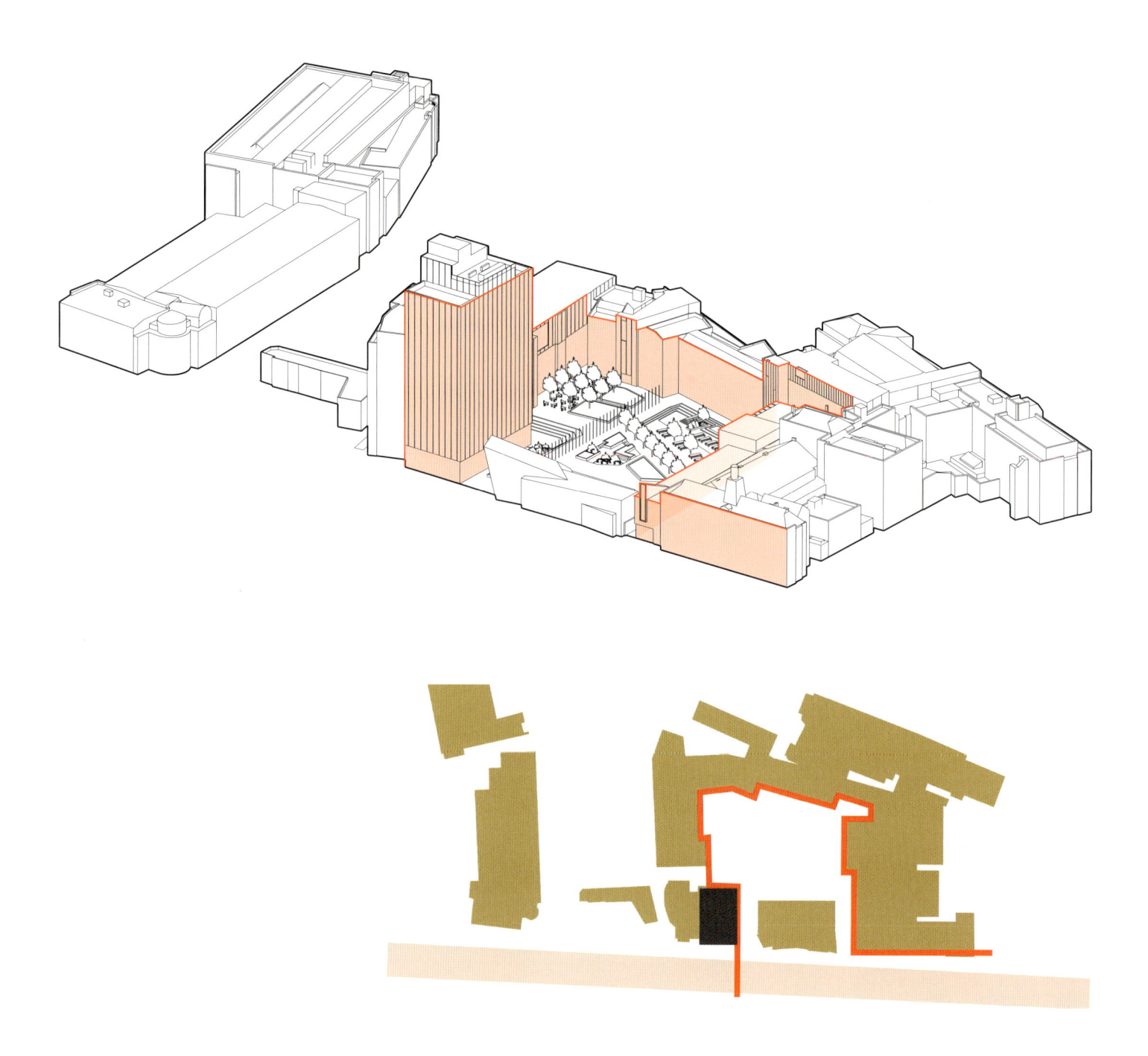

ABOVE
Plan and isometric drawing illustrating how the streetscape along Holloway Road is folded into the centre of the campus with the existing tower providing a visual anchor to both the main road and the new courtyard.

LONDON METROPOLITAN UNIVERSITY

The masterplan for the London Metropolitan University seeks to rationalise the current arrangement of space across the campus, in particular, the dispersed and often remote and hard-to-find locations of lecture and teaching rooms. The masterplan recognises a requirement for both distinct specialist spaces for specific activities and the need for shared teaching, lecture and commons spaces to bring efficiencies and higher utilisation. The masterplan has sought to achieve this by locating hubs of specialist facilities across the campus and in doing so to create a more legible environment.

These shared flexible teaching, tutorial and communication spaces are brought together into more visible and accessible locations, focused around a new central courtyard. To complement this strategy core activity spaces for entry, meeting, exhibiting, eating and drinking are also focused on the courtyard. The combination of these elements results in a much more engaging relationship between inside and out, private and public.

By the removal of some existing structures the campus can be made more permeable with the streetscape allowed to flow into the central courtyard. This encourages the courtyard to become a public space and thus creates a far better connection into the urban realm. The scheme then works with the current buildings surrounding this central courtyard to extend and repurpose them as well as opening them up to create a new and varied street frontage. In doing so the masterplan seeks to provide a more civic relationship between the university and the city.

BUILDING STORIES | 38

Located adjacent to the new Emirates stadium of Arsenal Football club, the site has excellent public transport links, with Holloway tube station and Drayton Park overground station just a few minutes' walk from the university. The site fronts onto Holloway Road, the A1, which is one of the busiest arterial routes into central London from the surroundings to the north.

RIGHT
Existing site arrangement illustrating the 'closed' nature of the campus.

RIGHT
'Reaching out and inviting in' diagrams illustrating new courtyard space (agora) bringing the public realm into the site.

ABOVE
The Campanile in Siena, Italy, provides a focal point to the main piazza.

In this he sets out that the building's exterior mattered more than its internal function, as the sacred high city of the Acropolis seen from afar formed a symbolic focal point of the state. The Parthenon was entered only by the few, but as an object in space it represented the collective consciousness of the many. In this sense architecture today, as then, is totemic, in that it serves as a shared symbol or emblem of a group of people. Where once the Athenians saw the Parthenon as the sacred protector of the city-state, today, in a world suffused with so-called iconic architecture, the gods may have been dethroned by the icons of capitalism, but the ability of architecture to unite the hopes and dreams of people remains.

In ancient Greece the secular world inhabited the space of the Agora, which was the market place, political forum, philosophical debating ground and courts of justice along with hosting all of the other multifarious affairs of public man. Above all the Agora was the political, economic and intellectual crucible of democracy. The great Stoa, a long colonnaded building that fronted the open space of the Agora, was without prescribed function but instead served the many kinds of human interaction that drove the state. Together with the other buildings of the Agora, the Stoa framed the central space, forming an irregular courtyard in which we find the origins of public space.

ABOVE
Existing tower at London Metropolitan University.

RIGHT
Conceptual visualisation of proposed re-cladding of the London Metropolitan University tower.

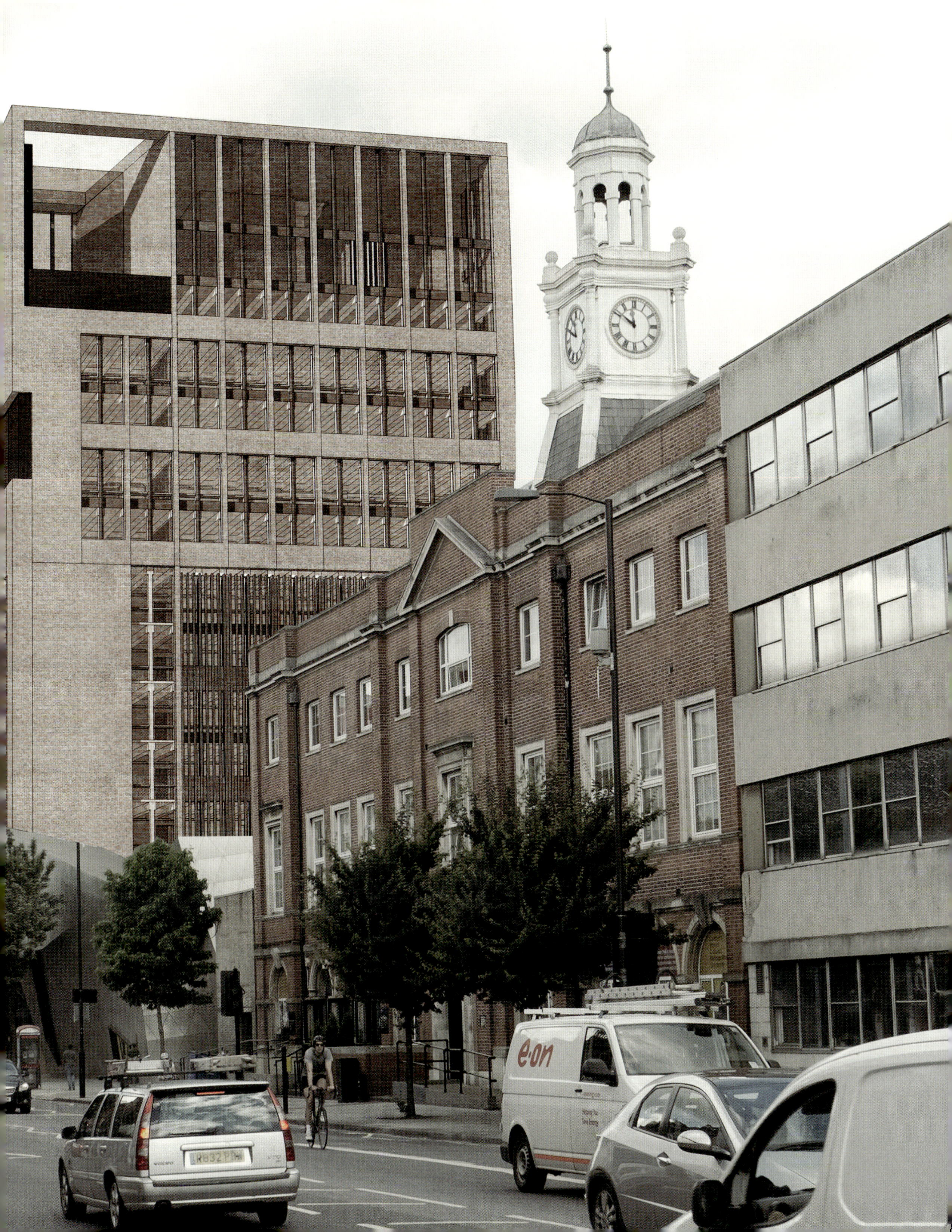
e·on

Architecture and the Digital Age

ABOVE
Two students working on the platform above the lecture theatre at the John Henry Brookes Building at Oxford Brookes University.

BELOW
Students working within the Abercrombie Building at Oxford Brookes University.

Where once the design of buildings was largely determined by invariant function, the impact of new technologies in the twenty-first century and accompanying revolution in the way people live and work has made for far less stable ground upon which to base architecture. The sociologist Zygmunt Bauman has observed that where once the industrial world was premised on the order and certainties of what he termed "solid" modernity, over recent decades human consciousness has rapidly transformed in the face of what he characterises as "liquid" life.[3] For Bauman the liquid modernity of the twenty-first century is one of uncertainty and ever more rapid change. The digital revolution has overthrown hierarchical social orders, and through a network of social media and instant communication people have found a new power and voice. The physical implications of this paradigmatic shift have been equally radical. Portable digital technologies have freed people from doing one activity, in one space, at one time, as more itinerant patterns of working and global connectivity have changed our understanding of community and regional identity. The full implications of these fundamental changes are still being played out but the challenges for architecture are ever more apparent.

Today the ideas of spatial determinism, once the bedrock of architecture, have been overthrown by a need for buildings that are more flexible in their day-to-day operation and able to respond to future, and as yet unimagined, uses. There is a new architectural awareness that if buildings are not to become rapidly redundant they will require a built in resilience that will enable them to respond to these changes. Yet in this lies a profound architectural conundrum. Often the spaces of ultimate flexibility are also those of least identity, and in their bland universality they lack the sense of place and belonging which is at the heart of meaningful human inhabitation. Paradoxically the need for places with which people can identify is ever more pressing as the nomadic life of the laptop and smartphone has been accompanied for many by a greater sense of individual alienation. Adrift in the network of the virtual world, the need to assert our physical presence in expressive places and to meet the deeply rooted sense of comfort that arises from being in the presence of others is ever more important.

ABOVE
Students working within the Design Workshops & Studios at Arts University Bournemouth.

RIGHT
A student working outside the lecture theatre at the John Henry Brookes Building at Oxford Brookes University.

People Being Heard

From the polis of ancient Greece we might consider how today the fall of public man in consumer culture has brought a cultural homogeneity; focused on the internalised world of the home, the television and latterly the internet it augured the diminution of the need for public spaces that once formed the focal points of historic societies. William J Mitchell in his books *City of Bits* and *e-Topia* predicted the digital age would bring about a whole new urban infrastructure.[4] The urbs, which had been the building stones which had founded the ancient cities of history, would be replaced in a digital world by bits, the discrete packages of data information. Mitchell's view was that an increasingly atomised yet interconnected digital world would do away with the high street and places of physical gathering.

But the human needs for the comfort to be found from the physical presence of others has seen a growth in the places of physical assembly. The event of cinema-going has not been replaced by streamed media, nor has the wish to be seen in public diminished the joy to be found in dining with others; the proliferation of coffee houses mirrors the eighteenth-century tradition of a public meeting place to conduct business face to face. In universities, libraries which were once the domain of silent study have become, in an age of online books and journals, the spaces where students meet to work together. In *The Ecstasy of Communication*, Jean Baudrillard observed:

> *The need to speak, even if one has nothing to say, becomes more pressing when one has nothing to say, just as the will to live becomes more urgent when life has lost its meaning.*[5]

Baudrillard's prescient but dark mirror of 1987 foresaw how today's technological revolution would result in a new form of human alienation equal to that of the industrial era, but one typified by passivity and ceaseless communication and information.

ABOVE
Images showing how library spaces have developed to respond to the changing demands of students and the impacts of technology.

TOP | 18th–19th century library
MIDDLE | 20th century library
BOTTOM | 21st century social learning space, Oxford Brookes University.

THE LISTENING PROJECT

The Listening Project is an ambitious oral history exercise undertaken by the BBC in conjunction with the British Library that aims to build a sound archive of our times for future generations to hear.

The RIBA competition asked participants to create a special Listening Pod to travel around the UK, to extend the geographical reach of this unique and important oral history project. The 'pod' had to break down into pieces small enough to be brought into normal office buildings through the doors and passenger lifts. Therefore, to create an integral soundproof structure, Design Engine used the form and geometry of a radial structure to allow wide compressible joints to be 'pulled in' and clamped into position to create an airtight interior.

The radial shells that form the exterior envelope form 'listening niches' to allow passers-by and visitors to engage in the project via built-in speakers. The pod comprises an outer 'protection' shell, resiliently separated from the inner 'acoustic' shell, which achieves a mass/spring/mass sound insulation system. Air is circulated within the exposed cavity providing attenuation by forming a circular labyrinth. The depth of the convex, fabric-covered surface to the interior space diffuses incident sound and provides absorption to the 'recording' environment.

BUILDING STORIES | 44

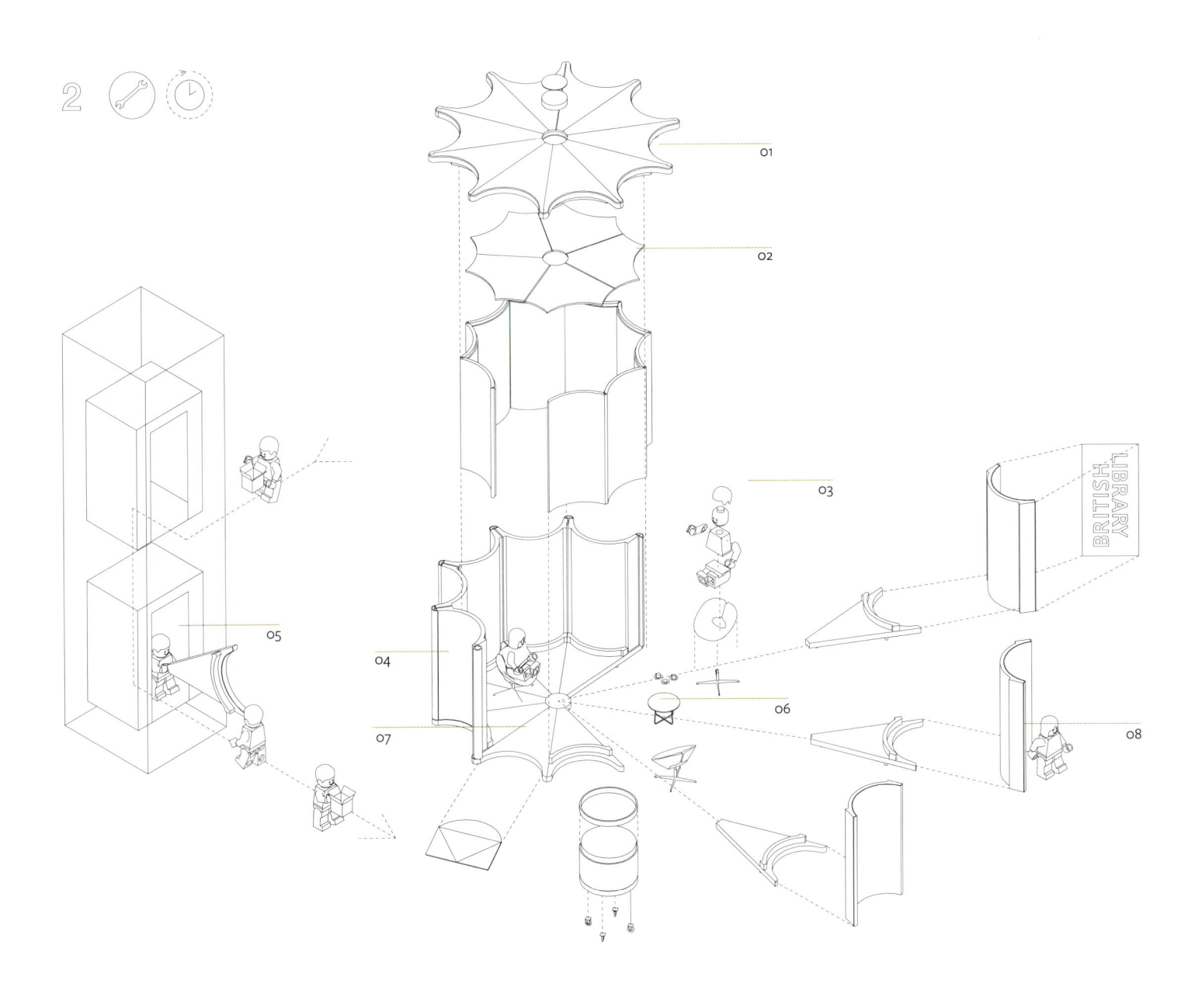

ABOVE & RIGHT
Competition images for the Listening Project.

01. Roof segments
02. Acoustic inner shell
03. People who like listening and talking a bit
04. Mirror-finish outer shell
05. Segments fit into lift
06. Tea; milk, one sugar, thanks
07. Floor panels on levelling feet
08. Speakers built into outer panels, to create 'listening niches'

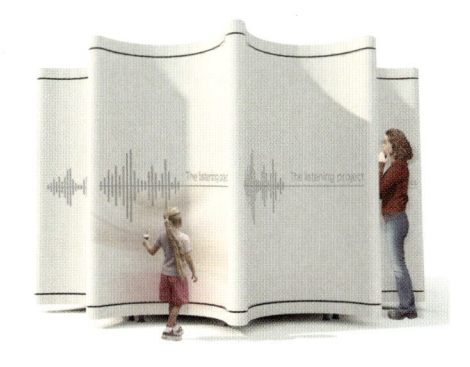

PEOPLE | 45

ABOVE
The new social learning space within the John Henry Brookes Building at Oxford Brookes University is a direct result of increased access to knowledge, which has created an increased demand for collaborative working and social interaction.

People and Community

ABOVE
The Byker Wall, Newcastle upon Tyne by Ralph Erskine was a milestone in creating community centred high-density housing. The vision of the Byker Community Trust is to maintain the Grade II* listed property as a high quality example of sustainable housing and services, where people want to live and work with a sense of pride in their homes and communities.

Architecture impacts on our lives in many ways. However, it is perhaps to the young or vulnerable that the built environment has an ever greater responsibility as the receptacle of the human life entrusted to it. Schools, hospitals or social housing schemes were seized upon by the post-war idealists who saw that social reform could be delivered through architecture. However, much of this idealism became a vehicle not for social inclusion but for the prototyping of formal architectural principles hypothesised by the Modern movement. Of these, the point block and radiant city of Le Corbusier or the megastructures of Metabolism, whilst exquisite as idea on paper, in reality too often became dystopian nightmares for the societies upon which they were imposed. One of the greatest lessons from history is that of Pruitt–Igoe in St Louis, Missouri, designed by Minoru Yamasaki, the architect of the Twin Towers of the World Trade Centre in New York. First occupied in 1954, the 33 low-income 11-storey apartment buildings were laid out on a strict Cartesian grid. The project, with all of its Corbusian Modernist tropes, was intended to improve the lives of its inhabitants, but within years of completion Pruitt–Igoe had become a ghetto of crime and social alienation. The architectural historian Charles Jencks famously pointed to the end of the Modern movement as taking place on 15 July 1972 at 3.32 pm (or thereabouts)—the time of commencement of the wholesale demolition of the buildings which had become socially uninhabitable.[6] The reasons for the failure of the project are many and complex, but underpinning its demise was a fundamental failure by the architect and commissioning authority to understand or engage with the tenants whom the project was intended to house.

The failures of architecture that arose from a disinclination to consult or often consider those that it would serve have provided a haunting and cautionary backdrop for architecture today. The work of the architect Ralph Erskine did much to reverse this failing, and his project to relocate an entire community from Victorian slums into a long, unbroken block of 620 maisonettes known as the Byker Wall, in Newcastle upon Tyne, was a landmark in community architecture. Erskine's project was completed in the 1970s and it has been a long journey for the principles of community engagement and social inclusion to be fully embodied into planning and architecture legislation. The 2011 Localism Act set into statute a requirement to consult with local community groups, and sought to value an architecture that both met the needs of those that it served and afforded those users a sense of having played an important role in the design process, giving them a sense of ownership.

CEDAR PARK CARE HOME VILLAGE

The Cedar Park Care Home Village for the Enham Trust based at Enham Alamein near Andover, Hampshire, is for a centre of excellence to support people who have suffered damage to their nervous systems, including brain injury and strokes, acquired through accidents or from neurological illness or virus. The project includes a new health and well-being centre, restaurant and meeting spaces. The masterplan proposes the regeneration of the Cedar Park estate, including a state of the art Neuro-rehabilitation Unit and the development of 81 new disabled accessible apartments. The project was developed in association with the charity and from the initial stages the end-users were engaged in the design process.

ABOVE
Visualisation of the Cedar Park Care Home Village.

RIGHT
Masterplan drawing of the Cedar Park Care Home Village.

Craft
Architecture: Art and Craft

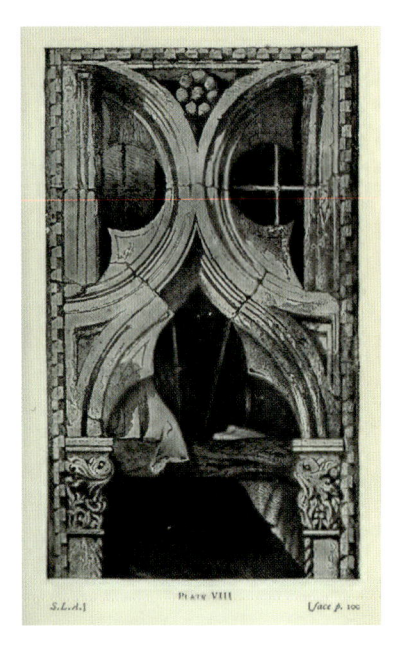

ABOVE
The Seven Lamps of Architecture, John Ruskin, 1849. Plate VIII—Window from the Ca' Foscari, Venice. For Ruskin, Venice embodied a world of craftsmanship and the joy to be found in making beautiful objects and buildings to the glory of God with one's own hands—qualities which he felt were being swept away by the dehumanising mechanised processes of the Industrial Revolution.

The nineteenth-century art critic John Ruskin saw painting and architecture in more than purely aesthetic terms and felt that the arts were a reflection of the moral and spiritual state of a nation.[1] Looking back over the history of art he felt that a profound shift had occurred somewhere around the Renaissance when artists had ceased to employ art for the honour of God and started to see themselves as gods. The resulting decline in moral standing had led to hellish, polluted cities and the terrible living and working conditions of the Industrial Revolution that was transforming the world around him.

A group of artists agreed with Ruskin and thought that the artists who succeeded Raphael had intellectualised art, placing it in the academy when it rightly belonged with the craftsman in the workshop. This they felt had corrupted art away from its original intentions of mirroring nature and expressing ideas of the heart, to the extent that the art of the time had lost any spiritual and creative integrity. This pre-Raphaelite brotherhood of artists included William Holman Hunt, John Everett Millais and Dante Gabriel Rossetti who under the patronage and critical support of Ruskin made paintings of exquisite detail that romanticised the medieval period, with subjects taken from the plays of Shakespeare or the legends of King Arthur. These they felt represented a society at one with itself and nature, governed by the moral laws of chivalry and honour. Similarly, Ruskin thought that medieval architecture held a moral integrity which was reflected in the way in which buildings were constructed by skilled craftsmen who found reward in honest labour, making beautiful things with their own hands. Ruskin fell in love with the city of Venice and set out the principles of medieval craftsmanship in *The Stones of Venice*, a three-volume treatise on the art and architecture of the city.[2] First published from 1851 to 1853, Ruskin describes "seven lamps", or guiding objectives, towards which architecture should strive. These are in effect moral categories which architecture should embody and for Ruskin these were to be found in the Northern Gothic of the thirteenth century with buildings like the cathedrals at Wells, Amiens or Chartres. Through the seven lamps of Sacrifice, Truth, Power, Beauty, Life, Memory and Obedience, Ruskin is at pains to show that the finished appearance of architecture is an embodiment of the process through which it is made, and in turn of the lives and beliefs of its makers, which derives from the joy that comes from crafting a fine material with one's own hands.

BUILDING STORIES | 50

ABOVE
The University of Winchester's St Alphege Building artwork in production. Here oak is burnt and then doused in water to give a charred effect to the face of the timber that retains the grain and texture of the material.

Craft and the Reform of Society

Whilst Ruskin provided a powerful criticism of industrial society, it was William Morris who took his remedy into practice. Morris found kindred spirits in the pre-Raphaelite brotherhood but, instead of tackling painting, applied these ideas to the manufacture of everyday household furnishings that he thought would bring authentic craftsmanship back into people's homes. His designs for wallpaper, textiles and furniture drew on the forms and patterns found in nature. These were all produced by reviving traditional skills and Morris, as good as his word, taught himself to weave and spin his own yarns. Morris intended these products to be accessible to all, but of course due to the high production cost they could not compete with the mass produced goods which he loathed. Ironically, today Morris's wallpapers and fabrics, many of which are still in production, command premium prices. But Morris's ideas were pervasive not least through his writing, which was of course published in Gothic script on hand-printed paper under his own Kelmscott Press. *News from Nowhere*, 1890, tells the story of a man who dreams of an Arcadian world of social equality and harmony.[3] This utopian socialist society was in truth Morris's dream of social reform, and his antidote to the industrialised world.

BELOW
The University of Winchester's St Alphege Building artwork in detail, showing the oak of the crucifix which both reveals the grain of the material and through a charring process, shines in the light reflected from the carbonised surface.

ST ALPHEGE BUILDING ARTWORK

William Morris dreamed of a world free from the mechanised and soulless industry that mass production had brought about. In the work of Design Engine there is a particular attention to the celebration of the craft of making. For the artwork on the St Alphege Building at the University of Winchester, timber and steel are finely wrought by the hands of those who have many years of expertise in shaping materials. The personality of the individual maker is embodied in the final artefact, and this unity of design and craft skill is to be seen throughout the work of the practice.

ABOVE
Fabrication of stainless steel rods which represent the 11 Apostles.

RIGHT
Construction detail of the crucifix.

The Art of Making

Architects, painters, and sculptors must recognize anew and learn to grasp the composite character of a building both as an entity and in its separate parts. Only then will their work be imbued with the architectonic spirit which it has lost as salon art. Together let us desire, conceive, and create the new structure of the future, which will embrace architecture and sculpture and painting in one unity and which will one day rise toward heaven from the hands of a million workers like the crystal symbol of a new faith.
— WALTER GROPIUS

Whilst Ruskin and Morris were nostalgic for the craftsmanship of a pre-industrial past, in Germany at the advent of the twentieth century Walter Gropius envisioned a radical reunification of art and craft that would drive the technological future. 2014 marked the 100th anniversary of the Deutsche Werkbund (the German Association of Craftsmen) exhibition in Cologne. It was the same year that it was first suggested that Walter Gropius should take over the directorship of the art and craft school in Weimar, the institution that was later to become the Bauhaus.

The Werkbund's aim was to bring high quality design to industrial products and advance Germany's then-backward manufacturing base. Gropius's vision, realised in the Bauhaus, was the dismantling of the historic divide that had vested design with either the academies as a fine art or with the craftsmen and the trade guilds. This new unity of art and technology would aspire to produce high quality products that would benefit society and bring economic prosperity to all.

ABOVE
Poster for the 1914 Deutsche Werkbund exhibition in Cologne.

ABOVE RIGHT
Images showing the stone blocks being handcrafted at the New British Embassy in Yemen.

BRITISH EMBASSY, SANA'A—STONE BLOCKS

The stone blocks of the enclosing wall of the British Embassy in Sana'a are handcrafted. The technique of shaping each block with a one-degree angle on the outer face gives the horizontal coursing a crisp white line when seen in direct sunlight. The technique is indigenous to the Yemeni peninsula and was an important part of the process of creating a new embassy, helping to ensure the building had a sense of appropriateness and relevance to the historic context. For the skilled craftsmen who craft and lay each block there is a sense of pride and empowerment in their work, as the vernacular tradition lives on through their labours.

ABOVE & RIGHT
Completed mud wall courtyard in the British Embassy gardens in Yemen.

ABOVE
Traditional mud walls at the British Embassy in Yemen under construction.

BRITISH EMBASSY—GARDEN WALL

The enclosing garden wall of the embassy utilises a historic tradition of building construction that comprises mud, sticks and straw as the primary materials. Locally sourced, these walls require great skill in both the mixing and forming of the wall. The ratio of wall thickness to height is determined by the structural characteristics of the materials when hardened and the capping detail, designed to bind the upper surface of this friable material together, is drawn from the vernacular traditions of building construction in this arid desert environment. The wall is built off a stone base to ensure stability. This stone base is lost with time as mud washes over it. When seen in the context of the surrounding mountains the walls resonate, as a unity with the surrounding landscape makes the new embassy uniquely of this specific place.

Entrance canopy to the British Embassy, Sana'a, Yemen.

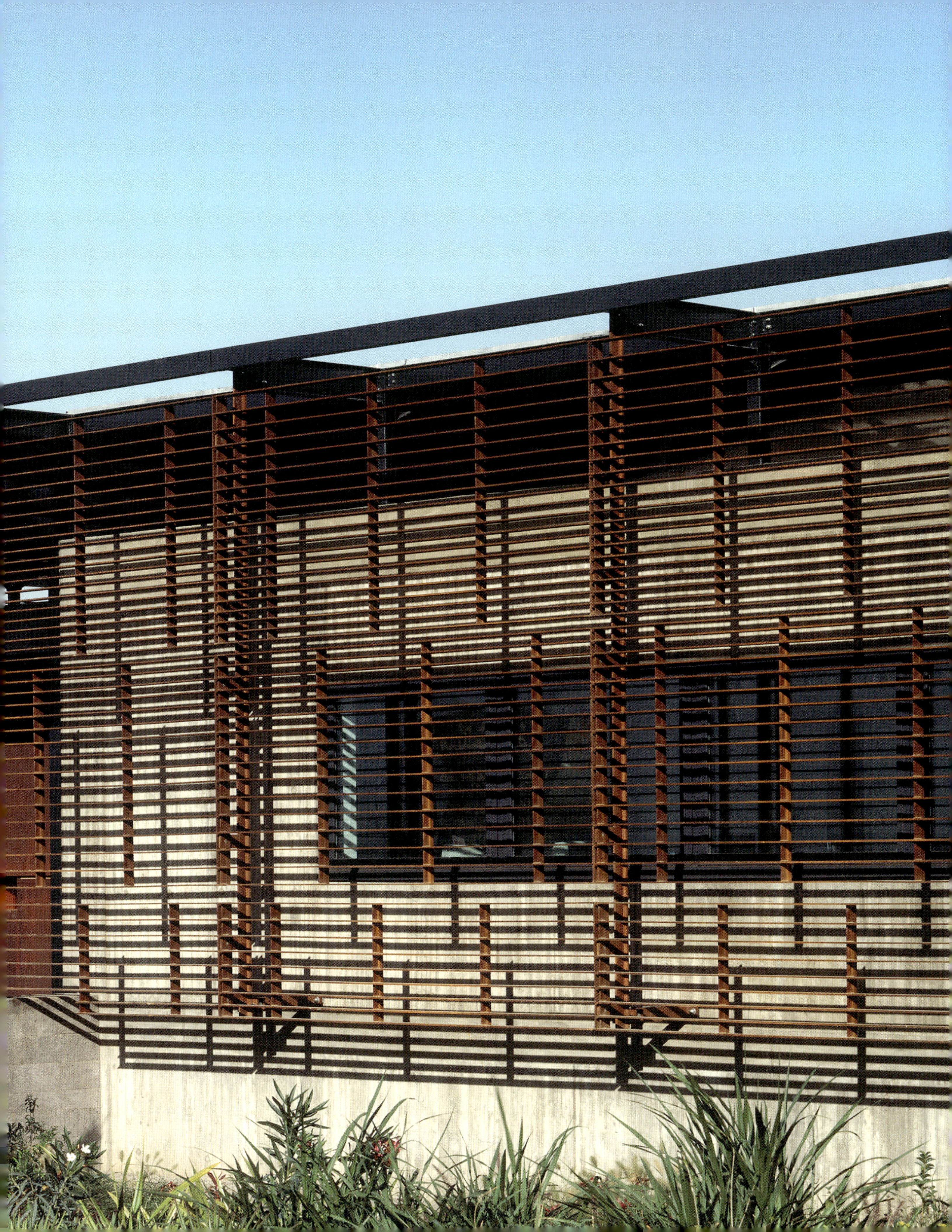

Craft and Form

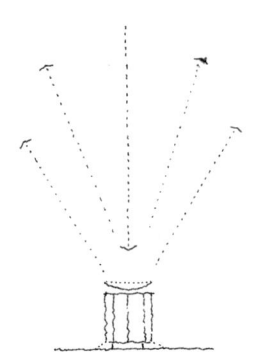

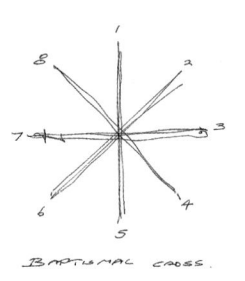

In the early days of the Bauhaus the way in which students learnt was divided into two seemingly opposing pedagogic methods. Firstly, an attitude of learning through doing was termed Weklerne, and it drew on the German Bauhütte, the medieval tradition of craftsmanship and the guilds which valued the action of the practised hand on fine materials. Secondly, Formlerne emphasised the creation of expressive forms and followed the romantic spiritual ideas of German expressionism, which was at the heart of Bruno Taut's crystalline vision.

Gropius enlisted the talents of Johannes Itten who, under the spell of oriental mysticism, turned the studio into something akin to a Buddhist seminary in which students were encouraged to express their emotions in an attempt to translate their inner mystical spirit into physical form. That is not to say Itten's experiments with abstract expression were without structure. Focusing on Light–Dark, Colour, Material, Texture, Form (expressive and subjective) and aspects of Rhythm, the basic course sought to free the individual's creative powers, to discover the materials which most stimulated their creativity and to convey fundamental principles, albeit very abstract principles, that would equip them for their future careers.

For the first semester the Bauhaus had almost no facilities, so Itten had to improvise and classes often took place seated on the floor. But in time students then proceeded to a series of workshops, each led by a master, where learning took place through practical experience. The workshops comprised ceramics, weaving, carpentry, metalwork, graphic printing, printing and advertising, photography, glass- and wall-painting, stone and wood sculpture, plastic arts, workshop and theatre. The masters included the likes of Lyonel Feininger, Wassily Kandinsky, Paul Klee, László Moholy-Nagy, Oskar Schlemmer, Josef Albers and Marcel Breuer. Only after successful completion of both Weklerne and Formlerne could students progress onto architecture.

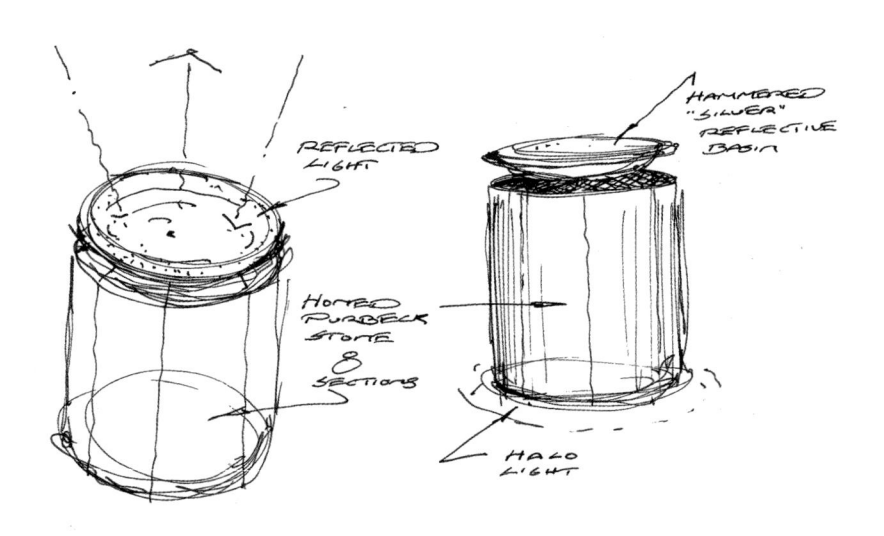

ABOVE & RIGHT
In representing the proposals for the font the drawing was an important tool for the exploration and expression of form. The essence of the reflective qualities of the mirrored bowl of the font is captured in an abstract watercolour painting; the greys and delicate blues of swirling reflected light take the form of an abstract image which evokes the Bauhaus ambition to capture an inner emotion.

BUILDING STORIES | 58

ABOVE
The use of drawing in representing the altar is evocative of the German expressionism of Erich Mendelsohn and his sketches for the Einstein Tower in Potsdam, Germany, completed in 1921. Mendelsohn's expressionist architecture sought to draw on the architect's subjective perspective and to capture this through distorted forms used to evoke emotional effect.

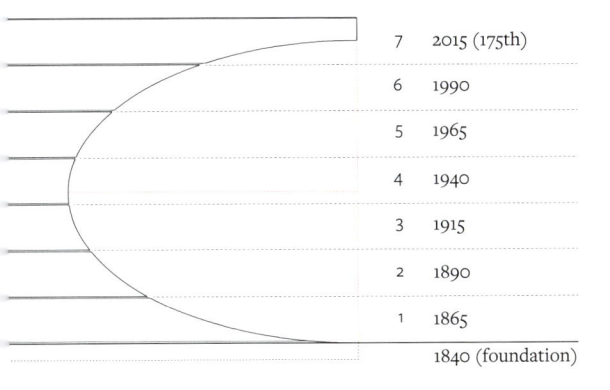

	7	2015 (175th)
	6	1990
	5	1965
	4	1940
	3	1915
	2	1890
	1	1865
		1840 (foundation)

ABOVE
The seven sections of the altar, representing seven 25-year time periods making up the 175 years. The seven sections also recall number imagery within the Christian faith.

WINTON CHAPEL—FONT AND ALTAR

The project to renovate and extend the University of Winchester's Victorian Winton Chapel is one of the most visible expressions of the celebrations to commemorate the 175th anniversary of the institution. The design for a new altar and font draws on strong forms and fine materials beautifully crafted. The font, a mirrored bowl balanced on a heavy stone cylinder, seems to float above the corona glow of down light giving it a metaphysical presence in the space.

In contrast to the font the altar of Portland stone laid in courses grows out of the floor, the sweeping lines leading the form upwards to a slender sacrificial holy surface. The Purbeck limestone speaks of the layers of geological strata from which the altar is formed. The altar and font stand in dialectic opposition along the axis of the nave, yet their use of parabolic forms and the weight of their respective bases upon which the sacred artefacts are delicately placed establish a dialogue across the space.

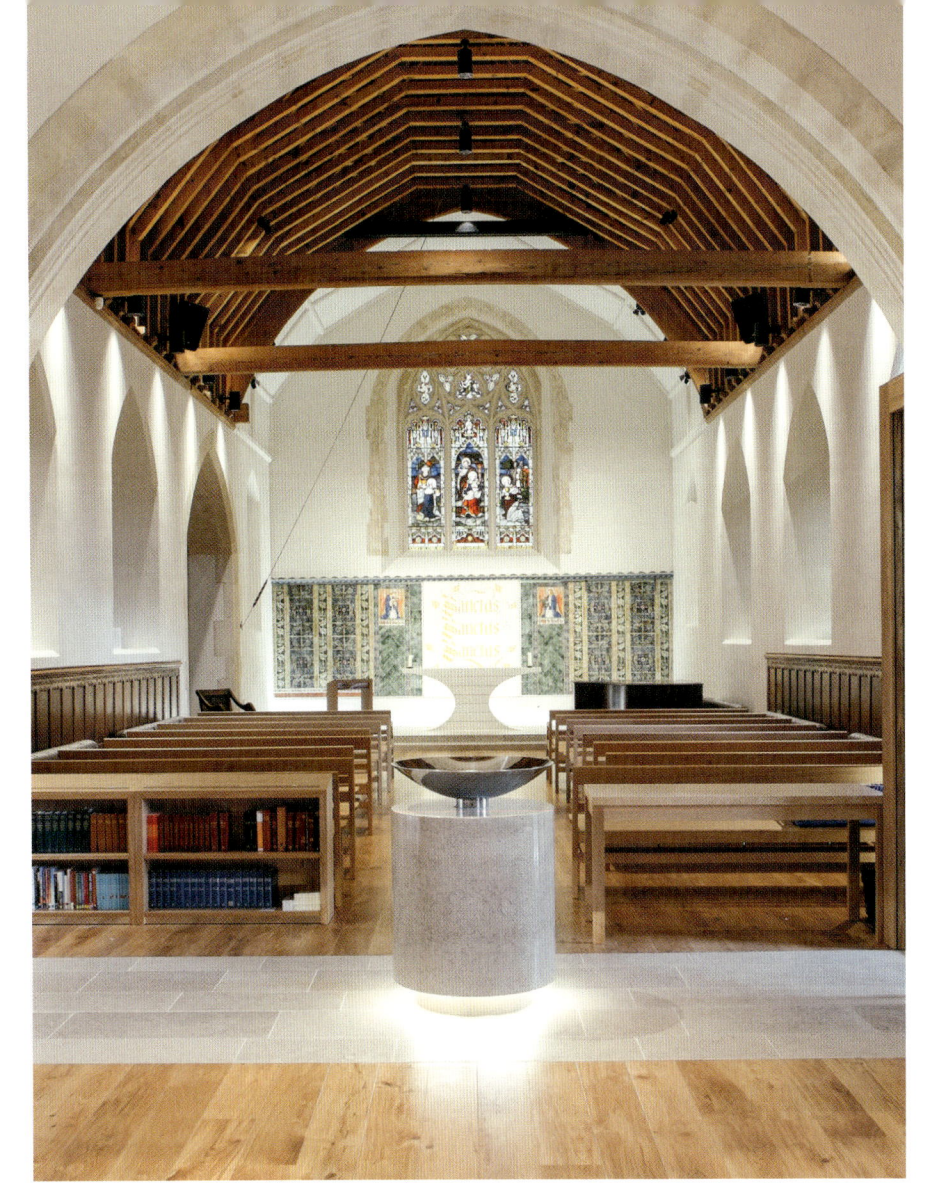

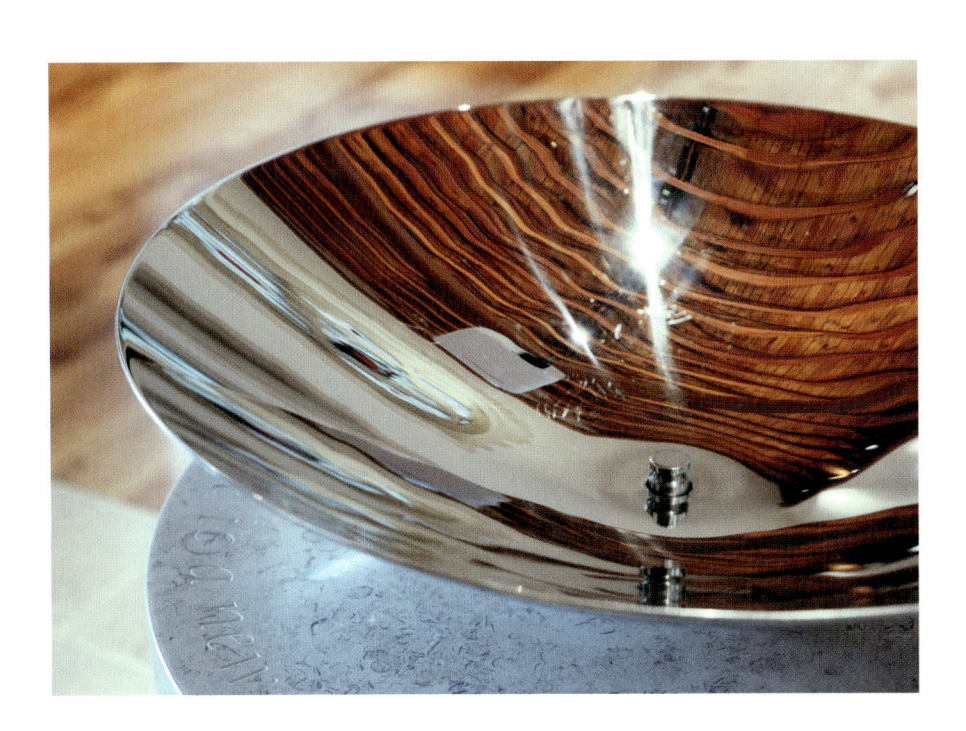

CRAFT | 59

Arrière-Garde and Avant-Garde

ABOVE
An example of a twelfth-century reliquary box.

At the beginning of the twenty-first century the relationship of craftsmanship to architecture represented many of the philosophical problems faced by Ruskin and Gropius. Whilst Ruskin and Gropius sought to grapple with the implications of industrial progress in an age of mechanical reproduction, today we face the challenges of the digital era. In a world of ever more rapid technological progress, the feeling of alienation that the virtual world has engendered across society mirrors the dislocation of the early factory workers. The need for individual identity and personal expression again competes with an obligation to embrace a universal technological future, resulting for many in mental tensions and a sense of cognitive dissociation; this then creates an impulse to seek refuge in the perceived safety of ideological extremes. In search of such certainty, the arrière-garde response of historicism mirrors the nostalgia of Ruskin for a return to the world of hands-on making, manifest in a rebirth of traditional skills in architecture. Proponents of this view have drawn heavily on phenomenology and a return to the nature of things, materials and the processes of shaping tangible material properties of architecture and focussed on their poetic possibilities to evoke human emotion and to create atmosphere, all deeply rooted in the human memory of experience. At the other extreme, avant-garde architects have sought to embrace the technological future and in particular the possibilities of digital design processes. The sweeping curves and amorphous forms of parametric computer aided design have resulted in buildings of otherwise unimaginable shape, whose increasing complexity is driven by the ever more sophisticated tools of digital representation and methods of digital manufacture. They have heralded an age of digital craftsmanship where the traditional skill wrought from many hours of practice of the hand on fine material find an analogue in the technical prowess required for the creation, manipulation and refinement of the virtual architectural model.

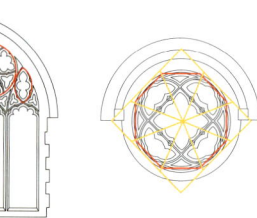

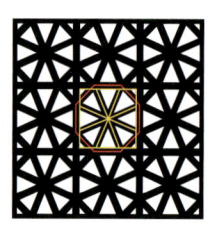

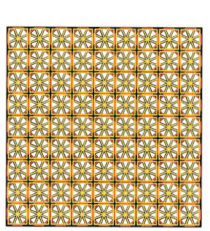

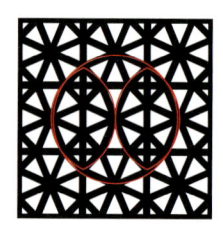

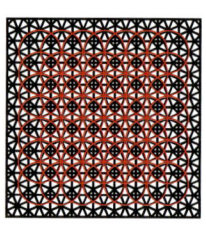

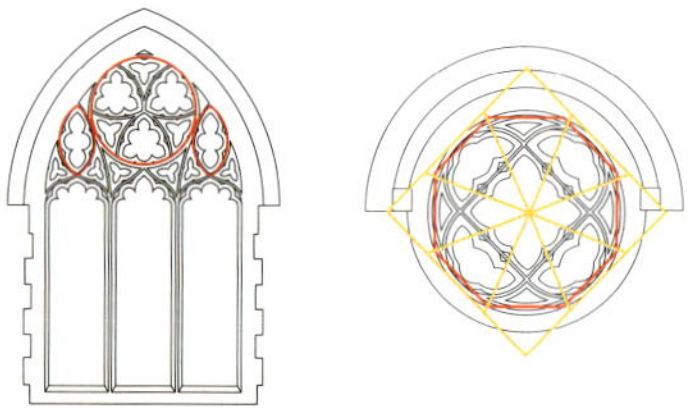

ABOVE & RIGHT
Abstracted patterns derived from the tracery windows of the main chapel.

WINTON CHAPEL EXTENSION, UNIVERSITY OF WINCHESTER

The Chapel extension uses a limited palette of materials. Delicate timber strips give vertical emphasis to the walls which are capped with a band of light that folds around the space, evoking the eternal homogenous folded geometry of the wall and roof. The horizontal band intersects a vertical shaft of light to form a crucifix and here the architecture and object merge so that the space itself can be considered as both building and object, a jewel-like interior of indeterminate scale. Both form and material are brought together into an expressive unity.

The Chapel is conceived as a reliquary box—the metalwork casket commonly used in medieval times to preserve and deify the remains of saints. These boxes often took the form of a rectangular base with vertical sides topped by two sloping top faces, meeting at a central ridge adorned with a raised strip and decoration. The box thus resembled a miniature house or tomb, and the lavish decoration of gold and jewels expressed the sacred nature of its contents.

BUILDING STORIES | 60

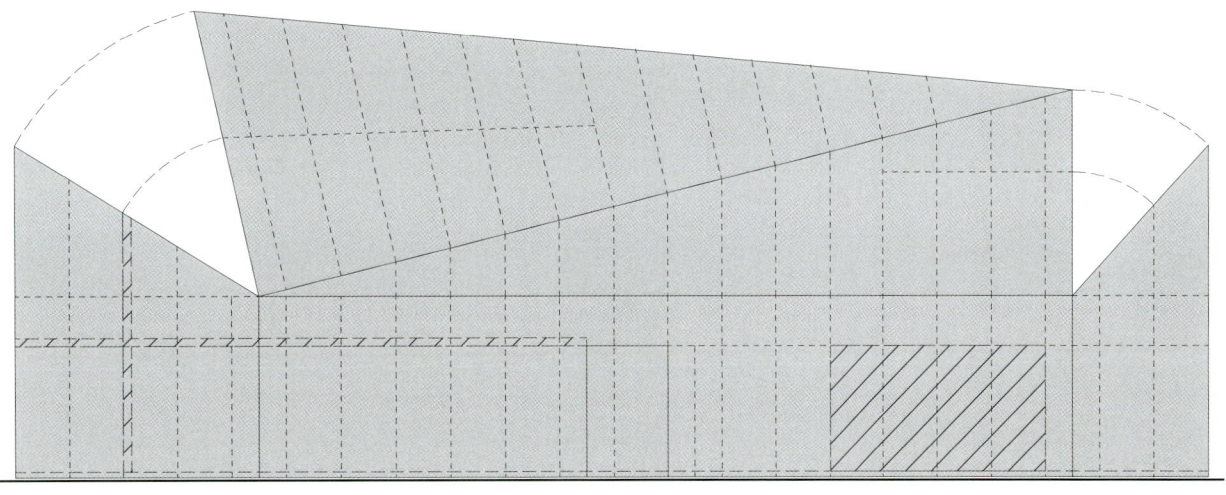

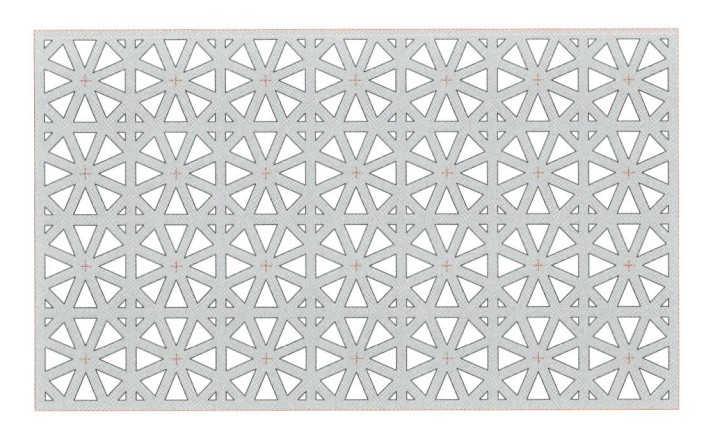

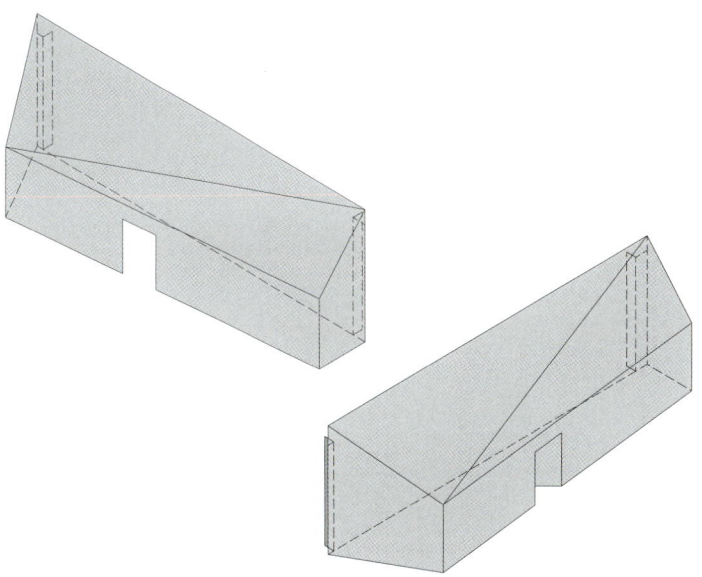

ABOVE
Fabrication drawing of the Chapel extension showing how it can be folded from a single sheet of paper.

BELOW
Development model of the extension including the abstracted pattern derived from the tracery windows of the main chapel.

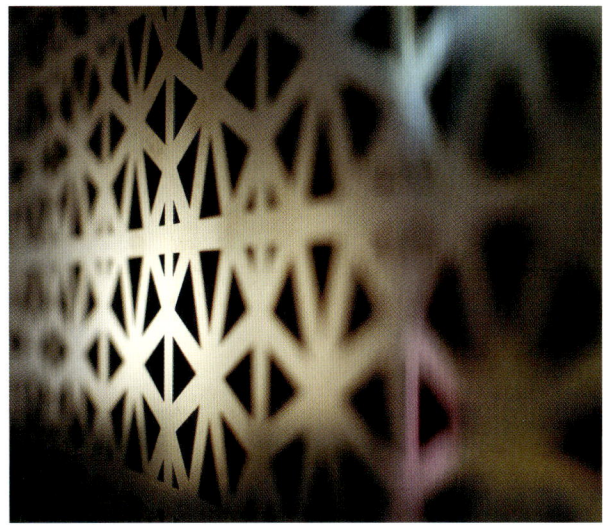

CRAFT | 61

ABOVE

Seen from inside the existing chapel, the stained glass windows of the Victorian structure are reflected into the new extension. The abstract qualities of the extension are juxtaposed with the figurative representations of biblical narratives in the refurbished chapel.

ABOVE RIGHT

External visualisation of cross-section through the chapel extension.

WINTON CHAPEL EXTENSION, UNIVERSITY OF WINCHESTER

The University of Winchester's Winton Chapel extension takes the form of a pitched roof structure which mirrors that of the existing building and allows light to penetrate into the perimeter exterior spaces. The ridge oversails the existing building's eaves line, creating a clerestory window that provides both light and ventilation at high level. To respond to the site edge the plan of the side chapel is tapered. This gives additional width to the chapel space that can be entered either from a discrete recessed north door or via the existing chapel interior.

This plan form creates a twist in the pitched roof bringing an intriguing geometric dynamic to the new addition which is wrapped in a diaphanous and textural surface that is continuous over both roof and wall, allowing the building to be interpreted at different distances and scales. The geometry of the Gothic tracery within the east and west windows of the existing chapel provides the source for a pattern that is both referential to the existing architecture and an interpretation appropriate for the twenty-first century.

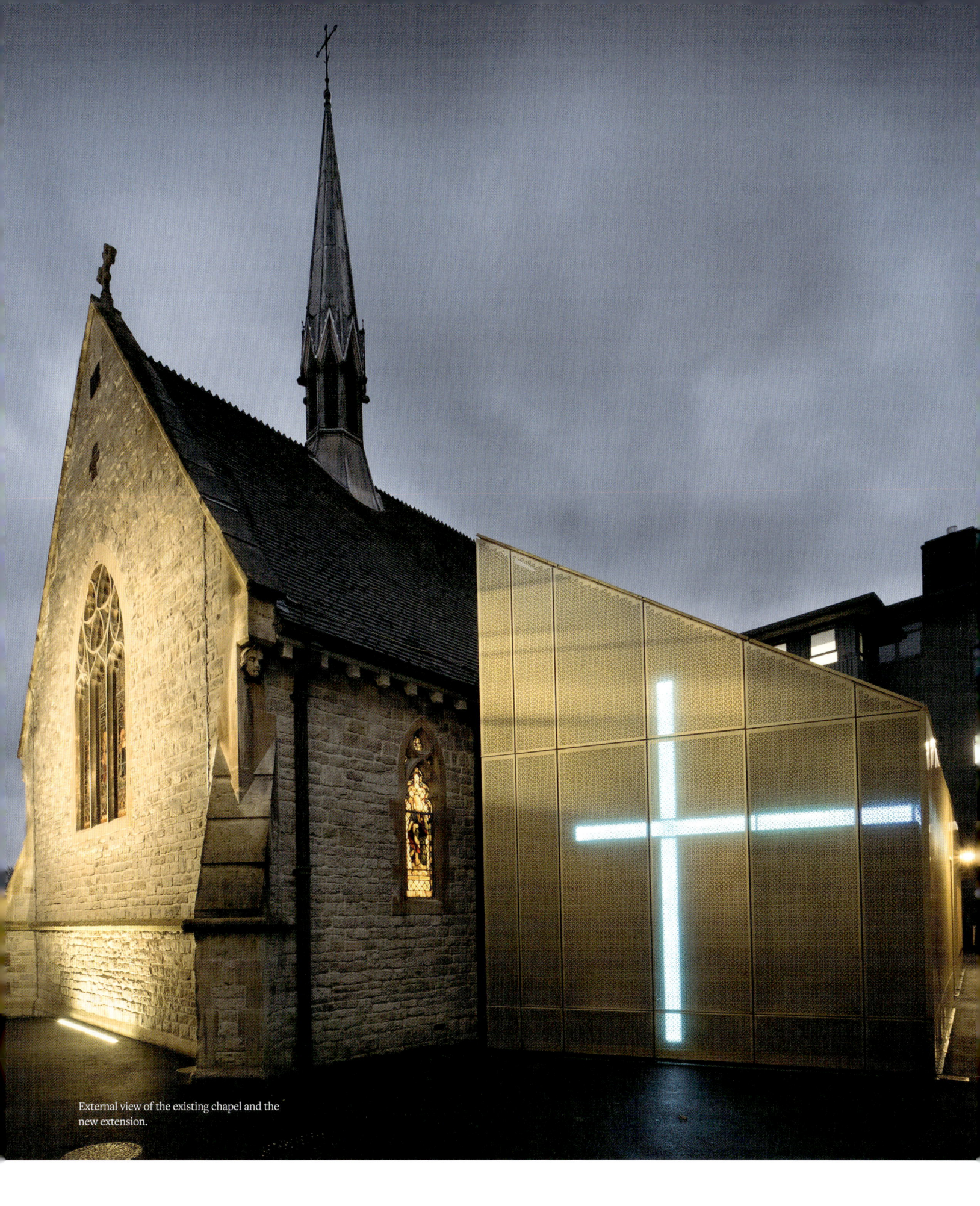

External view of the existing chapel and the new extension.

CRAFT | 63

Iteration and Refinement

In recent years two opposing views of architecture and its relationship to craft have emerged. On the one hand is a return to historic craft skills whilst on the other a wish to embrace the modern world of digital technologies. Too often these appear to be competing for architectural territory; however, these seemingly polar opposites might be simply the manifestation of the same concern with the way in which buildings are made. Technology today is not only part of the construction process but an integral aspect of the design process itself, with the craftsmanship of modelling, testing and refining architecture in the design studio extending continuously to the workshop and building site.

To elaborate this way of thinking, the etymology of the term 'techne', from which the term technology is derived, is informative. Techne is a term in philosophy which resembles episteme in the implication of knowledge of principles, although techne differs in that its intent is in the making or doing as opposed to disinterested understanding. In the classical world techne was most often associated with the craftsmanship, craft or art of how something was done; rather than the idea of abstract study of knowledge, techne was concerned with the application of knowledge through practice. This idea of application and practice is one of the primary roles of the architect. The architectural project affords the focus for directed action and this action is in itself a continuous process, the method of which flows consistently from the concept through to the realised building. Central to this process, which is at heart one of craftsmanship, is the need for testing, prototyping and iteration. It is the process of architecture and the art of this process becomes a crafted activity in its own right. The story of this process, the craftsmanship of making, thus does not differentiate the tools of the creative process but rather concerns itself with the story of how something is made and in this way the narrative, the story of techne, permeates all aspects of the architect's work.[4]

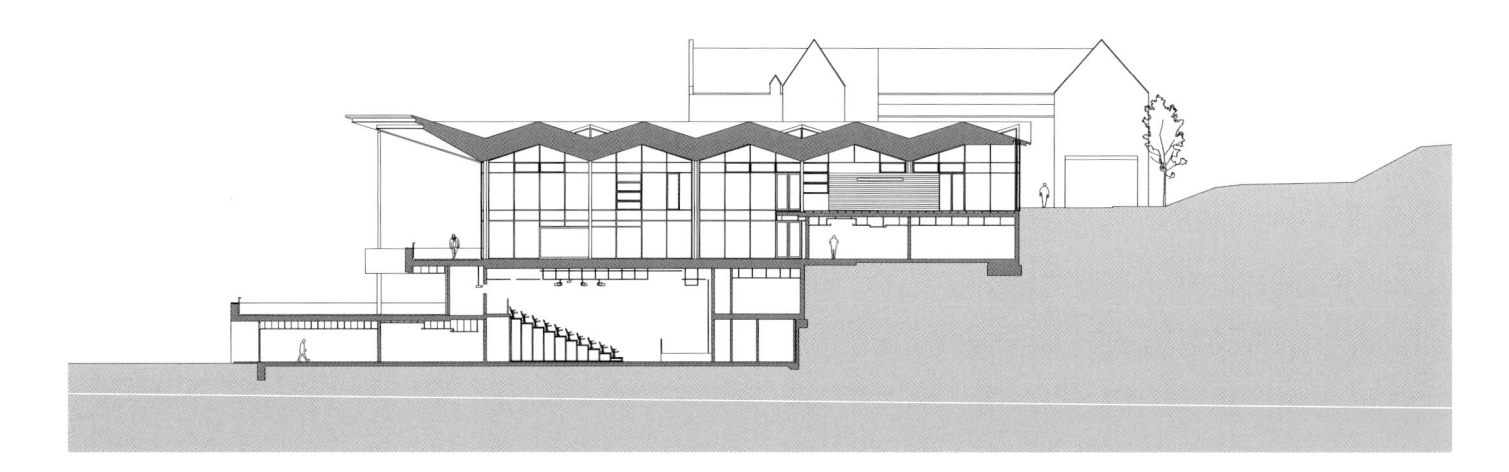

ABOVE
Concept models showing development options for the main roof to the University Centre at University of Winchester.

BELOW
Long section through the University Centre.

ABOVE
1:500 context model exploring relationship of roof and terraces to existing buildings and topography.

ABOVE RIGHT
Internal view of folded roof to Food Hall.

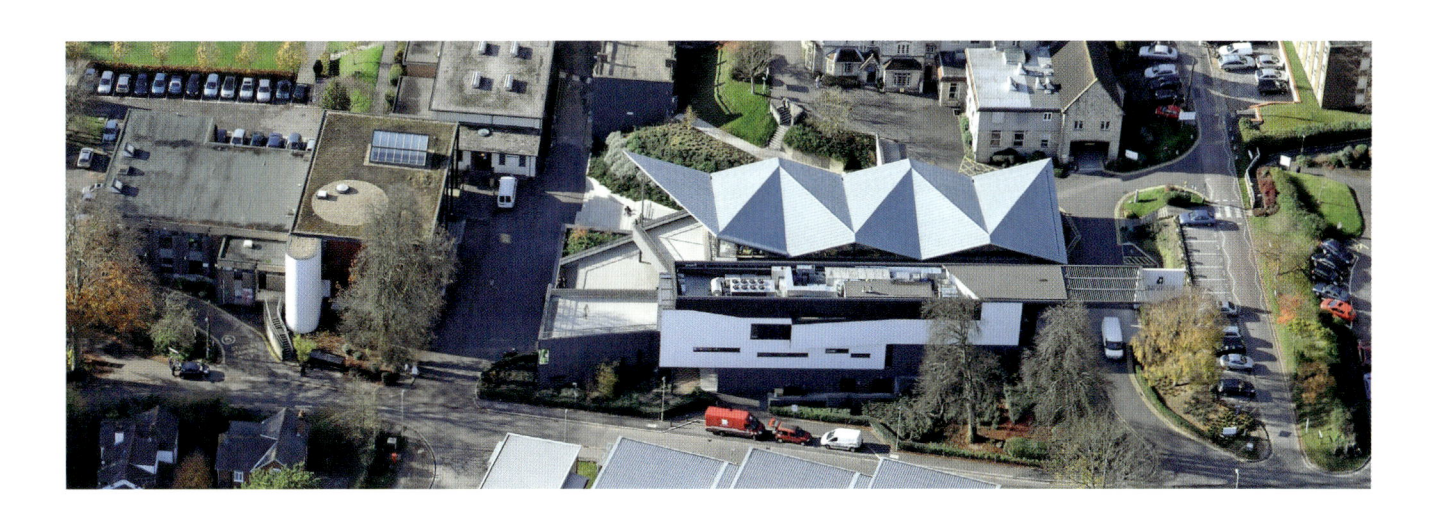

ABOVE
Aerial view of the completed University Centre at University of Winchester.

UNIVERSITY CENTRE, UNIVERSITY OF WINCHESTER

The University of Winchester University Centre uses the folded plane of an undulating roof that floats out into space above the steeply sloping site. The roof is a strong visual point of reference from around the campus and forms an important boundary between the university and the city. The roof is an exercise in the possibilities of geometric form developed from the folding of a single sheet, drawing on the folded geometry of origami, the ancient Japanese art of paper folding where intricate and complex designs are generated from a series of intrinsically simple transformations of the sheet. The sculpted form undergoes a series of iterations in the form of prototypes, with the depth of fold and angle of inclination varied. The final solution is tested for both its effect on the external appearance in the context of the surrounding campus and for its effect when viewed from beneath and inside the building.

ABOVE
View of University Centre at University of Winchester from the lower piazza.

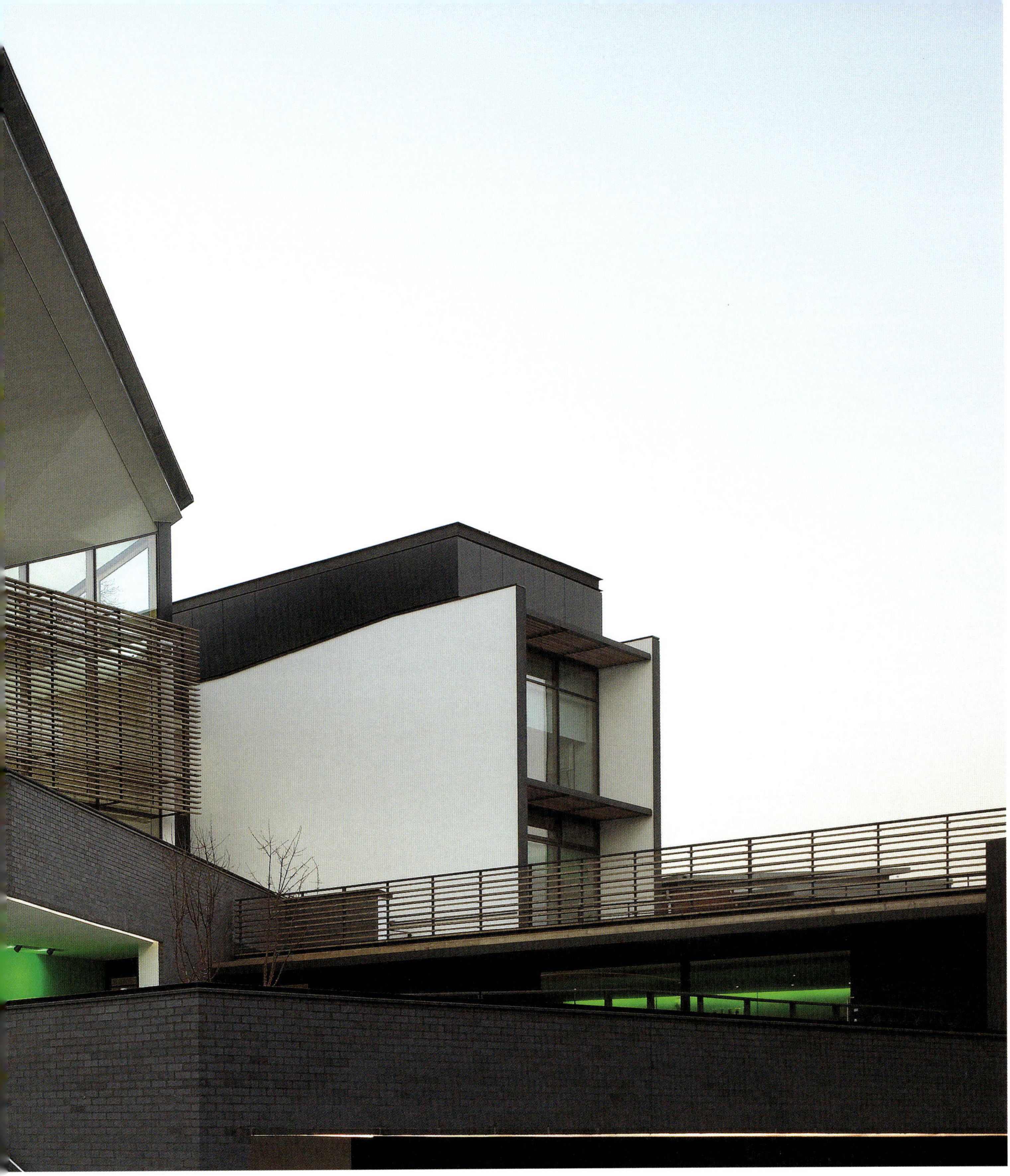

Sequence
Spatial Sequence

To experience architecture is to move through space. The way in which people move through buildings and the character of the spaces they encounter together form a sequence of experiences whose unfolding pattern gives each building a unique story. The spatial sequence through a building constitutes a particular narrative told through an orchestrated architectural arrangement whose events and structure make for a particular sequence of affective experiences.

The idea of architecture seen as an unfolding story, seen in perspective space from the viewpoint of the moving observer, was identified by Gordon Cullen in his book *The Concise Townscape*, 1961. Cullen prioritised architecture conceived from eye level rather than depicting the environment as a traditional plan and emphasised the idea of what he termed 'serial views', presented in sketchy perspective images as a sequence of freeze frame views through the eye of an observer moving through space.[1] Understanding distant landmarks that draw us towards them, the importance of light and shade along with areas of contained space contrasting with open vistas were what Cullen felt made for an engaging and visually rich experience. He also considered in some detail the textures and surfaces that made for a stimulating and tactile environment, enhanced through the devices of contrast and juxtaposition. All of this was built on a uniquely empirical approach to design, one that was concerned with buildings and spaces that had their origins in human experience rather than the abstractions of plan or elevation.

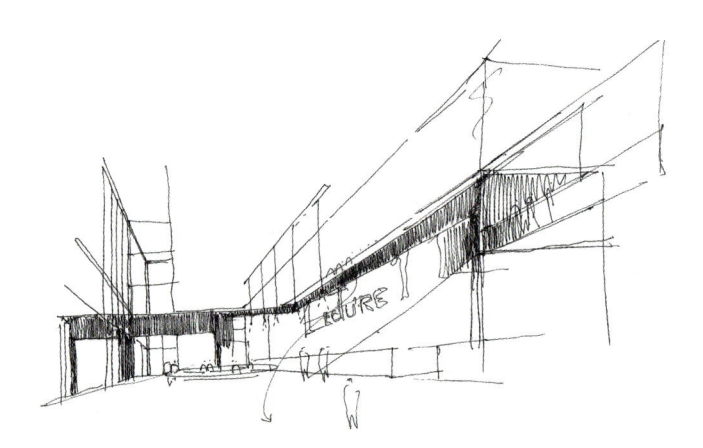

ABOVE
Sketch by Gordon Cullen.

ABOVE RIGHT
Conceptual sketch of ribbon in the reception area.

OPPOSITE
Reception area of the John Henry Brookes Building at Oxford Brookes University.

JOHN HENRY BROOKES BUILDING, OXFORD BROOKES UNIVERSITY

As with Cullen, the sketch perspective is a key tool in the work of Design Engine, seeing spaces firstly in perspective, as they would be experienced by the moving observer. This design method begins with the spatial quality from which the plan, elevation, section and other orthographic abstractions are then derived, rather than commencing from such abstractions and moving towards experience.

This design process is inductive in that it moves from specific instances, in this case observational sketches, towards a general conclusion of the plan. In contrast, rational planning commences with the abstractions of the overall schema and, following deductive steps, determines the instances of experience.

BUILDING STORIES | 68

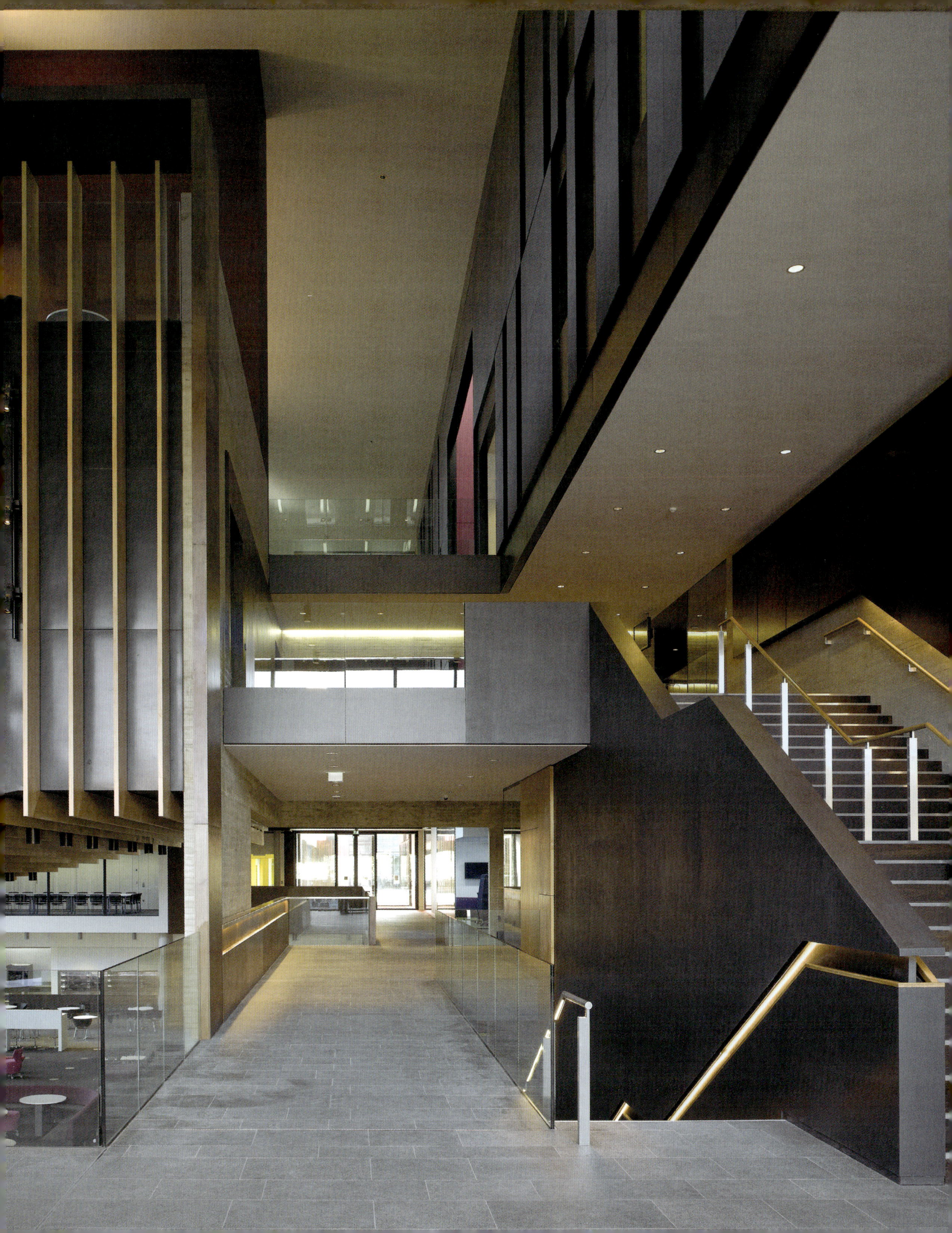

01
The colonnade element of the ribbon draws visitors into the campus and helps to give unity to the retail units behind.

02
The ribbon of steel crosses the atrium close to the entrance and links the outside of the buildings with the arrival spaces within.

03
Further into the atrium the ribbon reappears, guiding visitors to spaces further within the campus.

04
The ribbon terminates by wrapping around the food hall and finally forming a vertical chimney.

BUILDING STORIES | 70

01   02 03   04

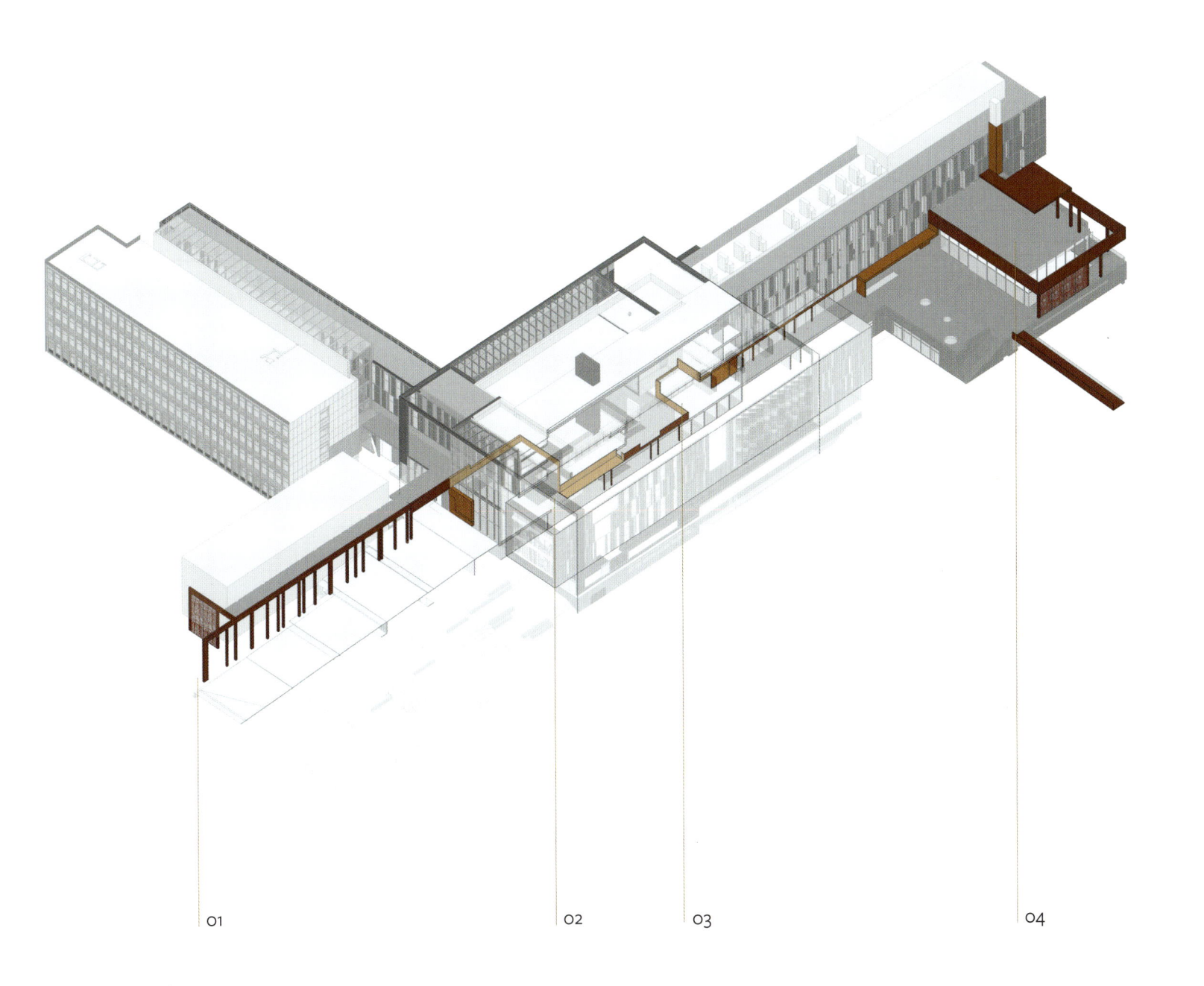

JOHN HENRY BROOKES BUILDING, OXFORD BROOKES UNIVERSITY

The principal point of entry to the new John Henry Brookes Building is set one storey above the existing Abercrombie Building and inner courtyard level. This required a change in level of 2.5 metres from Headington Road, in the process creating a gentle ramped approach to the building through a generous public piazza. On entry (at level one) you are then at the main circulation level and benefit from an elevated view across the forum, aiding orientation and legibility of the building, increasing the functionality of the forum space at level zero and crucially providing fluid movement to the Student Union, pooled teaching rooms and food hall.

To give clarity and emphasis to the journey from the stepped piazza into the new John Henry Brookes Building, inspiration was taken from Paul Klee's idea of 'taking a line for a walk'. The line is made manifest by the introduction of a ribbon of weathered steel. This helps to enhance the principal point of entry as well as reinforce the primary circulation route that leads through the building.

The building makes explicit its narrative sequence as a great rusted steel ribbon winds its way through the building. The ribbon changes scale, at once a towering colonnade yet elsewhere a handrail. These shifts in scale and purpose are met by a directional change in the route, at the point of transition from one narrative scene to the next. Each change in the progression through the building heralds the transition to new spaces or functions.

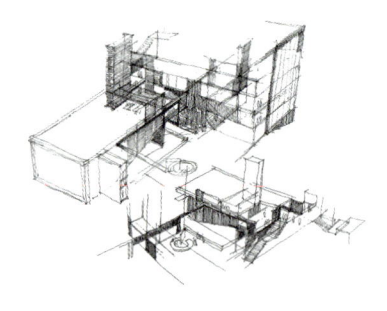

The Picturesque

ABOVE
Sketches explaining how the spaces connect throughout the John Henry Brookes Building.

BELOW
Long-section illustrating changes in levels through the building from the entrance piazza through to the food hall at the rear.

OPPOSITE
Concept model of the Corten Ribbon inspired by Paul Klee's ideas on 'taking a line for a walk'.

The idea of spatial sequence through buildings has its origins in the empirical tradition and in particular that of the English landscape garden. The great eighteenth-century gardens of Stowe, Stourhead and Rousham were in many ways a physical manifestation of the mythological stories of the ancient classical world popularised at the time in the work of the Romantic poets. The aesthetic appeal of sensory delight, variety and contrast was captured in Edmund Burke's melding of the sublime and beautiful aesthetic experience to the middle ground of what he termed the picturesque.[2] The Grand Tour and a fascination with all things ancient led not only to the classical revival in the work of architects like Robert Adam, but also a fascination with the epic allegorical stories told through landscape. Homer's *Odyssey*, describing the heroic journey of Odysseus, could thus be captured and viscerally experienced through landscaped gardens constructed to dramatise the unfolding narrative sequence.

To embody this narrative, the gardens included classical temples as station points along the route around the grounds, with seats framing picturesque views which copied the asymmetrical compositions of Claude Lorrain and Nicholas Poussin's allegorical painting. These canvases used the idea of fore, middle and background scenes to draw the eye deep into the painting, and great contrasts of light, texture and colour add to the drama and the artworks themselves. As these paintings drew the observer into the hidden meanings of the scene so too eighteenth-century picturesque gardens relied on mystery and intrigue, where having been presented with a framed vista the route onwards was often ambiguous, exciting the observer's curiosity. The scene offered and then denied was like the unfolding narrative of a great novel whose climax is hinted at yet constantly deferred, drawing the reader on with a sense of enquiry and surprise.

JOHN HENRY BROOKES BUILDING

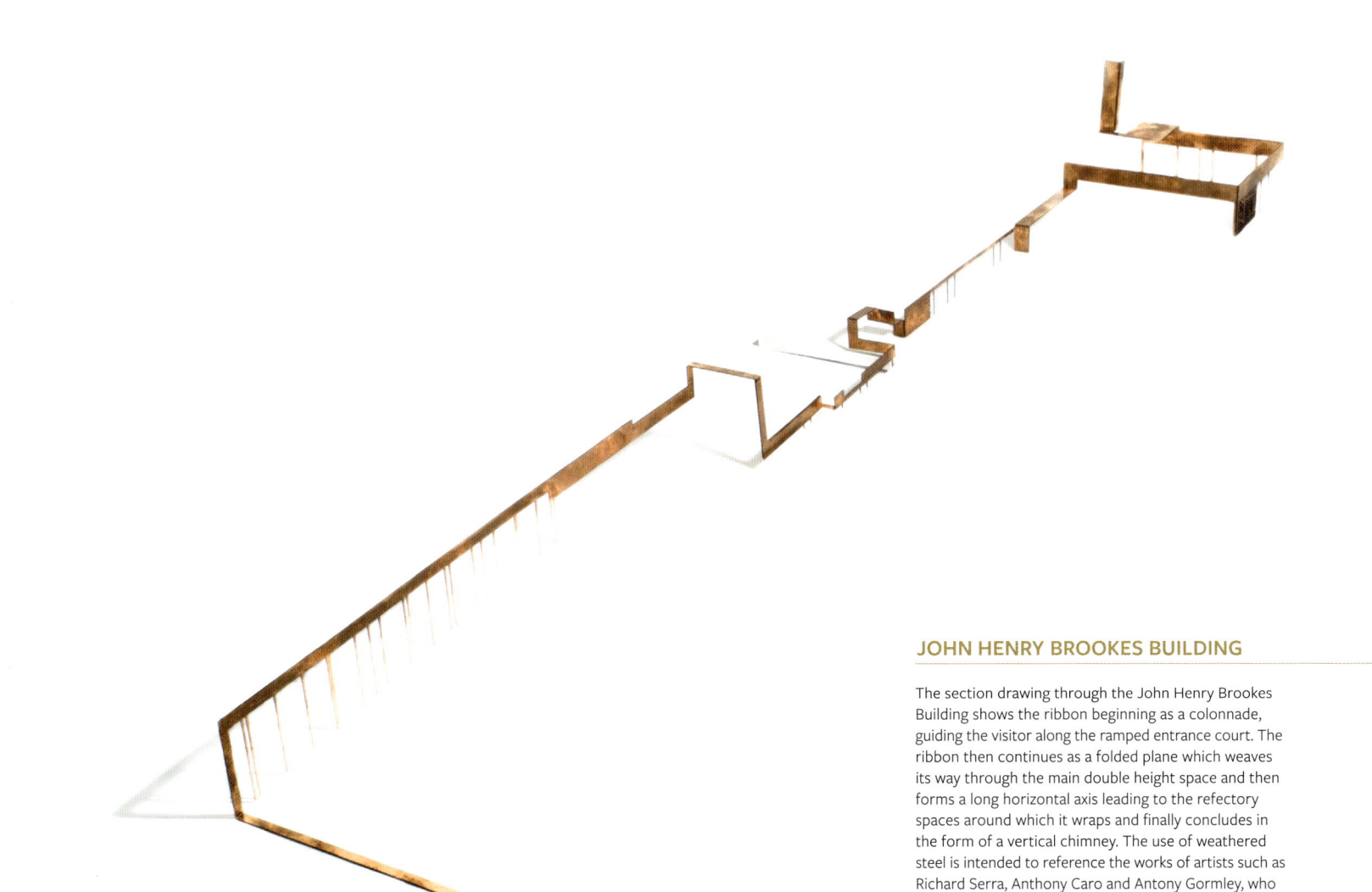

The section drawing through the John Henry Brookes Building shows the ribbon beginning as a colonnade, guiding the visitor along the ramped entrance court. The ribbon then continues as a folded plane which weaves its way through the main double height space and then forms a long horizontal axis leading to the refectory spaces around which it wraps and finally concludes in the form of a vertical chimney. The use of weathered steel is intended to reference the works of artists such as Richard Serra, Anthony Caro and Antony Gormley, who used the material in many of their public artworks.

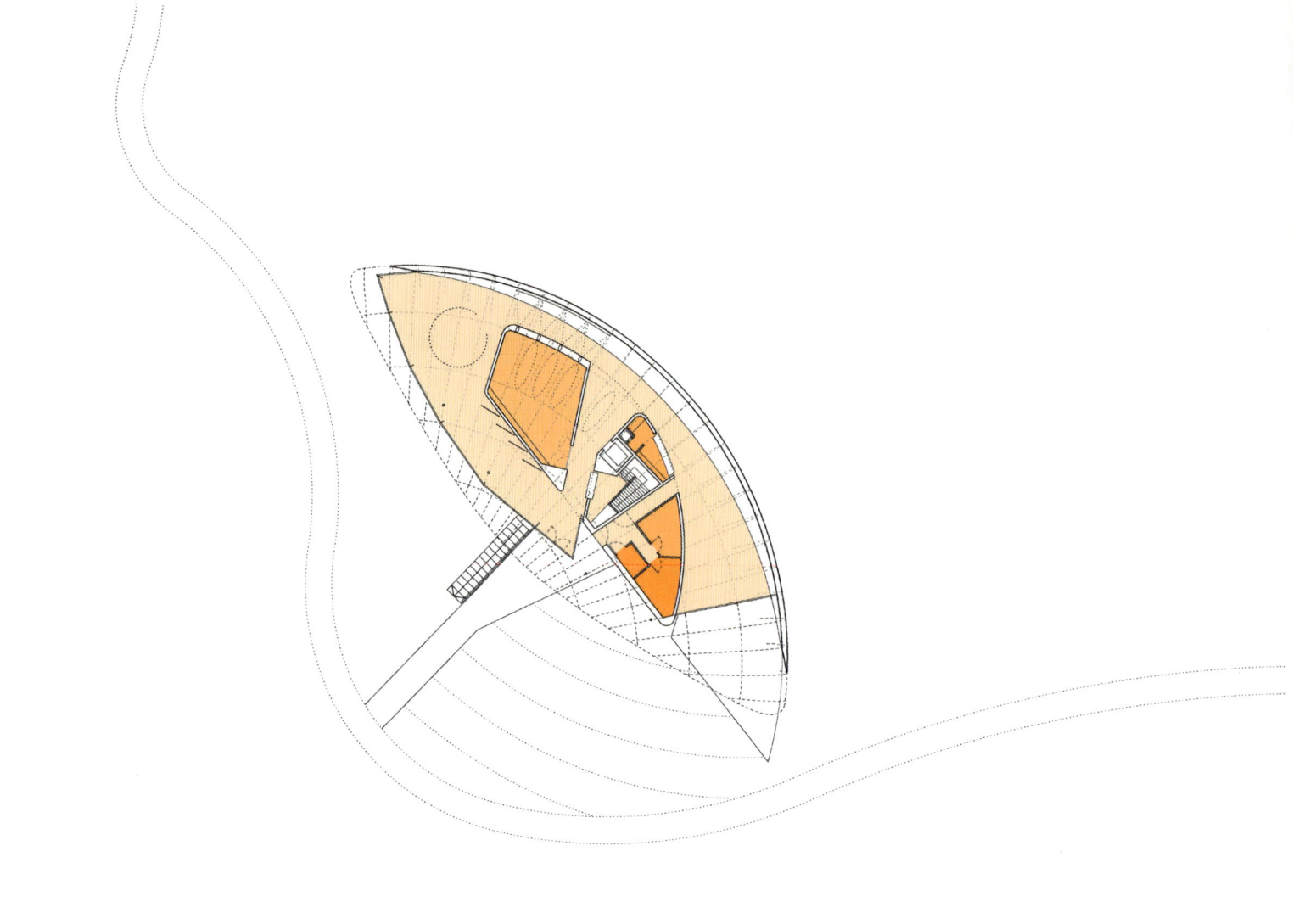

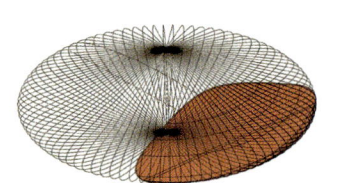

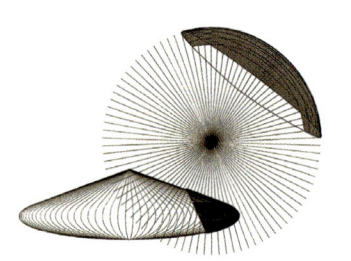

The English picturesque garden tradition was built on the idea of moving around the landscape with a carefully positioned series of temples, each carefully framed according to specific vistas where the viewing angle towards each element was considered as a painted scene captured in an enclosing border. Framing views and locating temples and follies formed series of unique events often with allegoric meaning. The journey between each temple set in the landscape formed a narrative sequence through which the visitor was led onwards along a storyline of unfolding events.

The framed landscape view was considered to relate to the cone of human vision, the region of the eye's perception which in humans extends at 30 degrees about a central point. This area of sight or field of view is central when considering the experience of architecture from the perspective of the moving observer.

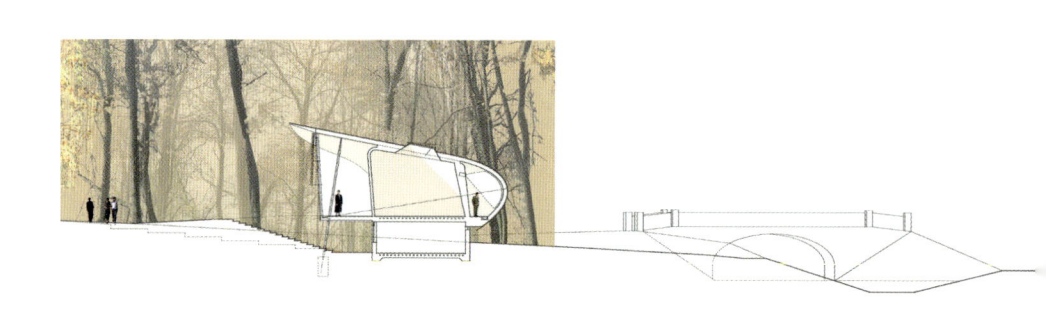

BUILDING STORIES | 74

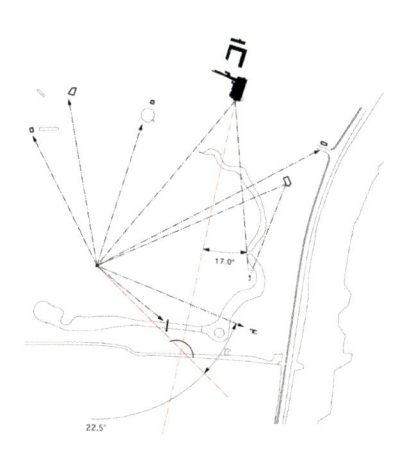

HERITAGE RESOURCE CENTRE, HARDWICK HALL PARK

Set within the grounds of Hardwick Park, the proposal for the new Heritage Resource Centre in County Durham provides a welcome departure from the generic. The form is designed using lessons learned from bridge building technology, each skeletal sector being clad in Corten steel for a naturally protected 'rust' finish. It is inspired by the kernel of a beech nut and reflects the surrounding woodland setting. The natural organic form also makes reference to the land art of the sculptor Andy Goldsworthy and its rusted steel skin evokes the serpentine curves of Richard Serra.

The building hovers above the landscape and forms a protective shell formed of an angular segment of a surface of revolution. This precise Euclidean geometry reflects the angular location of the centre from the important buildings and temples of the park. A series of Victorian follies are located on strict geometric lines from the house and, in order to avoid ambiguity, the new centre sits as a 'found' object in a wooded site, imitating the natural forms such as a seed pod. Its location responds to the geometrical logic of the park by using two acknowledged angles which have been previously identified as part of the fabric of the picturesque layout.

The overall orientation of the centre is placed on a 22.5 degree line radiating from the centre of the Temple of Minerva. The second ordering line is set at 17 degrees from a line radiating from the front of the hall through the fort grotto. This line serves two purposes; firstly to lock the position of the centre at the point where it crosses the 22.5 degree line, but also to order the internal orientation of the centre. People entering the centre are channelled through the entrance area at which point they are directly facing the front of the Hall and even though they are unaware of this it serves to reinforce certain aspects of the design of the park.

In spite of the fact that the design of the new centre uses certain geometric games to establish the location and orientation, it is not intended that this new geometry imposes itself in any other way on the closed system of the park. It is partly for this reason that the form of the centre has been designed as a counterpoint to the structures which exist, albeit in some instances as only marks on the ground around the park.

ABOVE
Initial concept sketch of 'seed pod' nestling within the forest at Hardwick Hall Heritage Resource Centre.

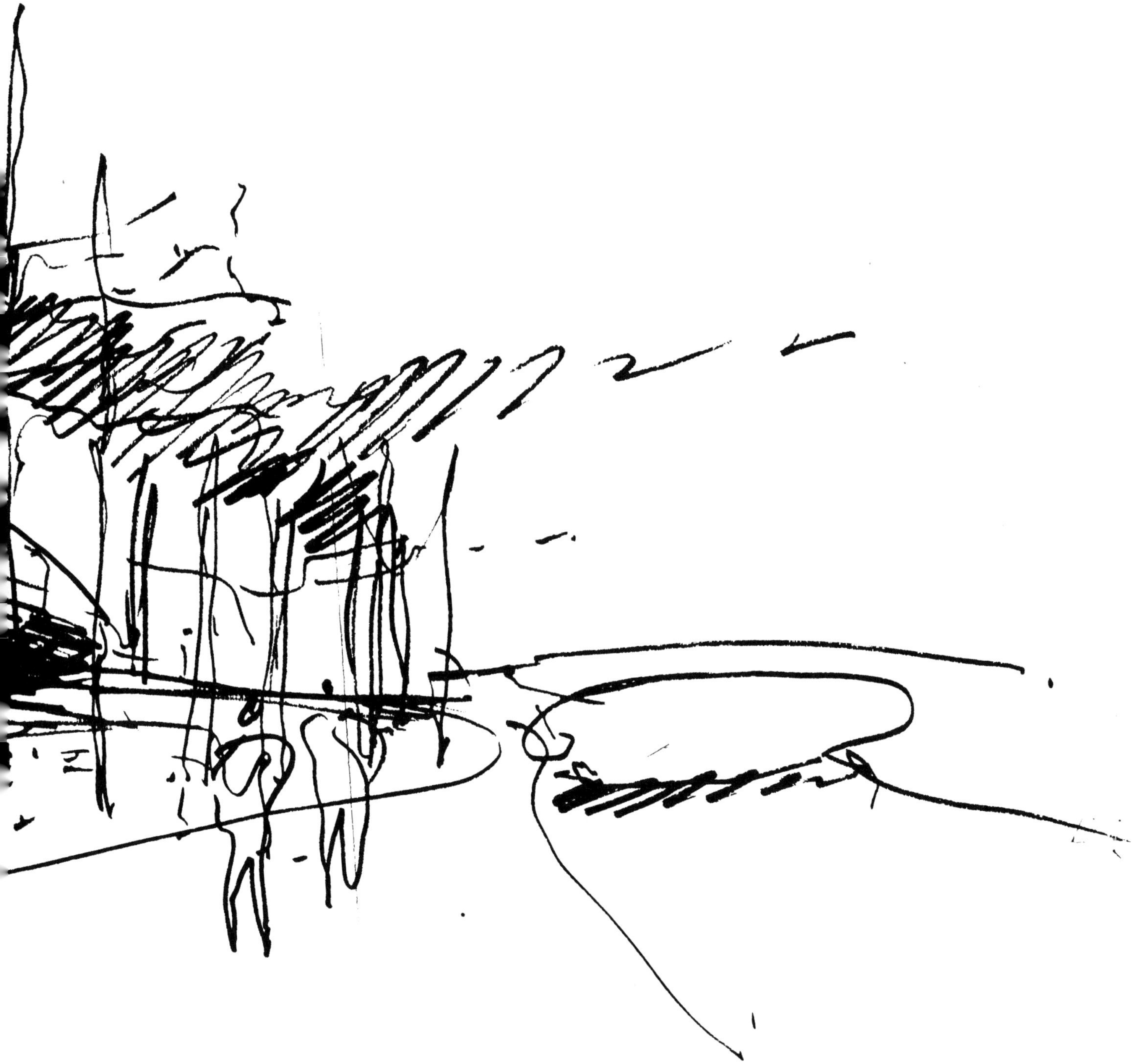

The Hierarchy of Sequence

For any spatial sequence to have meaning it requires a hierarchy of events. Some events are more important than others, and this can be emphasised by their duration and spectacle. Whilst each spatial experience might have its own character, the contrast between events through light, colour and volume gives a rhythm to the sequence, and as such each building story has a unique and carefully orchestrated pattern. To think of architecture in this way, as the idea of a journey punctuated by a series of events, is a metaphor of the building as a story and architecture as a poetic narrative, an unfolding drama or play whose rules of arrangement were first set out by the Greek philosopher Aristotle.

Aristotle's *Poetics*, 350 BCE, is the earliest surviving treatise on the theory of drama. Intended as a guide for the writers of literature and plays, Aristotle set out the rules for tragedy, epic poetry and comedy. Whilst Aristotle saw the poetic process as one of mimesis or imitation of real situations rather than that of invention in the mind or hypothesis, the structures that he described have strong parallels with architecture.[3] The purpose of drama according to Aristotle was to arouse specific affective emotions; he identifies pity and fear as the key elements of catharsis, through the experience of which in the form of drama one is purged of these emotions and thus afterwards in some way emotionally strengthened.

ABOVE
Context model showing the importance of the position of the new building within the context of the entire site.

OPPOSITE TOP
Exploded axonometric of the Learning Centre.

BUILDING STORIES | 78

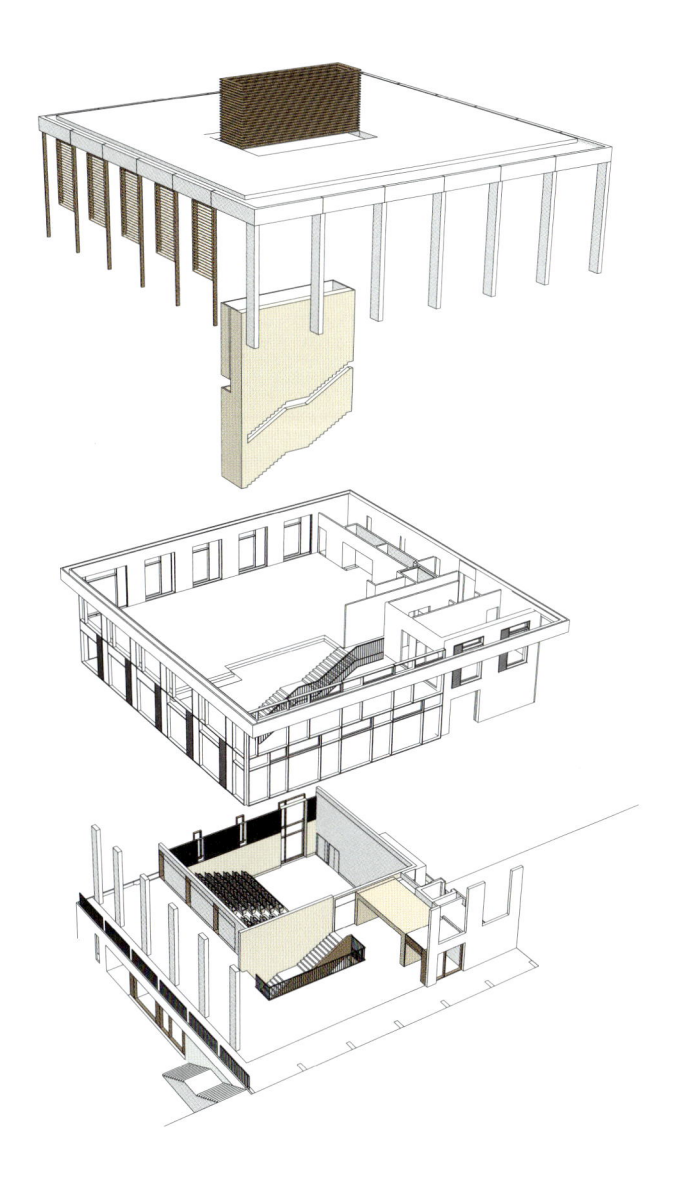

CENTRE FOR LEARNING, DOWNE HOUSE SCHOOL

The project for a new Centre for Learning at Downe House School is a search for a hierarchy of meaning. As with many campus plans which have developed in an incremental manner over time a sense of coherent narrative can be lost. Each building is like an actor in a play, and whilst each might have its own merits, the narrative of each to the other is absent and the whole assembly confused. In re-establishing a coherent story Design Engine have focused the campus around a colonnaded building which when seen in perspective from around the campus provides a visual and experiential locus. Sitting at the heart of the campus, it serves as a hub for the key spaces of learning and day-to-day activities: a new library, multi-purpose auditorium, teaching spaces, cafe, shop, resources hub and offices.

The Centre is a physical and visual draw into the campus from the main entrance and reinforces connections to the surrounding woodland which gives the school its unique setting. It is a moment of spectacle in the architectural drama of the school. Whilst modest in scale the colonnade frames the surrounding vistas and sits as a focal point in the frame of the campus.

01
View upon arrival at the school.

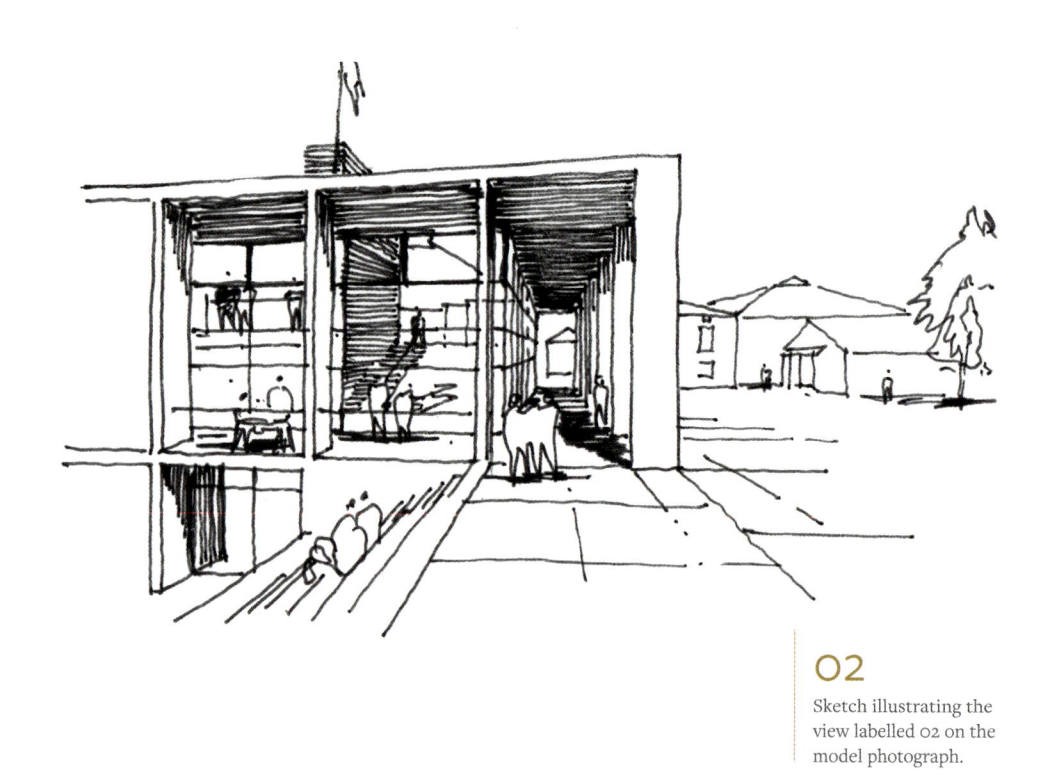

02
Sketch illustrating the view labelled 02 on the model photograph.

03
Sketch illustrating the view labelled 03 on the model photograph.

BUILDING STORIES | 80

04
Visualisation illustrating the view labelled 04 on the model photograph.

Aristotle identifies plot, character, theme, language, rhythm and spectacle as the key elements of play. Of these plot, rhythm and spectacle have clearly identifiable architectural parallels.

Firstly, plot comprises the arrangement of events or incidents on the stage and focuses on a series of defined events that occur in sequence. These events can be further defined as particular plot 'points', often when a character has to make a choice which is often a moral decision that will go on to influence future events, and there are clear equivalents in architecture where the choice of route through a building comes to influence the observer's future experiences. Rhythm sets the pace of these events as each character and the language they use develops at a unique pace which, when witnessed together, give the play a direction and impetus leading to a climax and the rhythm of the play creates its unique mood. In architecture this might be seen as the speed of a space, how fast we move through it along with the interfaces between various spaces as one architectural experience transitions to the next. For spectacle, Aristotle described the actors, set, costumes, lights and sounds as the means through which events could be highlighted and made memorable. Such spectacle often relies on visual impact or the feeling of the audience members that they are witnessing events of an impressive scale or of great human significance. Similarly, architecture uses moments of dramatic emphasis to give prominence to certain spaces whilst downplaying others.

CENTRE FOR LEARNING, DOWNE HOUSE SCHOOL

As a focal point on the campus the building provides a point of orientation and introduces a new hierarchy to the existing buildings. The colonnade or peristyle comprises a sequence of layered frames through which one walks. This layering gives the building a unique rhythm and changes the pace of movement, slowing the sequential experience and, without ostentation, provides a moment of spectacle within the sequence of spaces around the school.

The delicacy of the colonnade and lightness of the building intentionally contrast with the deep arcaded reveals of the foreground building. The visual weight of the foreground building is juxtaposed with the lightness of the new learning centre. The deep shadows of the semi-circular arcade are made more apparent by the brightness and delicacy of the new colonnade. As such, a narrative hierarchy is established so that each building can play its part in the overall sequential composition.

Processional Sequence

ABOVE
Procession at St Mary's Episcopal Cathedral, 1998.

BELOW
Cross section looking towards ante-chapel, showing the procession space and the courtyard with the Hawthorn tree.

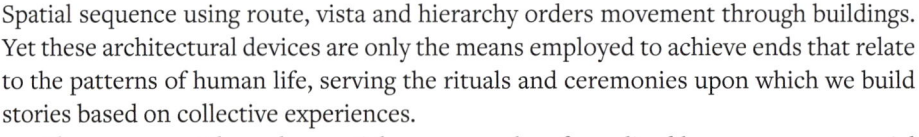

Spatial sequence using route, vista and hierarchy orders movement through buildings. Yet these architectural devices are only the means employed to achieve ends that relate to the patterns of human life, serving the rituals and ceremonies upon which we build stories based on collective experiences.

The movement through a spatial sequence when formalised becomes a ceremonial or ritual act by which we reinforce the structures of society that bind the individual to the collective. Rites of passage where architecture, ritual and procession are brought together persist in societies across the world. From the ritual celebration of birth through the ceremonial rites towards adulthood to the procession along the nave of the church in the marriage service, the spaces which serve to celebrate these stages of human life follow us even into death, and architecture plays an important role in formalising these passages. Buildings have equally been constructed to both serve and emphasise religious or societal hierarchies, and both buildings and objects have taken on a special role in formalising these structures that give order to society. The structure of our political framework is often directly reflected in the parliament buildings made to house debate and decision, whilst the orb and sceptre, crown and throne—the ritualised symbols of monarchy—find meaning only in the ceremonies and places of coronation. Symbolic acts of investiture are synonymous not only with the objects that symbolise status but with the venues, pageants and parades that take place in a specifically orchestrated route and sequence through space and, according to accepted patterns, they become elevated to events of collective significance and shared memory that place them above the everyday.

The tradition of ritual and procession persists across the history of architecture as one of the driving forces that shape buildings and spaces. From the times of ancient Greece to the masterpieces of the Modern movement in architecture the sequence of space employed as a processional device has been a powerful influence on the making of buildings.

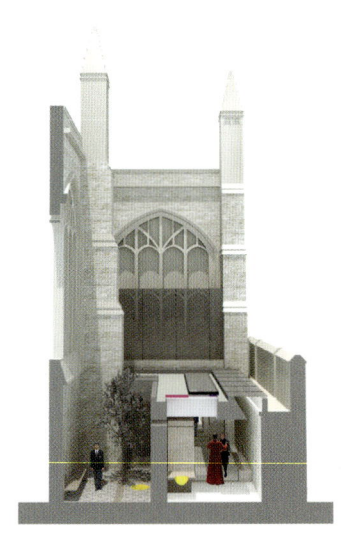

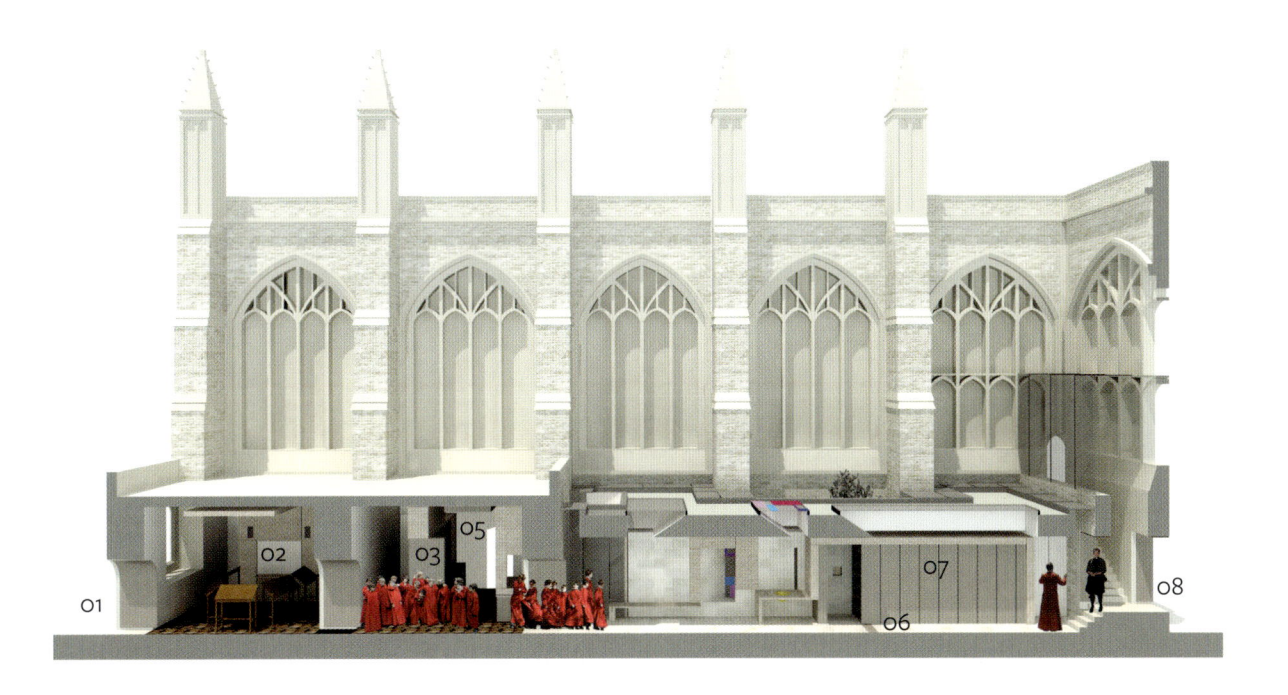

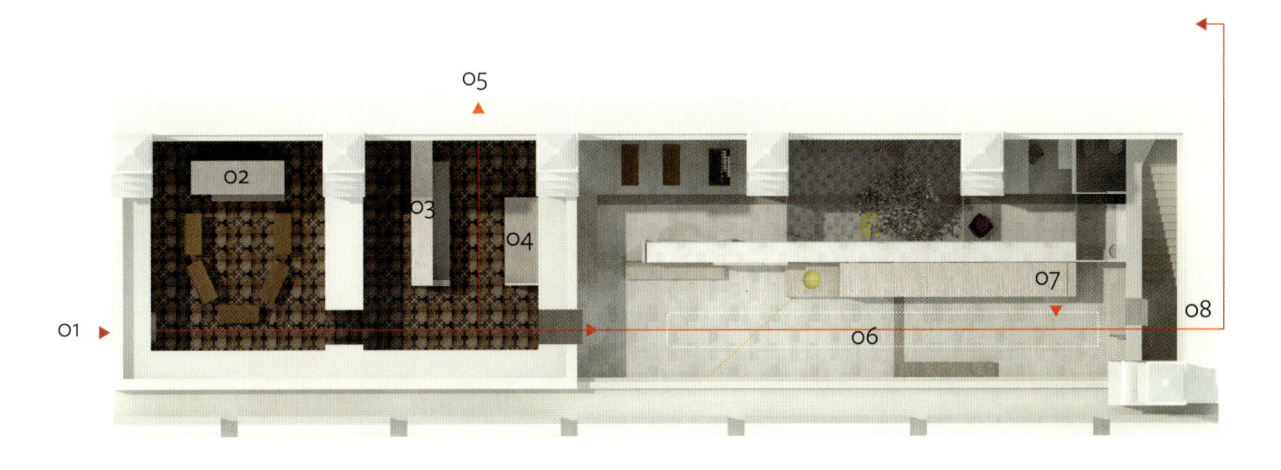

CHAPEL YARD, NEW COLLEGE, OXFORD

TOP
Long section looking towards chapel.
Bottom, plan layout demonstrating
the procession.

01. Entrance
02. Robe storage and choir change/song room
03. Chaplain's wardrobe
04. Vestments chest
05. Chaplain entrance at the altar end
06. Choir gathering/procession space
07. Sheet music storage
08. Choir takes music and enters at the back, walking up the aisles

The project for Chapel Yard at the New College, Oxford, comprises three spaces of song room, main vestry and existing Chapel. The spaces together form an experiential sequence which supports the needs of the chaplaincy and choir, as they prepare for service and commence through the processes of rehearsal, robing and procession. As this sequence is undertaken, so the atmosphere of each space adjusts the senses, in preparation for the performance at the service.

The song room represents the entrance space to the facilities. It is also the space which can be considered the first space in the experiential sequence that marks the preparations for a typical chapel service. The focus in this space is primarily one of gathering the choir to undertake practice.

The main vestry is also vital to the experiential sequence of preparing for a typical chapel service and the significant burden placed on this space to support a number of activities is reflected in the design of the timber-clad centrepiece to this room. The centrepiece separates functions within the room without completely dividing the space. The chaplain's vestry, being the main activity space, is intended to offer a place of calm and contemplation, as well as to support the pragmatics of preparing for a service. It incorporates a range of functional features including drawers and cupboards capable of storing the vestments and altar dressings.

Sequence and Promenade

The processional route to the Acropolis of Athens is one of elevating people, both literally and metaphorically, above the world of everyday affairs. The steps to the sacred citadel passed first through the monumental entrance gateway of the Propylaea, the culmination of the sacred way that led from Eleusis 18 km to the northwest and past the diminutive temple of Athena Nike, the symbolic protector of the city that it overlooked from the sheer walls of the Acropolis bastion. Having entered the sacred precinct the procession entered a level terrace occupied by the colossal bronze warrior statue of Athena Promachos from which led a ramp, passing on the left the Erechtheion and along the northern peristyle of the Parthenon, arriving at its eastern entrance portico. From there, processing up the steps of the elevated dais, and through two colonnaded porticos, one ultimately entered the east door and the inner sanctuary of the cella that contained the giant gilded statue of Athena Parthenos, the most venerated symbol of ancient Greek society. This elaborate ritual promenade embodied both the beliefs and cultural values of the golden age of ancient Greece, celebrated through the spaces and buildings through which its citizens processed.

Le Corbusier secularised the architectural promenade in his early houses.[4] The Villa Savoye is the culmination of the processional route that took the wealthy Savoye family from the polluted congestion of central Paris to the health-giving greenery of the countryside along the banks of the Seine at Poissy. Their journey by car was celebrated on arrival at the villa with a sweeping curve of the undercroft from where a gentle ramp zigzagged its way to the rooftop garden and a framed view across the river valley. Inspired by its Athenian predecessor, for Le Corbusier the architectural promenade was not only an arbitrary journey but rather a process of ritual purification where space, time and architecture were brought together to evoke a cleansing of both mind and body. In the device of processional sequence architecture reveals the capacity that the carefully orchestrated pattern of experiences, repeated and reinforced through building and route, can have in changing our emotional and psychological state, and in this architecture has the power to move not only our mood but our whole outlook on the world.

ABOVE
The route up to the Acropolis.

RIGHT
Detailed cross section through courtyard.

01. Hawthorn tree
02. Bench linking to oak cross
03. Rainwater collection dish
04. Rainwater hopper
05. Piscina set into joinery piece
06. Gathering/procession space

BUILDING STORIES | 84

The Hawthorn tree is a reminder of Christ's Crown of Thorns and is planted at the centre of an oak cross. The tree develops white flowers in summer and red berries in winter; both colours are prominent in New College's crest.

The sides of the roof perimeter are glazed in order that a minimal amount of construction is required to sensitively connect with the existing fabric of the Chapel and city wall and thus form an environmental envelope to the Chapel Yard. The perimeter glazing plays an equally important role in allowing natural light to play off the surfaces of the existing Chapel and city wall and suffuse the space within.

The centrepiece of bespoke furniture pieces brings versatility, flexibility and functionality to the spaces they serve, but they are also intended as crafted components which 'tune' their environment. Through careful design each piece will influence the environment to create its own unique atmosphere and character.

A central spine wall provides support to the cantilevered roof above. It also acts as an external wall to the courtyard and its stone surface is manipulated in response to the centrepiece element, which adorns it. A specially commissioned piece of stained glass by the artist Sasha Ward will be incorporated.

The spaces together should form an experiential sequence which supports the needs of the chaplaincy and choir as they prepare for service and proceed through the processes of rehearsal, robing and procession. As this sequence is undertaken, so the atmosphere of each space adjusts the senses in preparation for the performance at the service.

A cross is laid flush with the ground and occupies the full area of the Chapel Yard, appearing both internally and externally. Winchester College has generously pledged a tree from its land to implement this element of the building in recognition of the strong historic ties that exist between it and New College

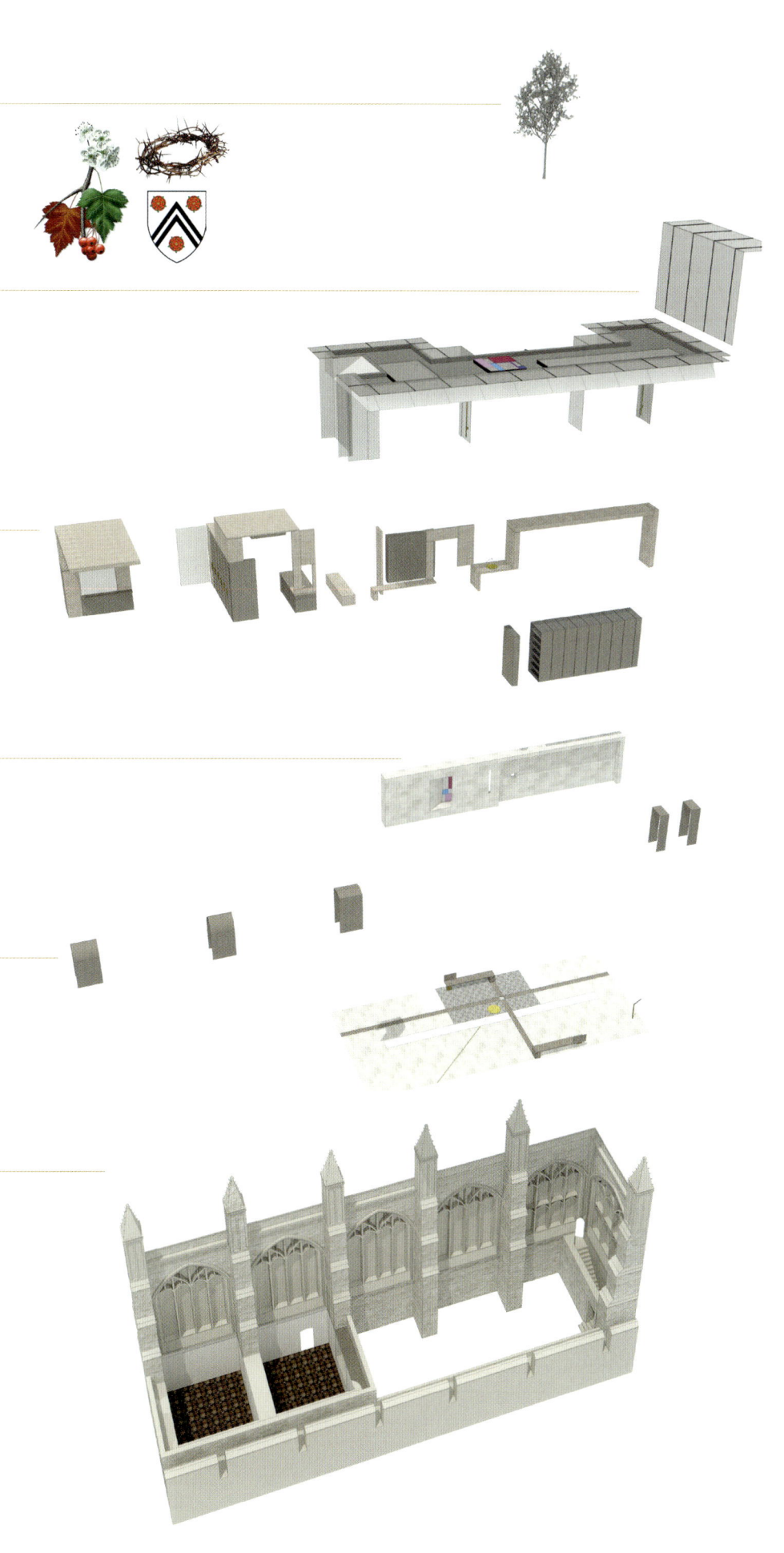

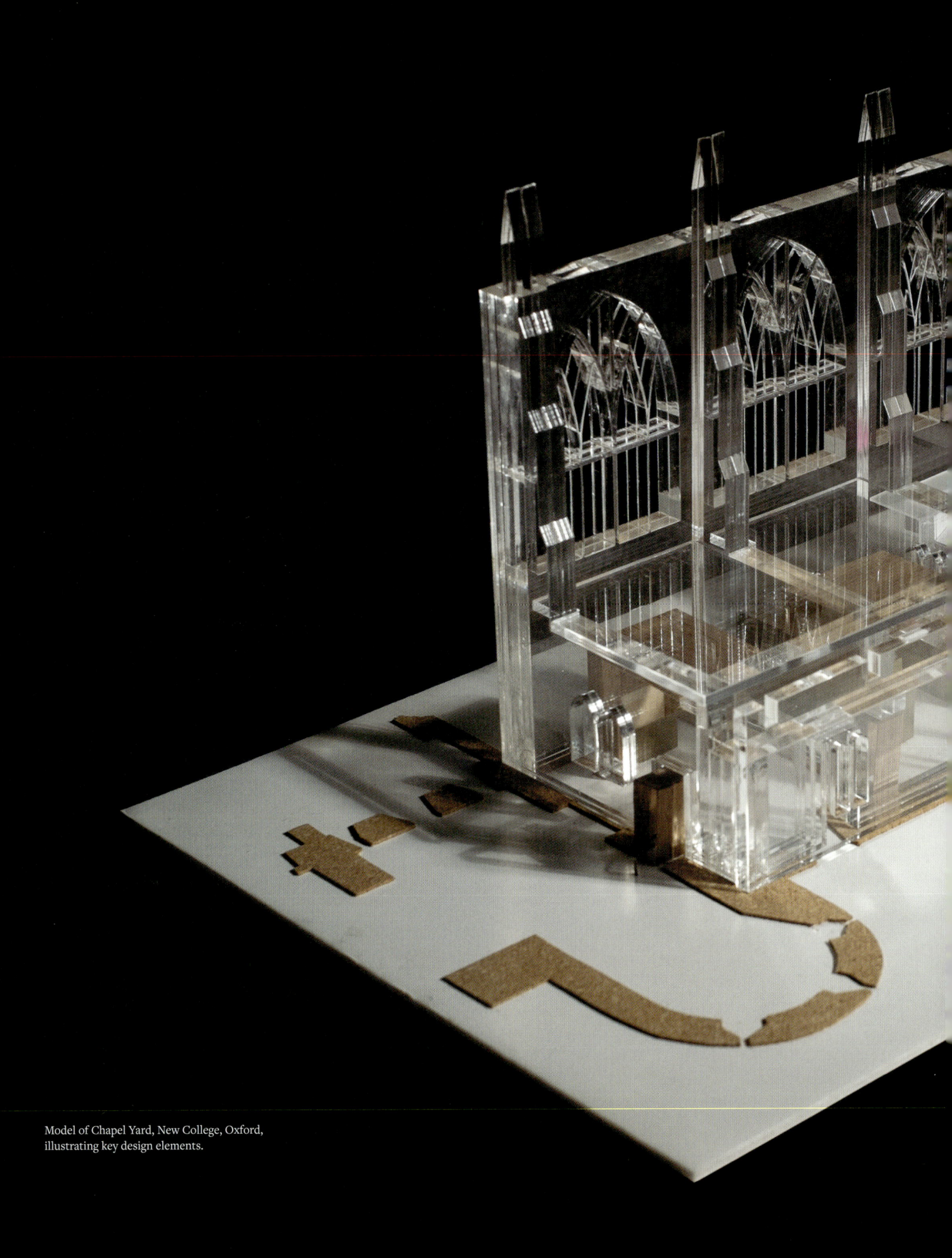

Model of Chapel Yard, New College, Oxford, illustrating key design elements.

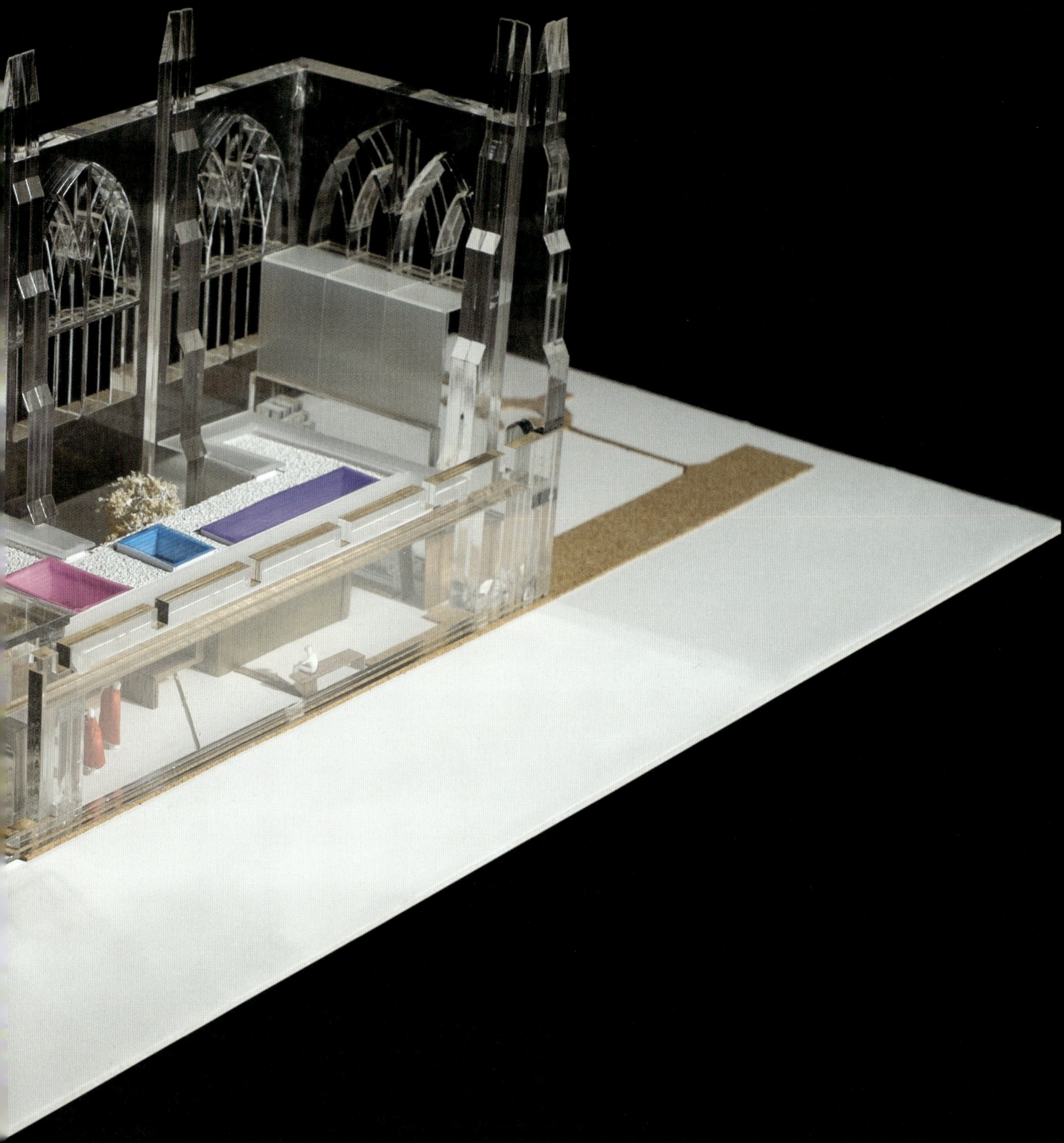

Wisdom

Past, Future and Present

Architecture is above all else an optimistic profession and to design is to hold a hope for a better future. Yet the creative act directed into the unknown future is forever built on the vestiges of the past, and too often architects have found the refuge of certainty in the architecture of history or futuristic prospects of tomorrow. Still, to be wise is to realise the impermanence of the past and the fragility of the future as we are inevitably forced to act in the ever passing liminal space of now. To know how to act requires wisdom and for architects this requires experience, knowledge and good judgement.

> *Gatsby believed in the green light, the orgastic future that year by year recedes before us. It eluded us then, but that's no matter—tomorrow we will run faster, stretch out our arms farther.... And then one fine morning—So we beat on, boats against the current, borne back ceaselessly into the past.*
>
> — F SCOTT FITZGERALD, THE GREAT GATSBY

RIGHT
The Ramboll Headquarters seen across an agrarian landscape.

OPPOSITE
Shows the relationship between the existing house in the distance, the new reception building and studios.

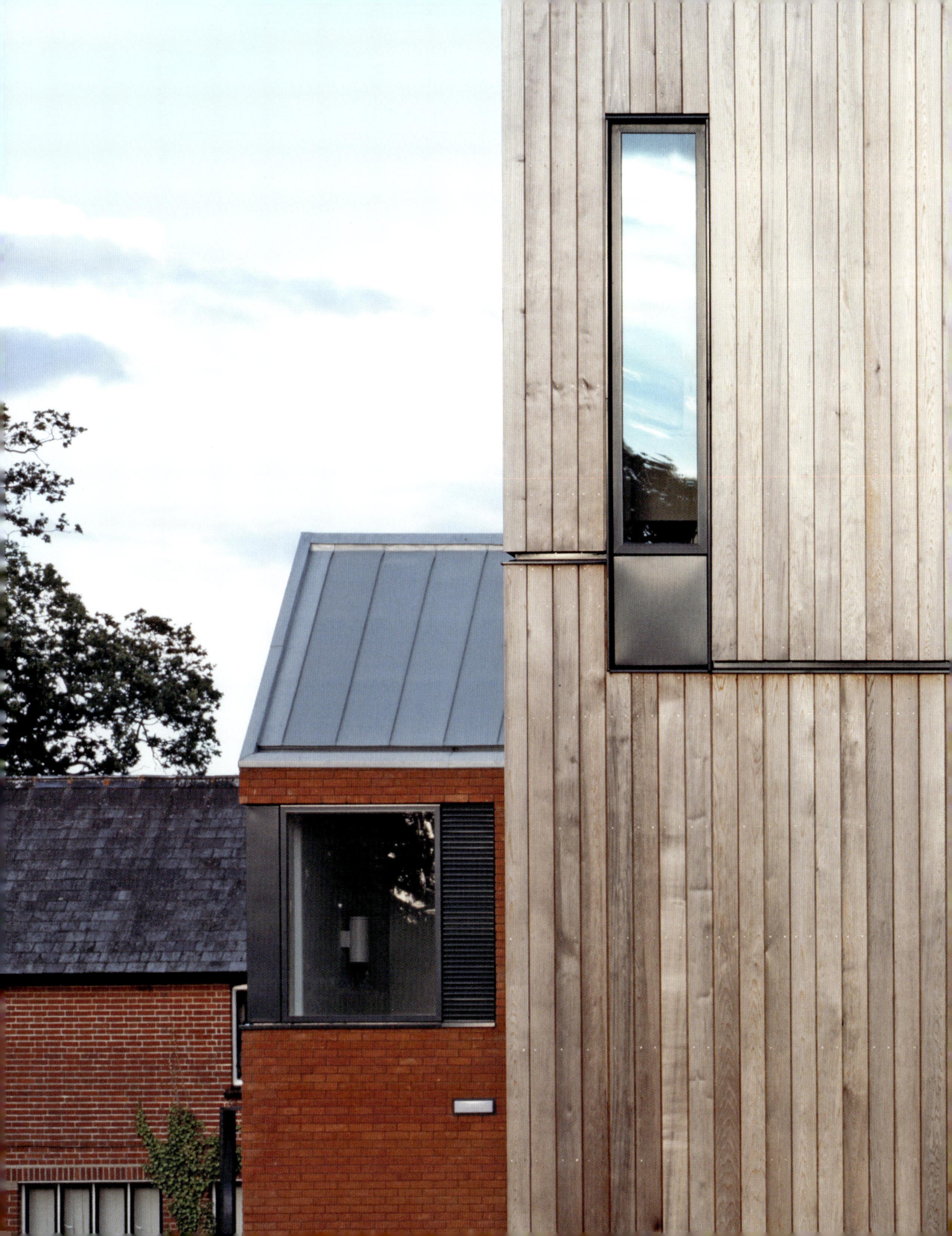

Past and Future

ABOVE
Typical elevation to the studios showing slot window arrangement.

Affirming a wise architecture firmly vested in the present contrasts with two opposing beliefs that have come to symbolise ecologically motivated building and, locked in two strangely opposing time warps, have sought to hold the high moral ground of wise and responsible architecture.

The first, a legacy of the twentieth-century obsession with the machine, is a belief in the ability of new technology to deliver utopia. Beginning with Filippo Marinetti's polemical Futurist manifesto of 1909, artists and architects rejected traditional forms and embraced the energy and dynamism of modern technology.[1] Antonio Sant'Elia's bold perspective sketches glorified the industrialised and mechanised city of power stations and transport interchanges. His and Marinetti's vision of the future lives on today in the High Tech school of architecture whose exposed structure, daring glass walls and visible services, once a celebration of the machine aesthetic, have now taken on the new role of symbolising environmental responsiveness through cutting edge technology.

In parallel with this faith in the future a diametrically opposed architectural historicism for a lost vernacular wisdom has emerged. In antipathy to futurology this belief holds that if we could recapture an authentic architecture that harmonised with nature, Arcadia could once again be ours. This is the ecology of timber, rammed earth and grass roofs, all used to evoke a sense of place and spiritual well-being. Architecture seen through this frame rather than utilising technological prowess to control the natural world is seen as working in hand with and as a part of the natural world. The ancient Greek mythology of Gaia, the primal Greek goddess of the Earth, has been evoked in architecture and science to see the earth as a complex self-regulating organism whose fine balance it is incumbent upon the human species to preserve and maintain.

These two shades of green design are in essence both metaphors, one mechanistic, the other organic. As architects once abrogated their aesthetic judgement of form to the needs of function, today equating ecological credentials, either vested in the future or in the past, with architectural merit seems to avoid the difficult question of what makes a wise architecture of today.

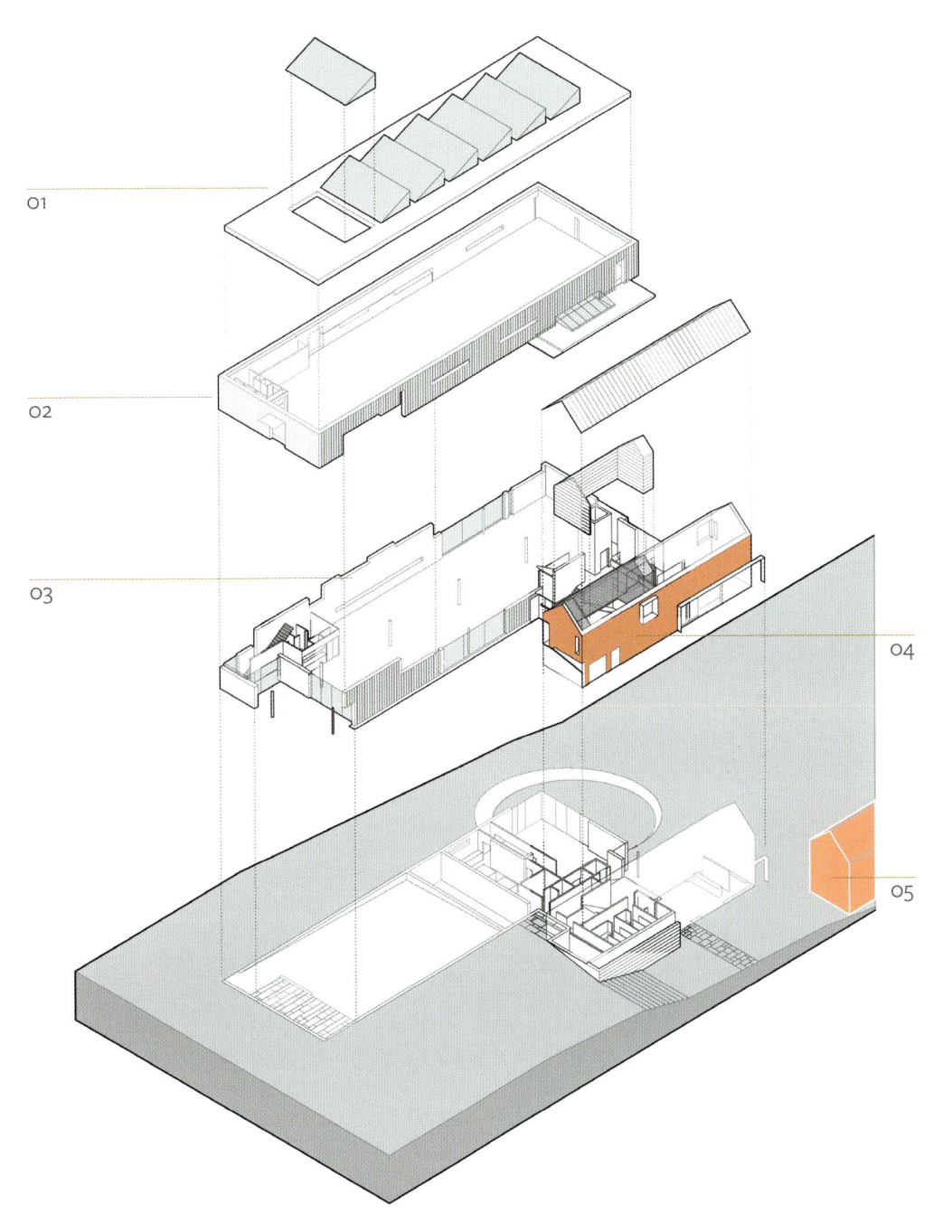

ABOVE
Axonometric of Ramboll Headquarters.

01. North light roofs
02. First-floor studios
03. Ground floor studios
04. Reception building
05. Existing house

RAMBOLL HEADQUARTERS, NETLEY MARSH

The Ramboll Headquarters in Southampton is a new low-energy headquarters building designed with a 'commercial green' strategy which minimises energy losses through the building fabric whilst ensuring a comfortable environment for those working in the building. The studio building provides open plan office space for 150 engineers. Design Engine has addressed the complex issues associated with the site topography and massing in a building of striking simplicity that comprises two linear volumes set at 90 degrees into the sloping site. The smaller, a brick pavilion, is of modest scale and provides the public face of entrance, lavatories and seminar room. The larger, cedar-clad volume, accommodates two floors of studios/offices with a restaurant tucked beneath at the lower end of the site. A glazed link between the two accommodates the changes in site and floor levels through a composition of half-landings, connected by wide flights of stairs that have a generous formality.

Externally the resulting elevation is controlled through the introduction of a meandering break line, the continuity of which unites the different window types and expresses the cedar cladding module. Providing a point of air ingress to floor plenums this fissure is both a pragmatic requirement and an abstract compositional device.

Against these dialectic opposites of blind faith in future technology and a romantic nostalgia for past building techniques, Design Engine has developed an approach to building that is technologically advanced yet embraces traditional wisdom. In doing so the context and building function are the principal drivers. This has resulted in some exceptionally sustainable yet understated solutions which have a pragmatic economy. It follows Buckminster Fuller's ideas of how to do more with less. Design Engine's ideas derive from an interdisciplinary research culture, with discussion focused more on 'why' a particular technical solution is required, rather than simply on 'how' an otherwise unnecessary condition can be resolved.

Universal and Particular

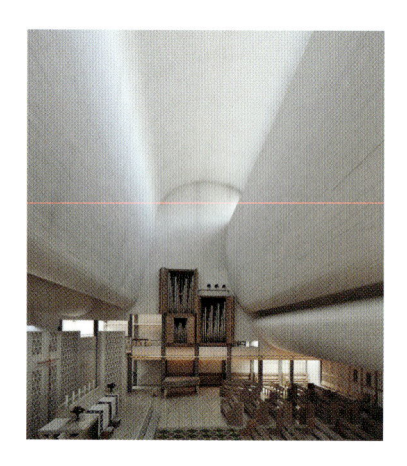

ABOVE
Jørn Utzon's Bagsværd Church in Denmark.

BELOW
Horizontal slots frame distant tree canopies which, from the seated position, provide important visual relief from the computer screen. Elsewhere larger windows are positioned next to meeting areas and draw attention to the picturesque views, whilst corner openings continue the internal diagonal spatial sequences out into the landscape.

In his seminal article of 1983, "Towards a Critical Regionalism: Six points for an architecture of resistance", Kenneth Frampton took up the challenge of the French philosopher Paul Ricœur who had posed the problem:

> How to become modern and to return to sources; how to revive an old, dormant civilization and take part in universal civilization.[2]

In this Ricœur had identified the powers of global capitalism destabilising local civilisation, customs, traditions and regional identity. Rather than an either/or dichotomy, Frampton adopted a both/and approach in which he set out the case for an architecture that could at once accommodate the particularities of regional identity whilst simultaneously seeing itself as a part of a global context. This approach, which might be termed contextual modernism, brings together at once the values of vernacular wisdom whilst accepting the universalising forces of the modern world.

To illustrate the idea of critical regionalism, Frampton famously analysed Jørn Utzon's Bagsværd Church in Denmark.[3] He astutely identifies how the building is universal in that it employs factory-produced panel walls and standardised components and outwardly rejects any familiar religious stereotypes. Yet the building's interior takes the form of cloudlike curves supposedly inspired by skies across the wide flat horizons of the Danish coast. In this way Frampton says that whilst the building is in many ways universal there is something very particular and unique about it, rooted in the particularities of its local context and responding to the qualities of light and the natural environment.

BUILDING STORIES | 92

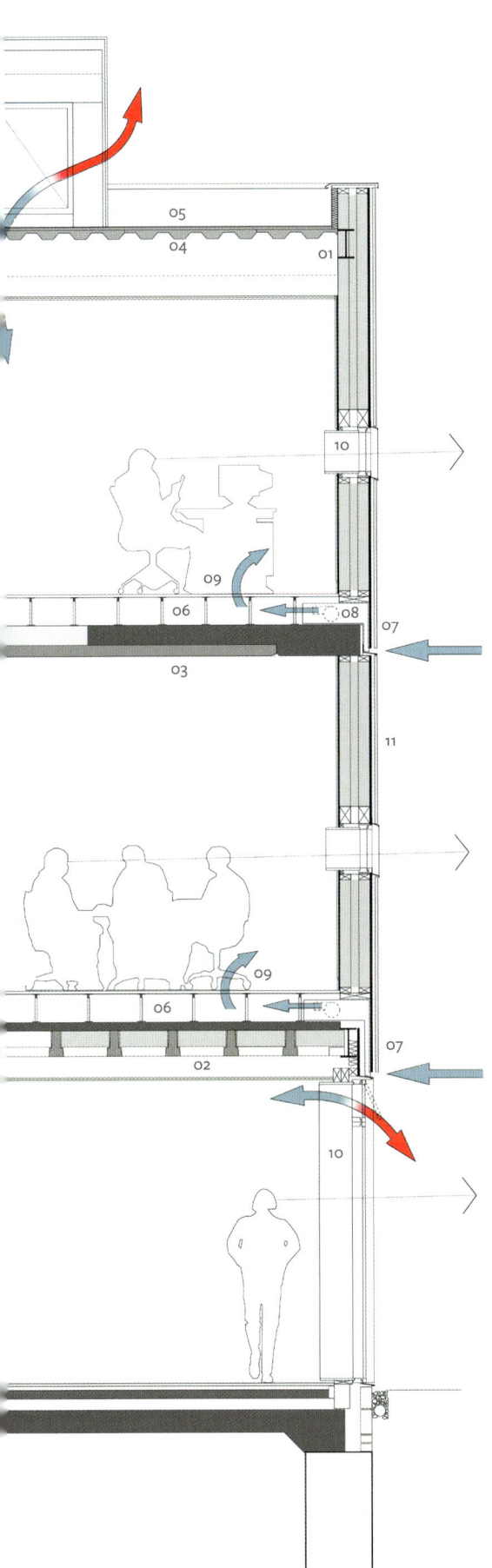

ABOVE
1:100 model of Ramboll Headquarters, detailing the north light roofs.

LEFT
Detailed section through the studios at Ramboll Headquarters.

01. RisSteel frame
02. Beam and block floor with 75mm screed
03. Pre-cast concrete shuttering with post tensioned concrete slab
04. Composite roof panel
05. Single ply flat roof membrane
06. Floor plenum
07. Air intake duct
08. Fan unit
09. Swirl diffuser
10. Velfac composite window system with PPC aluminium reveal
11. Cedar cladding

RAMBOLL HEADQUARTERS, NETLEY MARSH

This detailed section reveals the full importance of the inlet fissure through which very low-pressure fans located in the floor void draw air in through the cladding, discharging via floor grilles deep in the plan. This ensures year-round ventilation across the full depth of the floor plate and allows a night-cooling strategy to operate in conjunction with exposed thermal mass. In the studio, heating and cooling is provided by an innovative underfloor system that integrates within the raised access floor, using the tiles as the heat emitter. The underfloor pipework is served by a heat pump that delivers heating in the winter and cooling in the summer. This system also pre-conditions the supply air as it passes through the floor void. In addition to the wall openings the upper studio is day-lit by extensive north lights, with the sloping soffits that frame the passing clouds and provide a calm gallery-like interior; with this low-energy strategy, the building has a CO^2/m^2 rating of only 20 kg/pa, which is over four times better than current best practice and makes Ramboll one of the most energy-efficient offices today.

The overall effect of the studio building is in part that of a rural industrial appearance of farming machinery sheds and sits well in the context of surrounding agrarian landscape. However, the glimpsed sawtooth north lights to the upper studio and abstract fenestration pattern set it apart from any vernacular precedent.

WISDOM | 93

Vernacular Wisdom

ABOVE
Mojácar, situated in the south-east of the province of Almería in southern Spain, was used by Bernard Rudofsky in his book *Architecture without Architects* as an example of a model hill-town based on a vernacular architectural tradition that had developed over centuries.

BELOW
The Performing Arts Studios at University of Winchester.

The term 'vernacular' when used in architecture, at least to a modern audience, has always carried somewhat pejorative undertones. Often applied to historic and domestic building construction drawn from the use of local materials, it has gained some traction recently in respect of the sourcing of materials, but it has all too often been used to indicate the aping of regional construction techniques and more often the stylistic appearance of the buildings of a particular region.

However, the understanding of climate and location and the way in which the appearance of buildings through history has been influenced by local factors remains an important aspect of an architecture that has contextual relevance. The term vernacular has also held disapproving connotations for its application to everyday requirements and use of inexpensive materials. The history of palaces and temples that have throughout history represented the wealth and power of the few has too often delimited architectural discourse whilst the buildings that served the everyday life of the many have been overlooked or seen as less worthy of architectural attention. The Modern movement in many ways sought to overturn this hierarchy, only to impose a different kind of privileging that placed the intellectual avant-garde above the commonplace and familiar. Certainly this was the case made by Bernard Rudofsky in his book *Architecture without Architects*, 1964, where he stated that "Architectural history, as written and taught in the Western world, has never been concerned with more than a few select cultures."[4] In lauding what he termed the 'non-pedigreed architecture' of vernacular, indigenous and often anonymous buildings, he attempted to refocus architectural thinking on both the users and makers of buildings along with the beauty and sophistication that was to be found in hitherto unrecognised building traditions across the globe. Whilst Rudofsky's plea was for an appreciation of that which had been overlooked, the question for architects today is one of the application of hitherto disregarded traditions in the context of the modern world and universal building techniques.

PERFORMING ARTS STUDIOS, UNIVERSITY OF WINCHESTER

In the Performing Arts Studios at the University of Winchester the spaces are of a 'stripped down' aesthetic, chosen to meet the brief's requirements and to create a robust environment that promotes creative freedom for the users. The studios provide a flexible teaching environment for physical theatre and human movement. The intention was to create an expression for the building that has empathy with the teaching spaces within it but that is also responsive to the surrounding context and orientation. Much of the building perimeter is obscured from direct view due to the nature of the site location and its adjacencies to surrounding buildings. The design of each elevation is based on where it can be viewed from and the relationship to neighbouring buildings, along with the careful consideration of the dramatic effect of connecting those inside the building with the external environment.

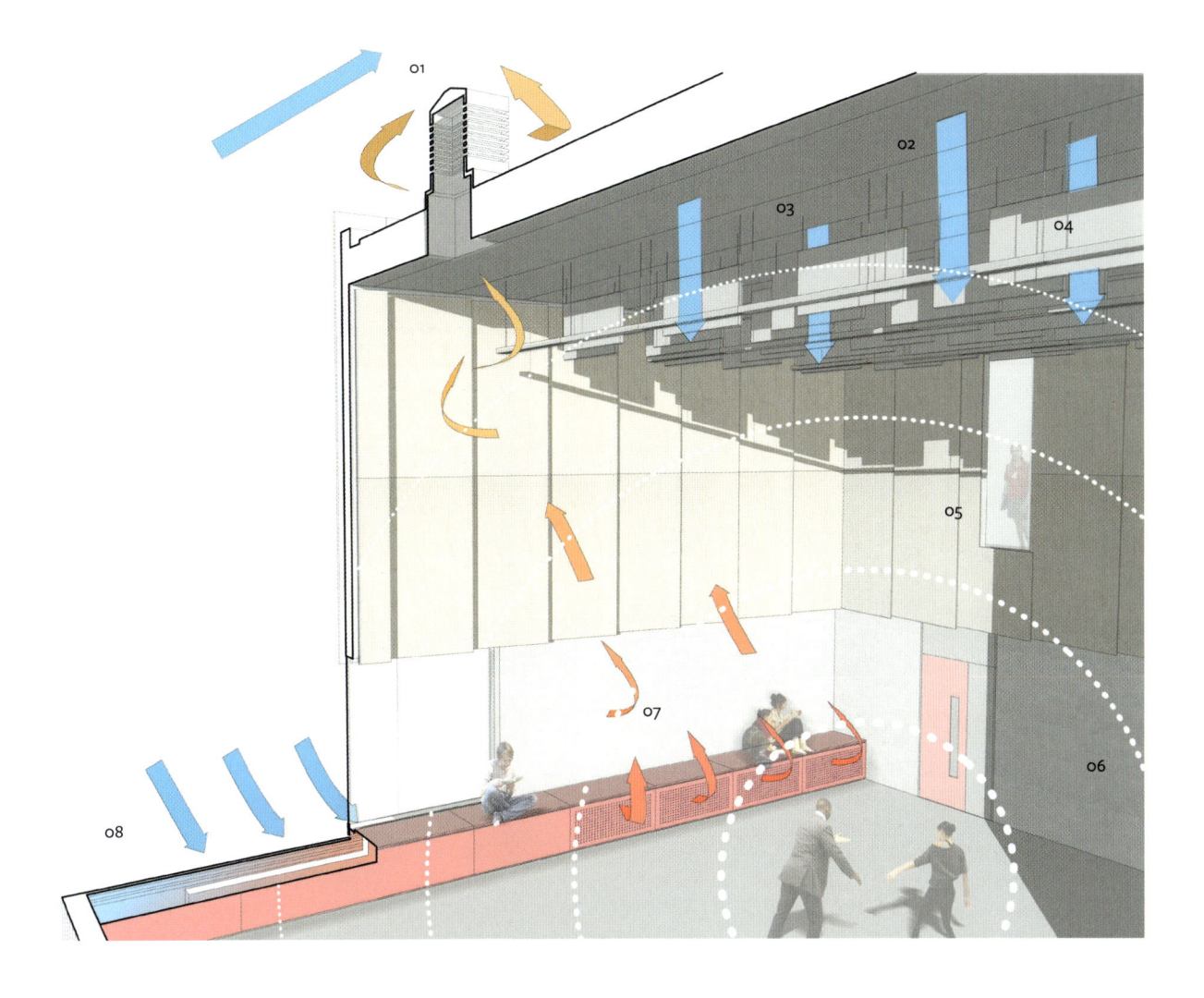

ABOVE

01. Rising hot air drawn out through roof by sound-attenuated ventilation stacks
02. Thermal mass provides tempered cooling during the day
03. Low-energy lighting
04. Acoustic absorption and reflection reduces reverberation within dance spaces
05. Internal windows give glimpses into the studios from the circulation spaces
06. Exposed blockwork at low level provides robust finish
07. Air is heated when required and distributed into the space
08. Air intake via a noise-attenuated seating plenum

RIGHT

Performing Arts Studios at University of Winchester. The long heating and acoustic plenum provides a place to sit for the performers in the studio space.

WISDOM | 95

East facade of the Performing Arts Studios at University of Winchester.

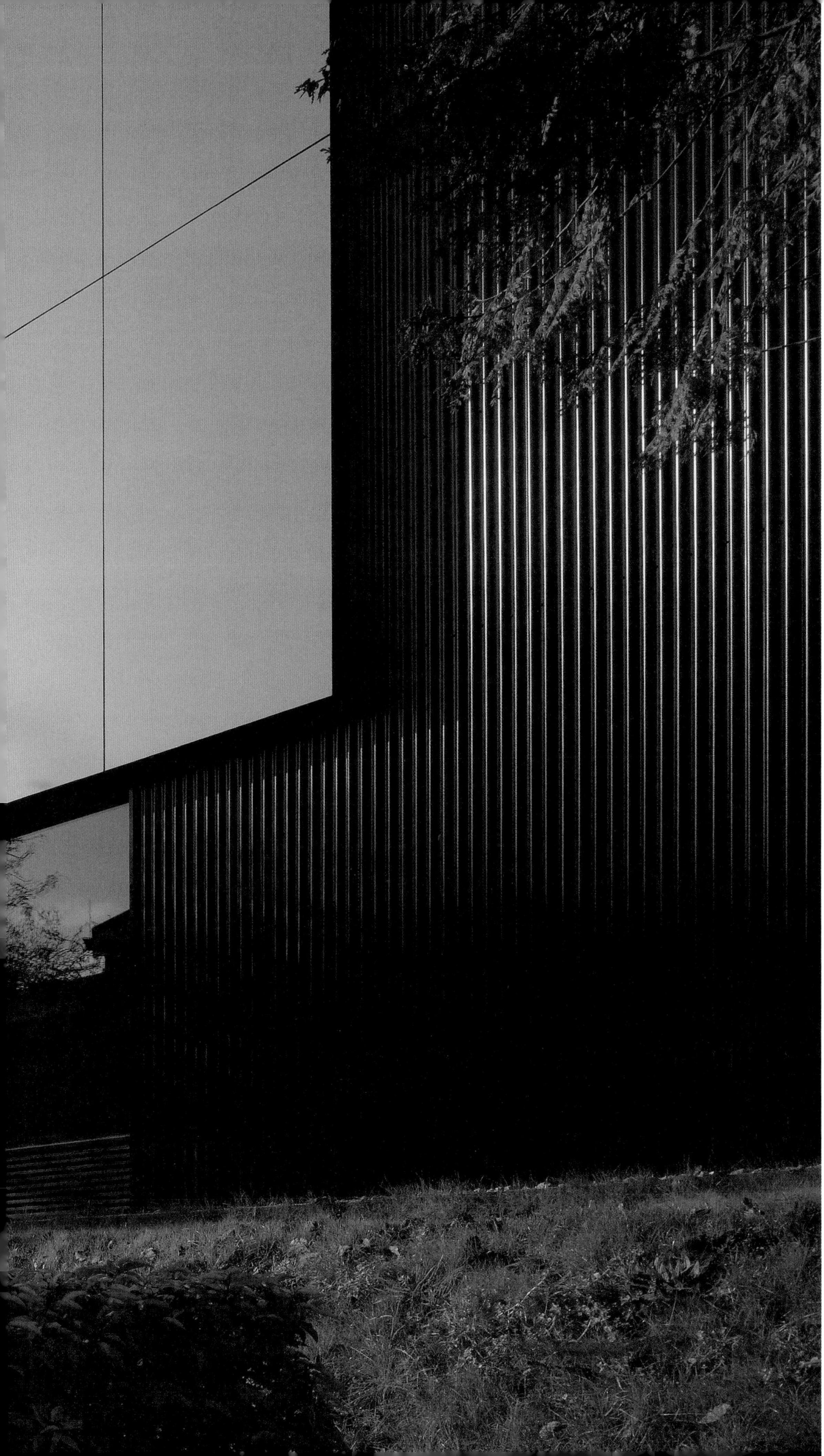

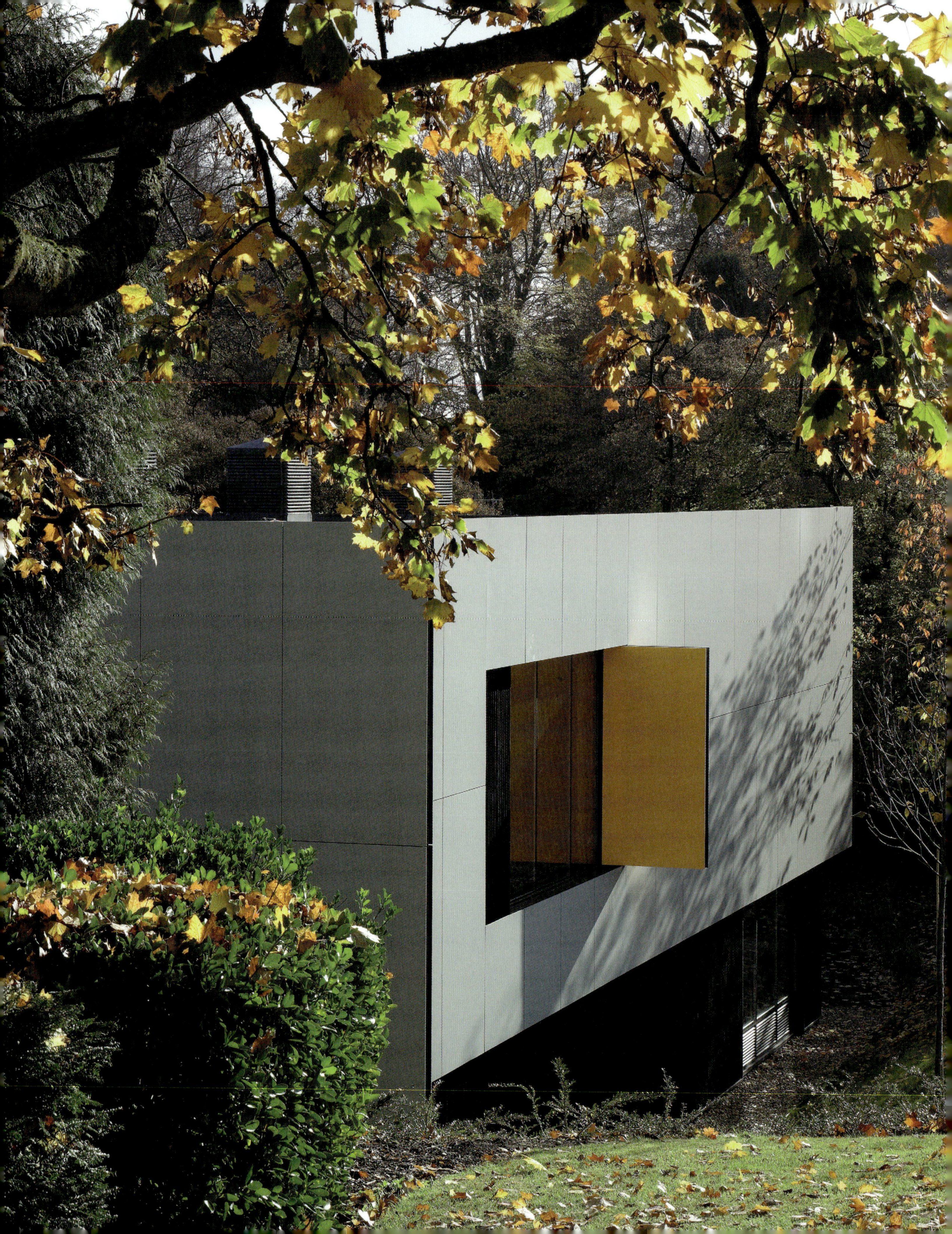

01

02

03

04

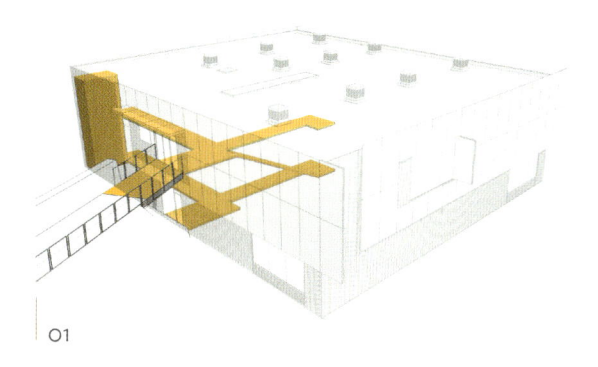

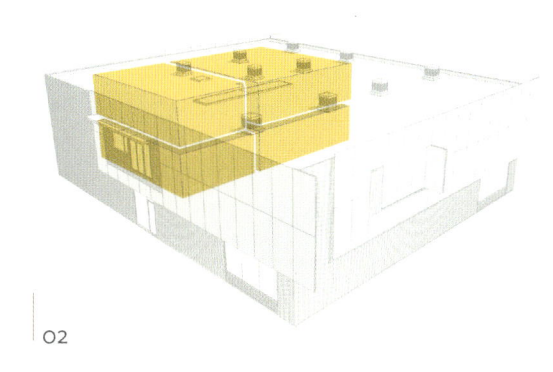

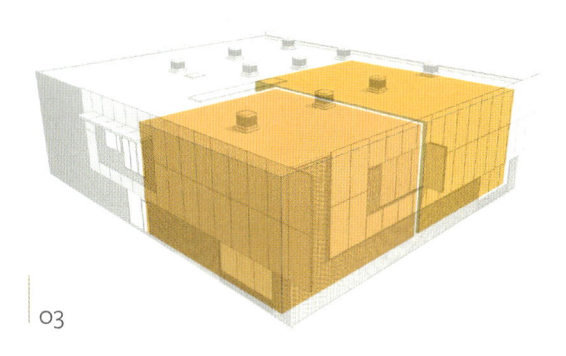

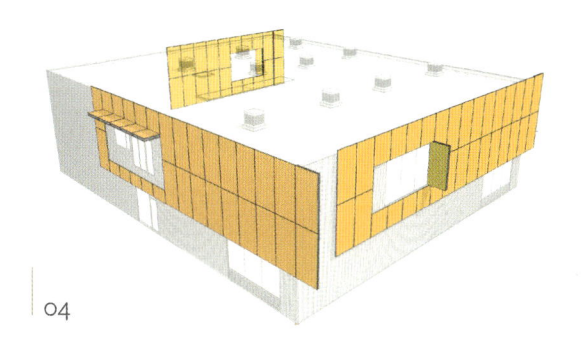

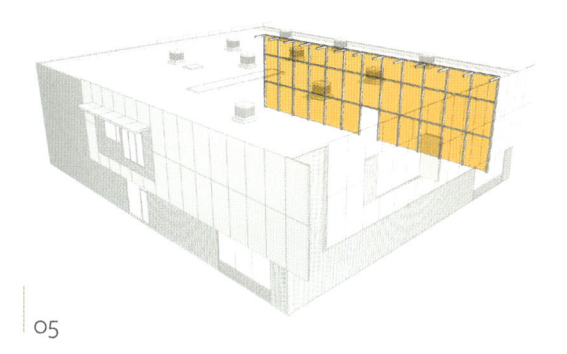

05

OPPOSITE
East facade of the Performing Arts Studios at University of Winchester.

ABOVE
Primary elements of the Performing Arts Studios at University of Winchester.

RIGHT
Double-height specialist studio.

01. Primary circulation
02. Multipurpose studios
03. Specialist studios (dance and drama)
04. Cladding panels respond to surrounding context
05. Green/planting wall

WISDOM | 99

Technical Wisdom

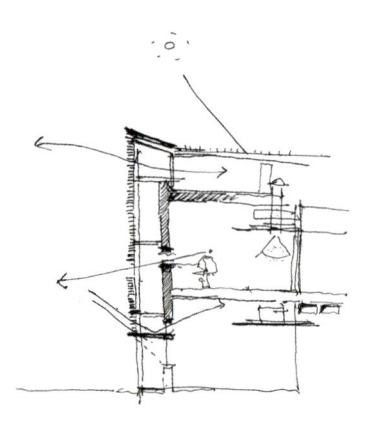

ABOVE
Sketch section of brise-soleil and the relationship to office spaces and protective mesh roof.

BELOW
The solar shading model shows how the varied spacing of the horizontal slats ensures good views from the office windows whilst cutting out late-morning sunlight.

Many of the lessons of how to respond to the environment of a particular location are to be found in traditional building techniques; however, new building types and the design requirements of the twenty-first century require new methods and levels of performance. The history of innovation in architecture is less one of radical moments of genius and more that of incremental development or applying familiar materials and methods in new and unfamiliar contexts. This approach to innovation relies on technical solutions derived from the transference of techniques and elements from outside of the architectural discipline.

The application of new and unusual methods of construction or the cross-disciplinary application of ideas into a new context is not new to architecture—much of the Modern movement was based on such radical ideas. Today the advent of powerful computing has given the possibility to test the efficacy of such innovation prior to its application. The developments in building information modelling and digital tools that enable the heating and cooling of a building to be tested with a high degree of accuracy have emboldened architects and clients to adopt systems that hitherto would have been seen as too unproven, and to apply these methods with confidence in their outcomes. This approach relies on the creativity and inventiveness of environmental and structural engineers working with architects, and the disciplinary boundaries of the professions have progressively eroded from their nineteenth-century origins.

07:00   08:00   09:00   10:00

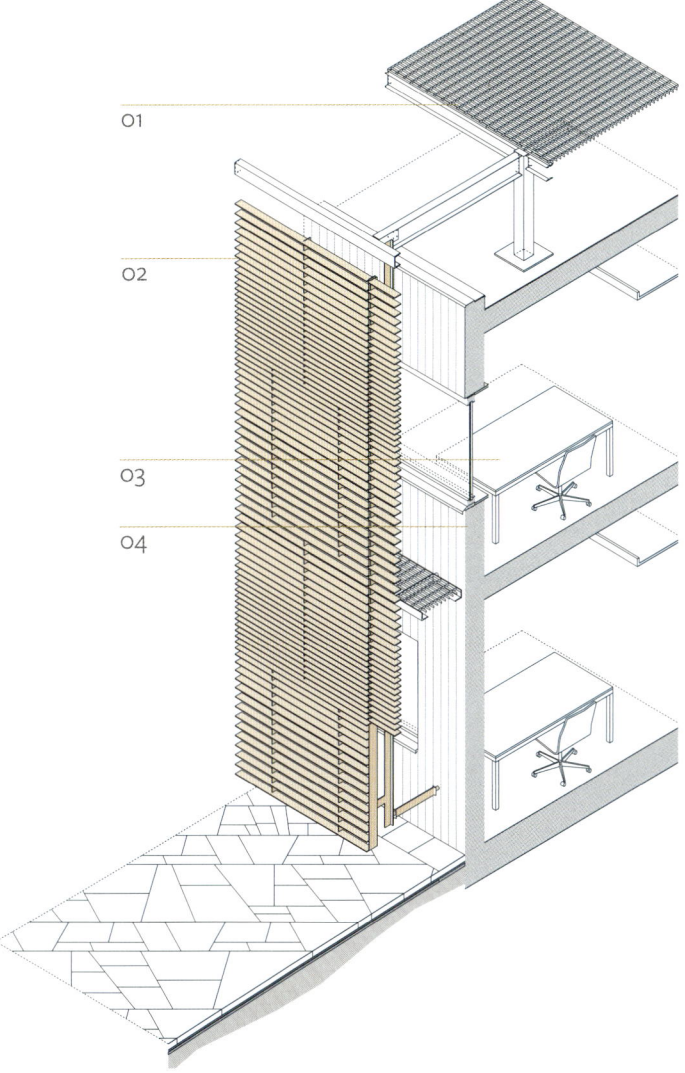

ABOVE
A typical portion of the building envelope showing weathering steel brise-soleil, canopy roof and concrete structure.

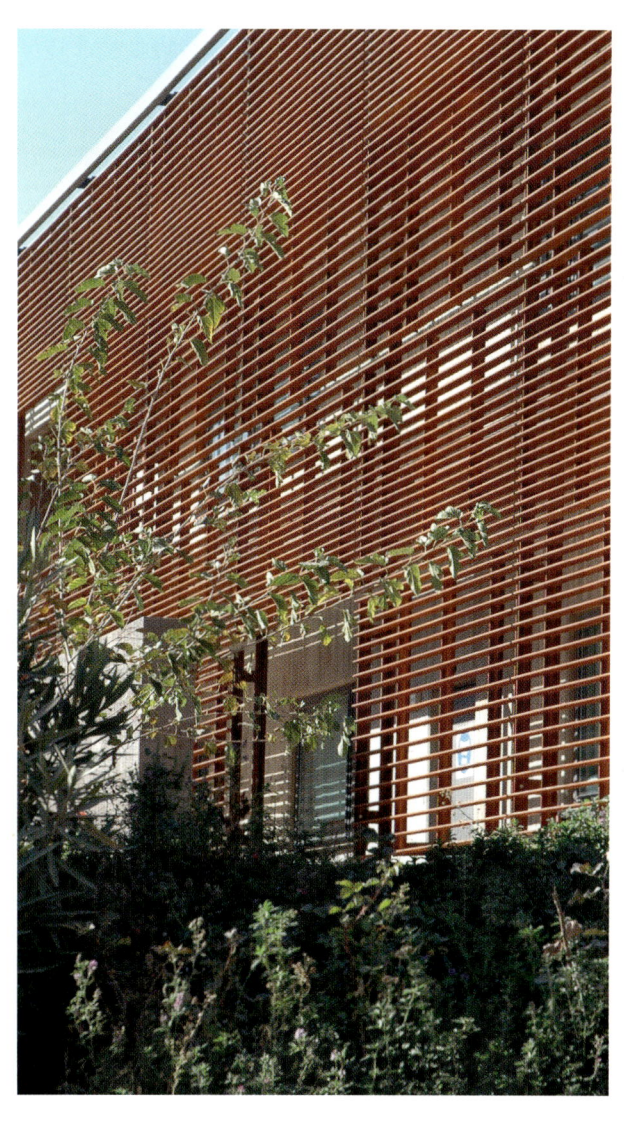

ABOVE
The external brise-soleil. The varied spacing of the horizontal slats ensures good views from the office windows whilst cutting out late-morning sunlight.

01. Mesh roof
02. Corten steel brise-soleil
03. Office space
04. Concrete wall

BRITISH EMBASSY, SANA'A, YEMEN

The climate in Sana'a offers a unique opportunity to create a lean engineering solution. Midday temperatures are moderately high throughout the year. In winter the monthly mean is seldom below 20 degrees centigrade and in summer the maximum temperature is almost always between 27 and 32 degrees. By designing the building to minimise solar-gain and by exploiting the cool night-time air, a secure, comfortable environment has been generated.

This is achieved by substantially shading the external walls and roof of the building. The brise-soleil, whilst protecting the interior from the late-morning and midday heat of the sun, allows the early morning sun to enter the building, providing valuable heat on cold mid-season and winter mornings. The concrete structure provides thermal mass, absorbing heat during the day and emitting it at night. The effect of this is enhanced by exposing the concrete soffit within the office spaces.

WARM AIR IN

COOLED AIR

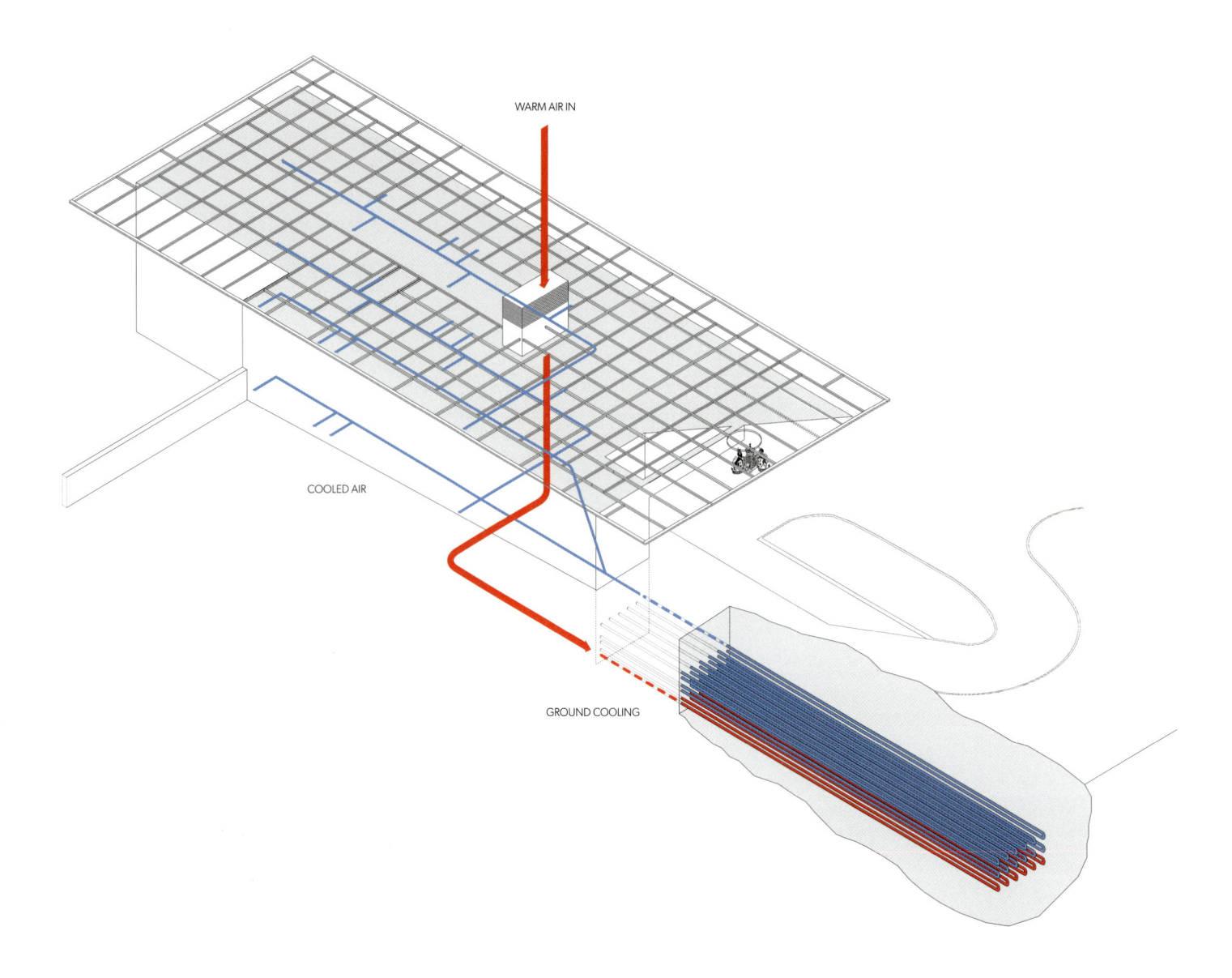

GROUND COOLING

ABOVE
Ancient Mesopotamian *qanāts*—subterranean channels and shafts used to transport and store water in arid climates—are today reimagined to provide underground cooling matrices for modern buildings. Thus a generation of scientists concerned with global sustainability are looking to the past for the methods, materials and designs that will reduce the environmental impact of mankind into the future.

The ability to model building performance dynamically has contributed to both the optimisation of mechanical systems and a new confidence in the efficacy of passive systems. Allied with developments in passive building technology such as photovoltaic cells and concerns over climate change, these new modelling methods have brought about a revolution in architecture.

Advanced computer modelling of building performance has also revealed some surprising results when turned on the architecture of the past. The vernacular architecture which was exalted by Rudofsky sat uncomfortably with the modern scientific paradigm. Indigenous architecture was built on empirical experience where methods of construction, structures and environmental control were developed over centuries through a process of trial and error. Indeed Rudofsky observed that the origins of much of this architecture were lost over the generations and, being undocumented and anonymous, any rational basis for the application of vernacular building methods, no matter how refined, fell outside of any scientific paradigm. It is in this context that much of vernacular indigenous wisdom was discounted, reliant not on scientific reasoning but based on what might be regarded as nothing greater than folklore. However, today these intuited solutions, when tested with advanced computing tools, are often found to be of extraordinary efficiency and economy.

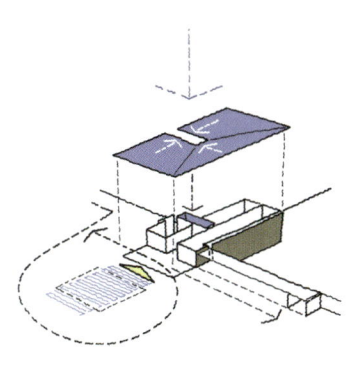

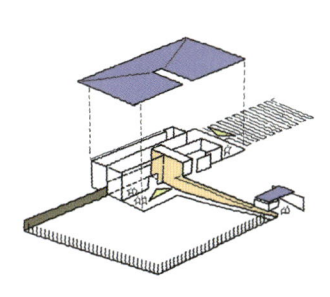

BRITISH EMBASSY, SANA'A, YEMEN

The amount of energy needed to cool the building is further reduced through the use of a low-technology ground cooling system. In the daytime, warm fresh air is drawn through a labyrinth of buried clay pipes before entering the internal spaces. In the process it is naturally pre-cooled, thereby reducing the amount of air-conditioning required.

Water is scarce in Sana'a, so the new Embassy has been designed to use it efficiently. The roof of the building acts as a rainwater collector to supplement the mains supply for irrigation. Grey water from hand basins is also used for irrigating the garden—there is an ancient precedent for this in the *bustans* (market gardens) of Sana'a, which are usually irrigated with grey water from the ritual ablutions of a nearby mosque.

This radical pragmatism (it goes to the root) has led to what they term a 'commercial green' approach. Central to this is recognition of the building envelope as the primary moderator of the internal environment, with the consequence that any low-intensity, low-energy building services solution hinges on the design of the external fabric.

OPPOSITE TOP
Labyrinth axonometric showing how warm daytime air is fed through the clay pipes that have cooled through the night.

ABOVE
Concept sketches showing the labyrinth and parasol roof for collecting rain water.

RIGHT
Construction of the labyrinth of buried pipes, which pre-cool air entering the building.

Old and New

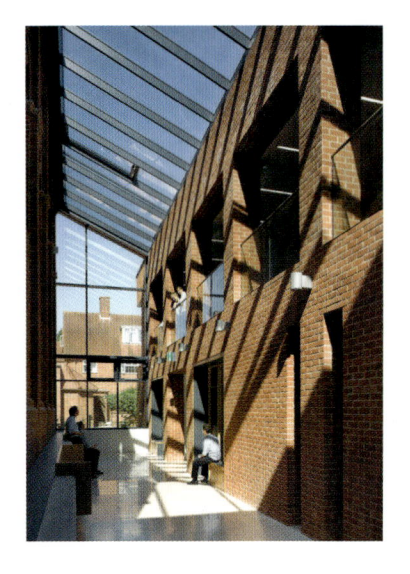

Working with existing buildings requires a particular kind of wisdom. The relationship between that which exists and that which is made new forms a special dialogue through which the reciprocal relationship of material presence establishes a new and powerful story.

Understanding the history of a building is a process of unearthing memories and stories, of delaminating the overwritten narratives that time has cast into stone. To read the character of a historic building is to understand how that which exists came into being, the hopes and ambitions of those who made it along with the techniques and materials of its construction. For such an investigation the examination is scientific, a dissection that reveals the anatomy of that which exists beneath the skin of appearance. But the investigation may be analytic; the understanding which arises from such a rigorous process is one of prioritising in order to decide upon how to design; to decide upon the best way to bring the past back into the present and how the relationship between that which is old and that which is new requires a clear strategy. Whilst aspects of restoration, conservation and preservation may form the basis of the treatment of the historic structure, the central question for the architects is how to relate the new to the old.

ABOVE
View of new atrium between the restored rackets court and the teaching wing

BELOW
View of the restored rackets courts

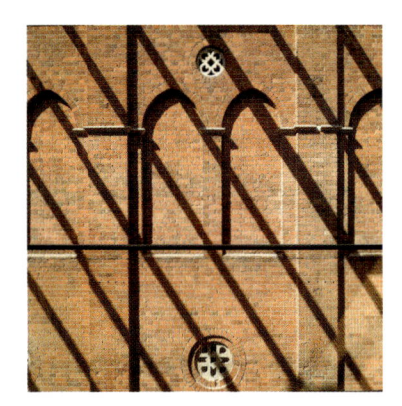

CLOCKTOWER COURT, RADLEY COLLEGE

Clocktower Court, Radley College, situated between Kennington and Abingdon, Oxfordshire. Established in 1847 by the Rev William Sewell, it now accommodates up to 684 boys. As well as addressing a number of important issues for the College, the project also represented a unique opportunity to improve the environment of Clocktower Court and realise its potential as a civic space in the heart of the College campus.

The project comprises ten history and politics classrooms, a social centre and cafe and extended art teaching facilities including a new double-height gallery. Woven between the existing historic buildings, the work is a knitting together of old and new buildings. The new development places the classrooms as a linear building over two storeys in the same orientation as the racket courts. The lower storey is a brick colonnade, which offers a new covered entrance route, taking pedestrians away from the existing roadside route that swings around the front elevation of the racket courts.

The end elevation of the classroom building is deliberately played down to allow space for artwork and to avoid competing with the more ornate frontage to the racket courts. The roofs of the classrooms are deliberately pitched so as not to conflict with the roof of the racket courts and as a result they offer a sculpted space internally to the upper classrooms.

BUILDING STORIES | 104

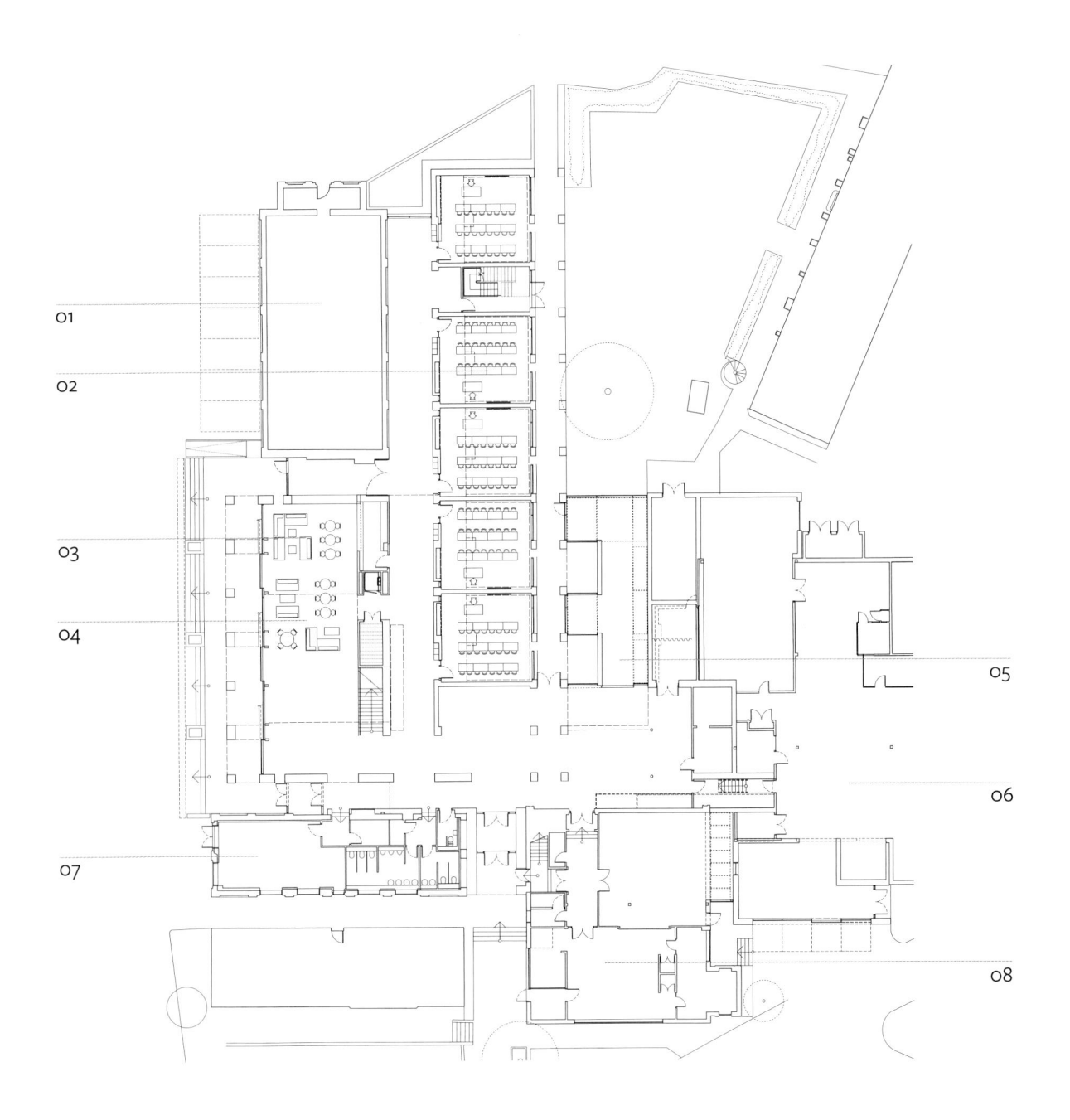

ABOVE
Clocktower Court at Radley College, ground floor plan.

RIGHT
Clocktower Court at Radley College, site plan.

01. Existing rackets court
02. Teaching rooms
03. Cafe
04. Forum/atrium
05. Sewell art gallery
06. Existing design technology
07. Refurbished old fives court
08. Existing art department
09. Clocktower Court

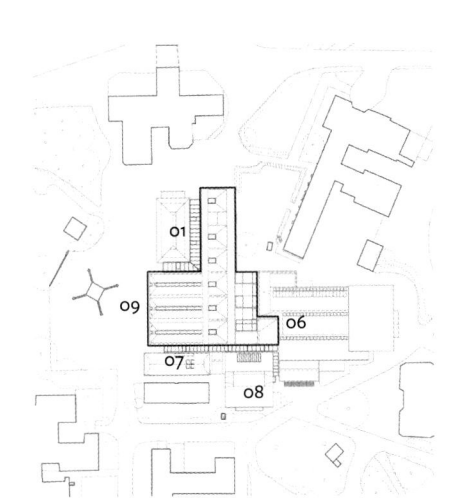

WISDOM | 105

Restoring Wisdom

ABOVE
Giorgio Grassi's restoration of the Sagunto theatre, Valencia, Spain.

The work of the Italian architect Giorgio Grassi stands as a powerful model of how to work with existing buildings. As part of the Italian rationalist school, also known as La Tendenza, Grassi's work is often considered the most extreme in its rigorous simplicity and sometimes severs architectural clarity. However, against his often austere new buildings many of his projects involved working with existing structures whose essential properties Grassi sought to preserve. Most notably, his project for the remaking of the Roman theatre in Sagunto, Spain, of 1985 embodies much of his profound thinking on the architecture of reconstruction.

For Grassi the project begins with a stripping away of the incidental elements of architecture that a building has accrued over the course of its life. The goal is that of first revealing and then completing the architectural framework, the disposition and massing of parts that constitute a given building type. This is done without recourse to artifice or nostalgia but rather with a searing clarity that seeks to strengthen the idea that once existed and through the vagaries of time has been lost or concealed. In completing the ruins at Sagunto, Grassi employed the greatest economy using the most minimal of means to complete the theatre. To Grassi only those elements of architecture that were indispensable to the original intention were required and the completed work was the logical outcome of his theoretical process. This approach of revealing only, as it were, the bare bones of the architectural typology and eschewing all but that which is absolutely necessary resulted in an extraordinarily beautiful and sublime reconstruction of the Sagunto Roman theatre. The resultant work is one of extreme rational clarity in which new and old are in essence the same elements of the unified totality, through which the underlying essential formal structure of the historic building was exposed. The school of rational architecture of which Grassi was a leading light has today fallen somewhat out of fashion, yet Grassi's ideas of revealing the underlying anatomy of architecture remain an enduring and wise ambition.

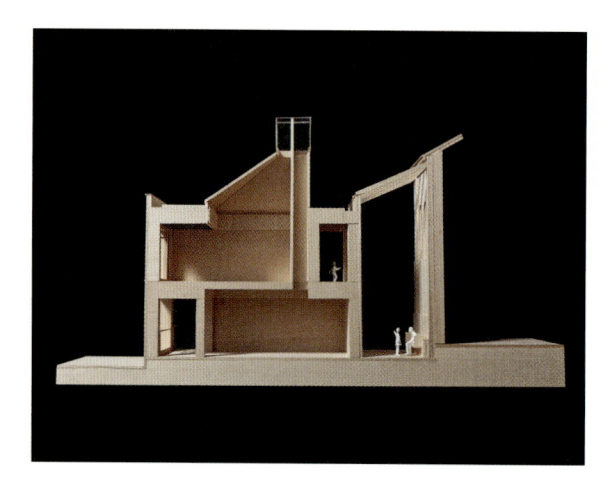

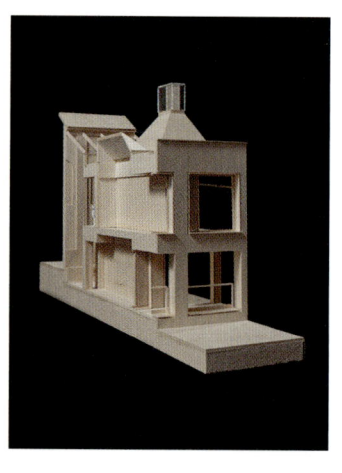

RIGHT
Section model exploring the relationship of the new building to the existing rackets court as well as the wind and light chimneys to the classrooms.

BUILDING STORIES | 106

ABOVE
Entrance view onto Clocktower Court showing the restored rackets court on the left and the new colonnade.

BELOW
Typical interior of a first-floor classroom.

CLOCKTOWER COURT, RADLEY COLLEGE

The project for Clocktower Court at Radley College follows the ideas of Giorgio Grassi in that its aim is to reveal the underlying architectural logic of the existing historic buildings which make up the site. Given the importance of Clocktower Court, the development deliberately placed the civic activities to engage with this space. The elevation of this part of the new proposal is colonnaded in brickwork, and proportioned so as to moderate the scale difference between the monumental racket courts and the more domestically scaled old fives court building. Through a process of paring away the extraneous accretions of time, the form of the racket courts and Old Fives Court at either end of the complex is revealed. The typology of these unique buildings informs the grid of the new teaching rooms, social space and art gallery as new and old buildings are united in a timeless quality that enables them to relate in harmony with each other.

The models (opposite) show the relationship of the classrooms with the upper classrooms shifted to the left to create a covered arcade below and a circulation corridor and gallery at first-floor level. The classrooms are capped with light and ventilation stacks, which drive the passive ventilation systems to the two-storey building. The new building is set away from the elevation of the rackets court to create a tall atrium space for the exhibition of artwork. The atrium is topped with frameless glazing, across which the old and new brick structures enter into a reciprocal dialogue.

ABOVE
Main elevation of Clocktower Court at Radley College.

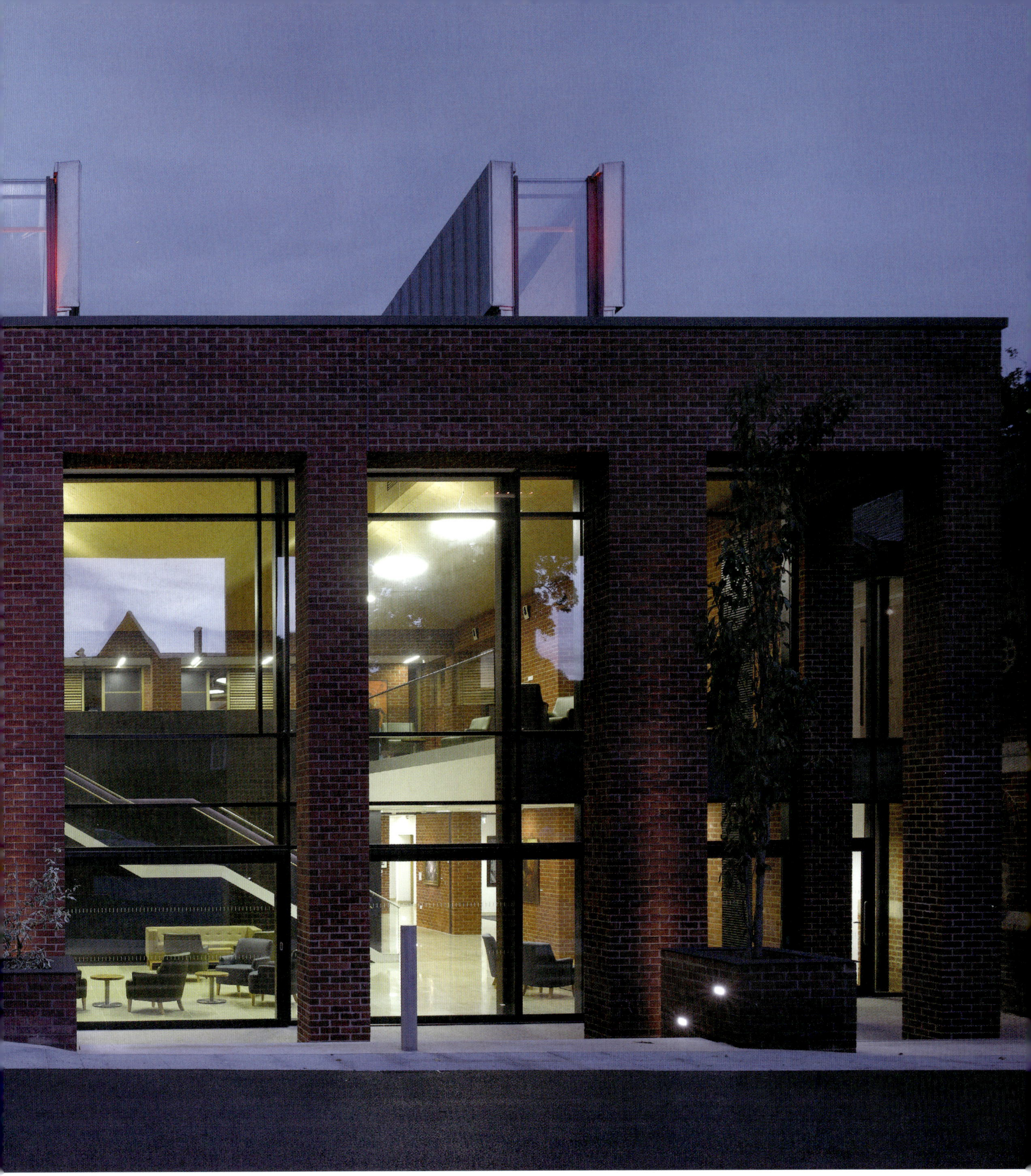

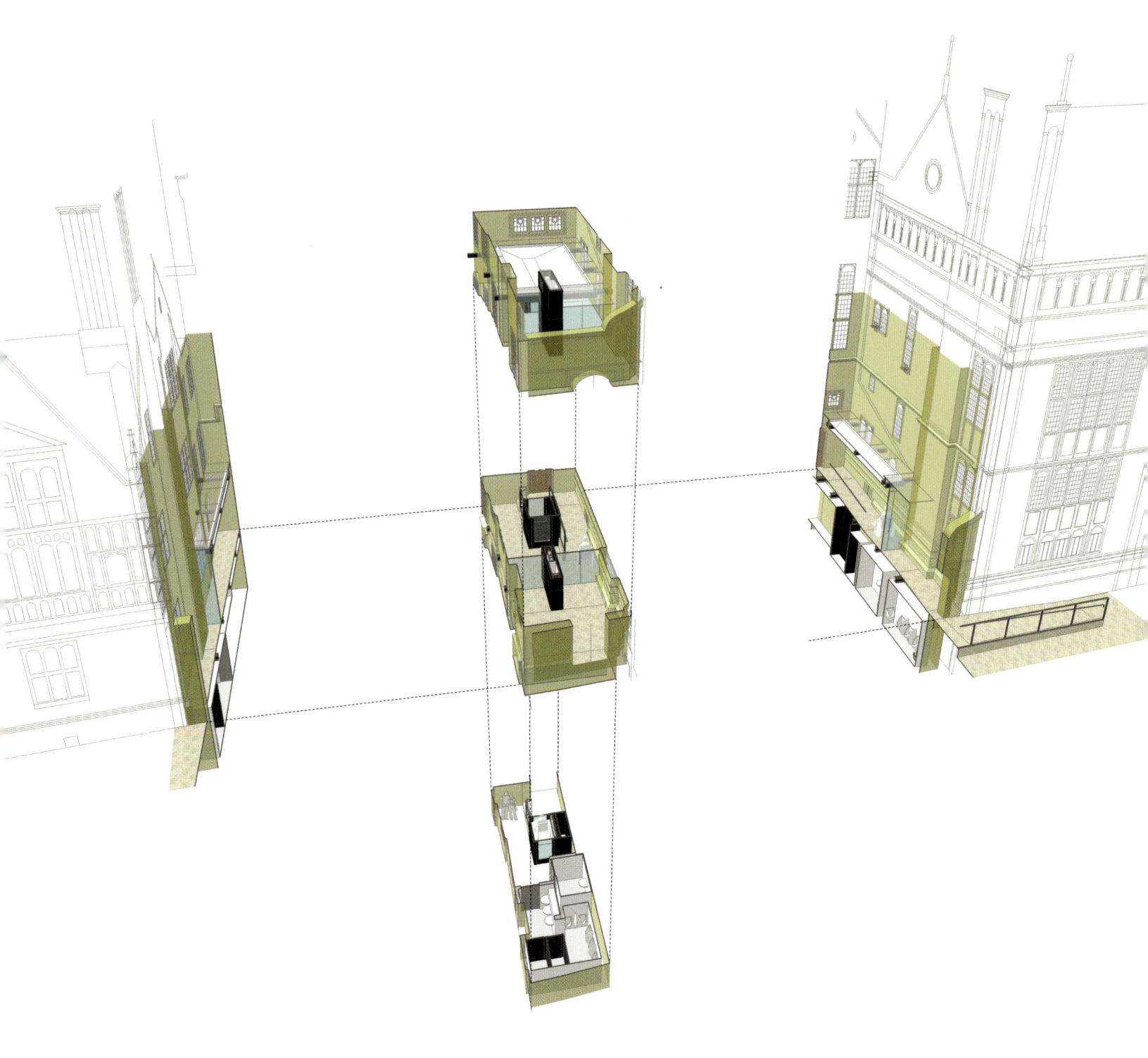

ABOVE
Exploded axonometric of Examination Schools insertion.

OXFORD EXAMINATION SCHOOLS

The existing Grade II listed University of Oxford Examination Schools building suffered from a lack of DDA-compliant access for disabled persons. The proposal took a redundant split level courtyard, squeezed between the Examination Schools and the Ruskin School of Art and inserted two pieces of 'furniture' within this very restricted space; one object contains a new lift and the other object allows light and ventilation to the toilet facilities in the basement. This new entrance also offers disabled access links between both buildings, from which neither had previously benefitted.

BUILDING STORIES | 110

Layers of Wisdom

The master of this relationship between old and new structures was the Italian architect Carlo Scarpa. Born in Venice, Scarpa grew up acutely aware of the layers of history that constituted the island city, from its Byzantine origins along with its fragility against the ebb and flow of the Venetian lagoon. He saw the city as a form of palimpsest, with each generation writing its own unique layer on the strata of inhabitation, and this sensitivity to architecture being subject to the vicissitudes of time gave his work a unique temporal quality. The power of Scarpa's work is that it speaks to us of the changing nature of the present—built on the complexities of the past, yet pressing inexorably into the uncertainties of the future. For the Castelvecchio Museum in Verona, Scarpa captured this fleeting moment with the existing Renaissance palace frozen in partial decay, into which he inserted a series of overlapping planes of walls and floors. The purity of each plane brings into sharp focus the fragmented and partial nature of the old castle. The contrast continues with Scarpa's use of raw materials as the weight of cast concrete is set against delicate steel handrails. Into the space of dialectic interplay between old and new, weight and lightness, Scarpa places the visitor and the artefacts of the museum.

ABOVE
Ancient and modern: the Castelvecchio Museum, Verona, northern Italy. Restoration and interventions by Carlo Scarpa, between 1959 and 1973.

RIGHT
Internal views of the captured space between the Ruskin School of Art and the Examination Schools at the University of Oxford.

Surface

The Free Facade and the Problem of Surface

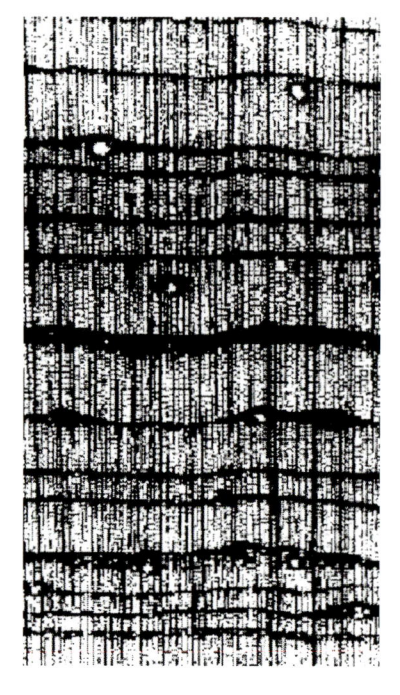

In the architecture of today the facade provides many opportunities to manipulate surface as a distinct architectural element, but this might not be possible had it not been for the ideas of the pioneers of the Modern movement who developed the notion of relieving the facade of its load-bearing requirement. Le Corbusier's "Five Points for a New Architecture" as set out in the journal *L'Esprit Nouveau* and later in his seminal book *Vers Une Architecture*, 1923, revolutionised the way in which buildings were made, almost 100 years after he postulated these ideas for a mechanised system of building.[1] Even today architects are still trying to reconcile the consequences of his design concepts. Le Corbusier's skeleton structure of a grid of concrete columns with rafts of reinforced floor plates, as demonstrated in his Dom-Ino frame, has become the standard model for building construction the world over. The same concrete frame and lightweight non-load-bearing intermediate walls subdividing space from structures are now ubiquitous, but perhaps Le Corbusier's legacy has been most problematically played out in what he felt was the logical corollary of this form of construction, that which he termed the free facade. For, once the facade had no obligation to communicate the tectonics of structure and was free of such requirements, what other meaning could the elevation convey? This problem was first addressed in the steel frame high-rise buildings of Chicago and Manhattan at the end of the nineteenth century, and by Louis Sullivan who coined the phrase 'form should ever follow function' in his book *The Tall Office Building Artistically Considered*, 1896.

ABOVE
Image of a pine cell structure used to create the frit pattern on the library facade of the John Henry Brookes Building at Oxford Brookes University. The pattern was chosen to reflect the extensive use of pine trees in the fabrication of paper.

RIGHT
Photograph of the inside of the new library showing the western facade, whilst under construction.

FAR RIGHT
Computer model of sawtooth facade which was developed to avoid overlooking nearby residential neighbours.

OPPOSITE
Photograph of the western facade to the library showing both the pine frit pattern and the sawtooth blade configuration.

JOHN HENRY BROOKES BUILDING, OXFORD BROOKES UNIVERSITY

The skin of the John Henry Brookes Building is instrumental both in knitting the campus together in a homogenous way and in creating a range of environments conducive to each unique use. Conceptually, the skin has been used to refer to the values of Oxford Brookes University. As an inspiration, detailed research was undertaken into incorporating images of the cellular structure of trees into the building's skin, in reference to the university's strong environmental ethos. Poetically, these images speak of the building blocks of the natural environment and its understanding through scientific research.

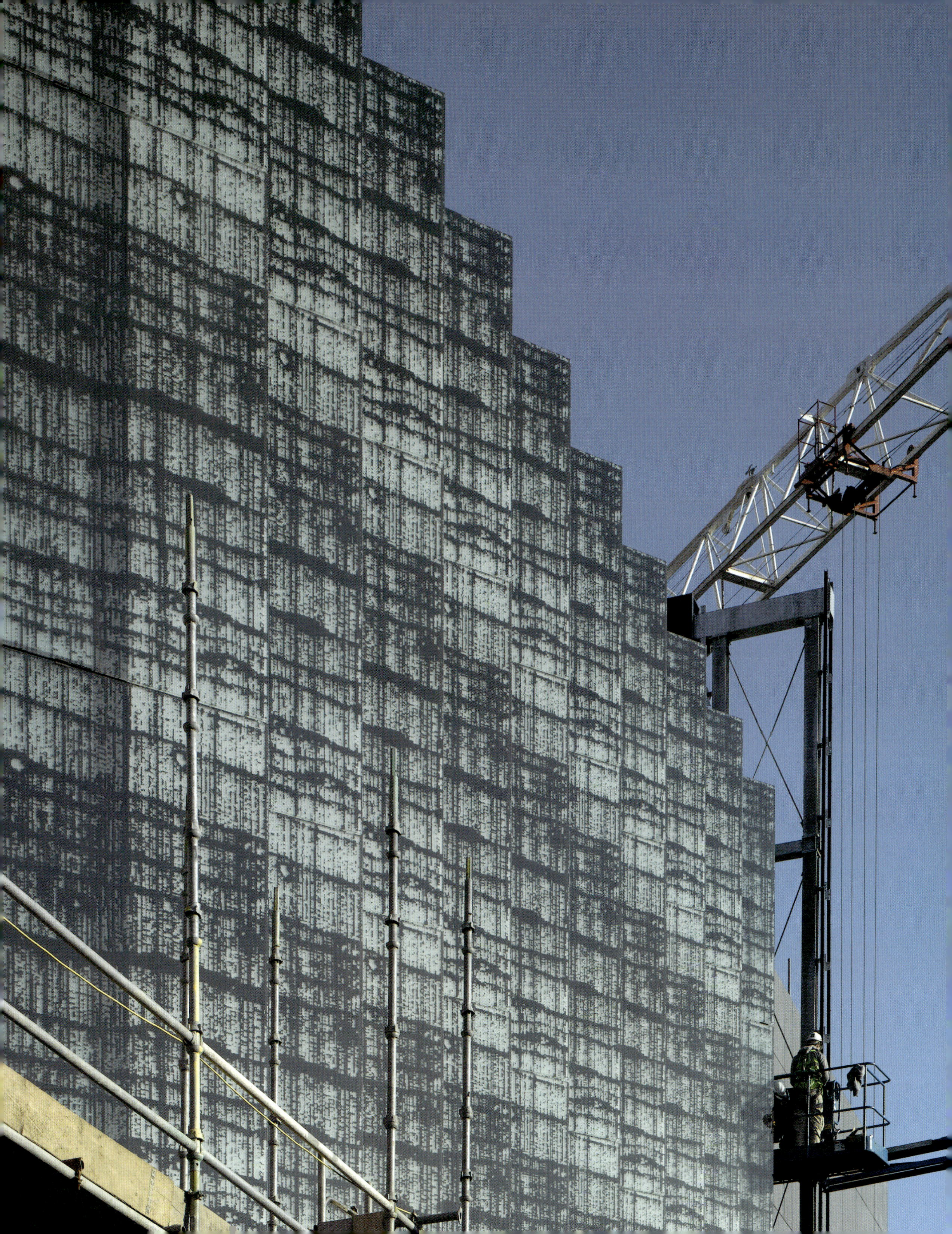

Surface Follows Function

ABOVE
Images of the cell structure of timber were sourced from Oxford Brookes University's Faculty of Life Sciences. Three timbers were selected: oak, pine and lime. Oak has been used for the skin of the forum, pine for the sawtooth blades of the library and lime for the weathered steel screen to the food hall. In each case a clue has been left in the building or landscape as to the species.

Louis Sullivan considered the aesthetic problems that arose once the facade of a building lost its structural significance. Its only functional requirement from this point became the role of a skin, mediating between the external and internal environments and transferring wind load back to the supporting internalised structural frame. The facade was thus denied its historic role as an expression of the vertical transfer of forces, and all of the lintels, arches and mouldings that it once necessarily entailed now faced erasure, reducing the facade to a curtain hanging on the outside of the building. Sullivan wondered what form this new face of a building should take, and what it would express. How, he asked, might we reconcile the functional needs of the interior with the requirement of a building to bear some external representation, while yet retaining a sense of honesty? The history of this problem is in many ways the history of twentieth-century architecture.

JOHN HENRY BROOKES BUILDING, OXFORD BROOKES UNIVERSITY

Design Engine has developed a particular approach to the problem that Sullivan identified; whilst accepting that the internal function will always impact in some way on the external form of the building, Design Engine celebrate the poetic possibilities that buildings' function affords. To do so they interpret the use of the building, its context and history, to develop a facade which tells a story through allusion, which makes for a surface rich in meaning. Employing a process of abstraction, the surface is particular and unique, using shifts in scale and pattern which make poetic reference to the building's use. In practical terms the patterns are rescaled to respond to the orientation of each facade and the need for solar shading, yet each surface tells a story and when read together the surfaces of the building make for a lyrical interpretation and meaningful expression.

Surface Scale

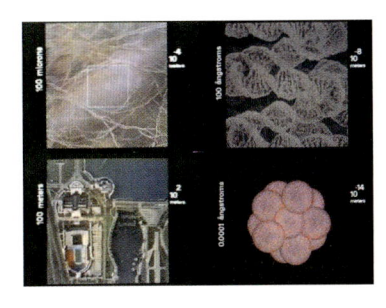

The great Romantic poet William Blake, famed for his visual artistry with words, alludes to the cosmic continuity from the smallest element to the most vast galaxy in the famous opening lines of "Auguries of Innocence". The shifting scales of architectural appreciation from the overarching concept through to the tiniest construction detail have this same continuity. The use of microscopic cellular structures rescaled to the glazing surface patterns or fretwork in steel panels brings to the fore the otherwise unobserved underlying structures that underpin the world around us.

> *To see a World in a Grain of Sand*
> *And a Heaven in a Wild Flower,*
> *Hold Infinity in the palm of your hand*
> *And Eternity in an hour.*
> — WILLIAM BLAKE, "AUGURIES OF INNOCENCE"

Blake's shifting scales were reinterpreted for the modern age in a short film written and directed by Charles and Ray Eames in 1977, titled, *Powers of Ten: A Film Dealing with the Relative Size of Things in the Universe and the Effect of Adding Another Zero*. Beginning with a one square metre overhead frame of a man and woman picnicking in a Chicago park, the camera draws away in intervals that see the frame of reference reduced by a power of ten, framing the park, the city, the earth and ultimately the scale of the observable universe. The film reverses direction from this cosmic perspective, zooming ever inwards, passing the original frame into the realm of negative powers of ten to show the cellular, elemental and atomic structure of the reference point. Similarly, this rescaling of the structures underlying the world around us is an architectural device employed when considering matters of surface to reveal the invisible structures that are the foundations of our world.

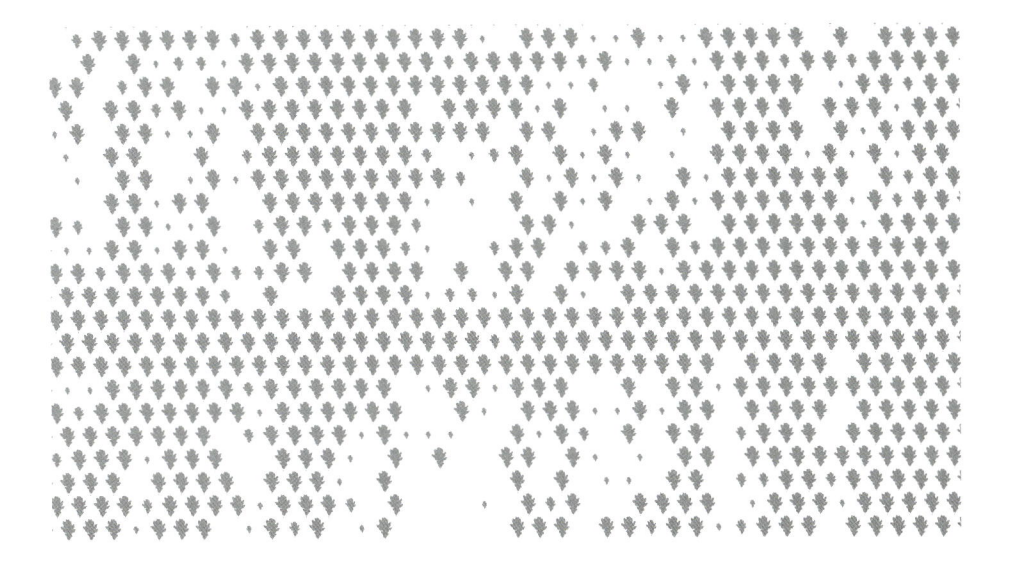

ABOVE
Frames taken from the film *Powers of Ten: A Film Dealing with the Relative Size of Things in the Universe and the Effect of Adding Another Zero* shows the camera zooming out from an original frame of reference.

ABOVE & RIGHT
The glazing of the central volume at John Henry Brookes Building is etched with a repeated oak leaf pattern. The leaf, repeated many tens of thousands of times, was found in nearby South Park and digitised; the degree to which the pattern, in each case, reduces solar gain has been factored into the analysis of the facade performance.

John Henry Brookes Forum Space at Oxford Brookes University.

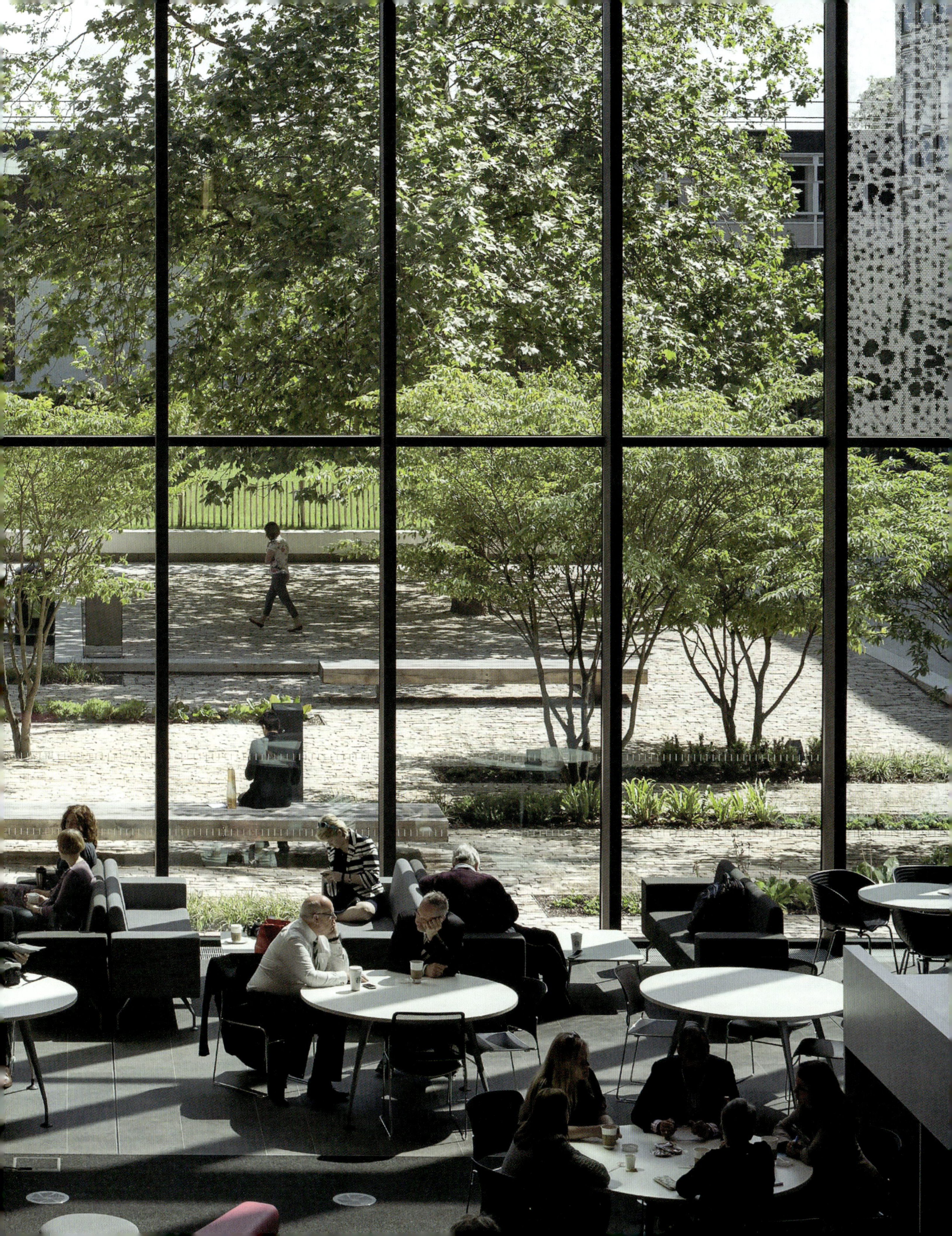

The Origin of Surface

ABOVE
Photograph of woven wooden strips which form the support structure for one of the earliest forms of wall construction, dating back over 6,000 years.

The term 'fabric' when associated with architecture is commonly used to describe the material elements from which a building is made. The elements of fabric comprise a series of surfaces: the walls, roof and floor materials which combine to create the enclosures which mediate the internal environment of human habitation from the external atmosphere. The stories which these surfaces tell are as much a part of us as the clothes we wear, our second skin; through history the tertiary skin of architecture has played an equal role in communicating who we are.

Gottfried Semper in his book *The Four Elements of Architecture*, 1851, set out a case that architecture starts from primitive origins and has its roots in construction, particularly the elements of the hearth, roof, enclosure and mound which he associated with ceramics, carpentry, weaving and stonemasonry respectively.[2] The wall he felt was a fundamental aspect of architecture as enclosure, being both a vertical means of protection, spatial definition and boundary designation. However, in its origins Semper describes the building skin as a fabric and attributes its making to the wall fitter or Wandbereiter, the maker of mats and carpets. Lightweight infill walls covered in woven fabric are to be found in some of the earliest forms of shelter such as wattle screens, where a woven lattice of wooden strips daubed with soil, clay and animal dung make enclosing infill panels, as exemplified in medieval timber frame buildings. Semper felt that wicker work was the essence of the wall, viewing the architectural elevation as a fabric screen that paralleled the woven garments which clothe the body and used the term *Bekleidung*, meaning clothing or attire, to describe the facade of a building as an aspect of dressing. To see the enclosing fabric of a building as analogous to the garments that cloak the skin brings to the fore the importance of the external communicative role and cultural significance of this fabric; something distinct from mere environmental modification which carries the poetic communicative possibilities of the building's surface.

JOHN HENRY BROOKES BUILDING, OXFORD BROOKES UNIVERSITY

A constant point of reference throughout the Oxford Brookes University building is a ribbon of weathered steel, which runs from the colonnade at the John Henry Brookes Building through the library and terminates at the food hall. At the end of the ribbon and facing a parkland of mature trees the ribbon delaminates from the glazed facade of the food hall to form a free-standing solar screen that wraps around the building.

The pattern cut into the Corten steel is derived from the cellular structure of the surrounding trees. This microscopic structure is multiplied by many powers of ten and draws attention to the otherwise invisible structures that underpin the surrounding environment. It casts a shadow whose porosity is reminiscent of the woven lattice screen which Semper felt was the origin of the wall.

Unlike the woven wicker screen that Semper described, here weathered steel does not require any protection such as paint, but instead forms a protective layer of oxidised material, which prevents further corrosion from occurring. The use of weathered steel is intended to reference the works of artists such as Richard Serra and Anthony Caro. The use of steel also serves to differentiate Oxford Brookes University as a modern institution, with material chosen to contrast with the stonework of Oxford University, its more historic counterpart.

ABOVE
At the John Henry Brookes Building at Oxford Brookes University, the weathered steel ribbon delaminates from the side of the food hall to provide a solar-protecting patterned screen and colonnade.

RIGHT
These drawings describe the fabrication of the patterned weathered screen element. The lime tree cell structure pattern has been chosen to reflect the predominant tree species in this location of Oxford.

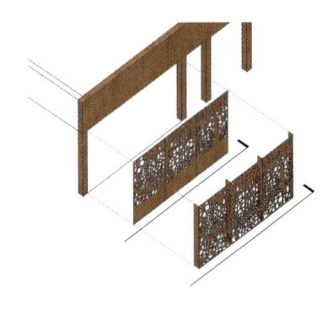

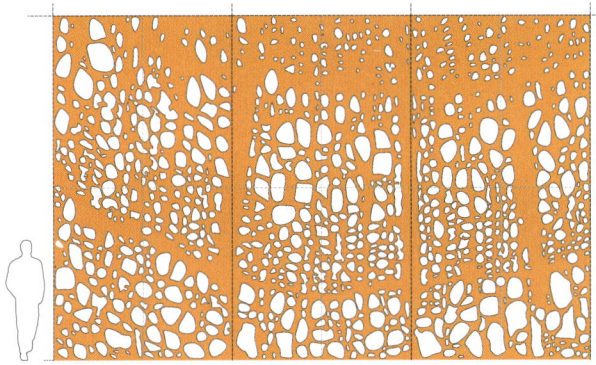

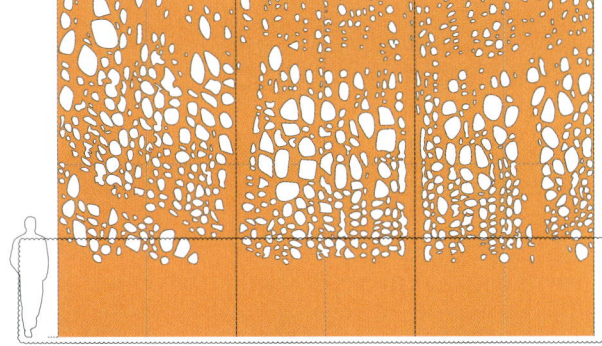

SURFACE | 119

Meaning in Surface

ABOVE
Photograph of Gdansk shipyard which provided the inspiration for the use of weathered steel to fabricate the outer shell of the new theatre.

ABOVE
The Last Judgement, 1467–1471, by Hans Memling, which is on display in the National Museum, Gdansk.

RIGHT
Visualisation detailing the southeast view of the theatre and its relationship to the city wall.

Every surface of a building is meaningful, each tells a story and, whilst a high level of abstraction may be employed, the surface and in particular the elevation is an important architectural device used to communicate ideas about the building's use and its location. In this way the facade is a semiotic device used to symbolise ideas and values. Since modern architecture dispensed with much of the facade's requirement to convey structural and tectonic meaning, the question of what the external appearance of architecture conveys has become ever more important. The ubiquitous glazed box of spandrels and mullions that has come to convey the corporate world and High Tech architecture predominantly appeals to values of rational efficiency and business prowess. Alternatively, straw bale or rammed earth construction along with green roofs and solar shading are seen as in some ways carriers of values about sustainability and ethical concerns. These questions are inherently linked with what a building symbolises and are bound to the semiotics of architecture. The Swiss linguistic theorist Ferdinand de Saussure defined the structure of semiotics and sought to understand the way in which language, in its broadest sense, including words spoken and written, along with images and sounds, is used to communicate ideas.[3] Much architectural thought has been invested into the ideas of semiotics to understand the rich history of architectural semiology and how buildings either overtly or latently communicated ideas.

Central to this discourse is the issue of overt and covert meaning. In a very direct sense, much of classical architecture made direct reference to the people, gods or battles for which it was built, either as places of worship or memorial. In this way the relationship between building and meaning was strongly established and ideas clearly denoted. However, such very literal bonding between the sign and that which is signified can result in a lack of subtlety and in many ways excludes the observer from incorporating their own meanings into the work. Using an approach which rather than employing denotation relies more on connotation, where meaning is suggested or implied, makes for buildings of enhanced richness. Creating surfaces of intentional symbolic ambiguity engages the observer and recognises that we each create our own unique interpretations of the world—our own personal stories through which we find meaning in that which surrounds us.

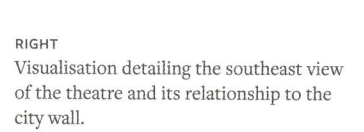

BUILDING STORIES | 120

RIGHT
Model showing side elevation with fading Shakespearean text.

BELOW LEFT
A sample used to test the transparency of the external skin.

BELOW RIGHT
Laser cut elevation of weathered steel showing Shakespearean text.

GDANSK THEATRE

The Gdansk Theatre was a competition-winning design, which provides a fresh interpretation of the Elizabethan Theatre by using new building technology, environmental systems and auditorium design to complement the inherent familiarity and intimacy of the old scale and proportions. The building provided a strong and clear narrative of the understanding of the history of Gdansk and the memory and importance of the Theatrum to the city. The Gdansk Theatre embodies its history in three ways. In conceptual terms the outer skin of the building is composed of two commodities that are strongly associated with Gdansk: steel and amber. The amber was referenced due to the abundance of the precious material washing up on the shores of Gdansk and is represented by a lightweight translucent polycarbonate curtain wall. Laser-cut steel panels, which could be fabricated in the shipyards of Gdansk, form a rainscreen cladding. The laser-cut pattern uses text of varying weight; as the letters grow fatter the text gradually becomes indecipherable until the facade becomes totally opaque. The text consists of phrases from Shakespeare's plays, selected to reinforce the metaphorical depiction of the universe in the building; at the base of the facade are quotations relating to darkness and evil ("stars, hide your fires; let not light see my black and deep desires"), and at the top are quotations relating to the sun. It is the same cosmic order that is powerfully represented in Hans Memling's *Last Judgement* in the Gdansk Muzeum Narodowe.

The roof of the auditorium was designed to be retractable to allow open-air performance in summer. Emblazoned with the coat of arms of the city, in its open form it becomes a signal announcing the performance of a play, just like the flags and trumpeters of Elizabethan times.

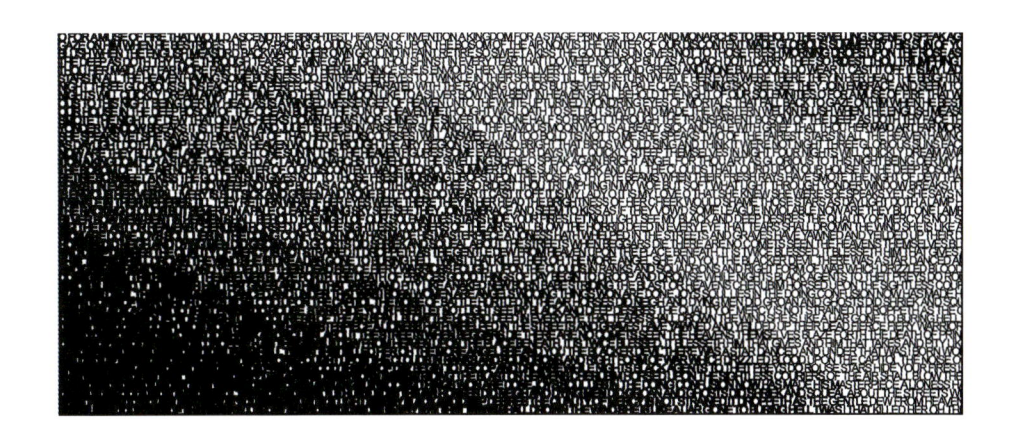

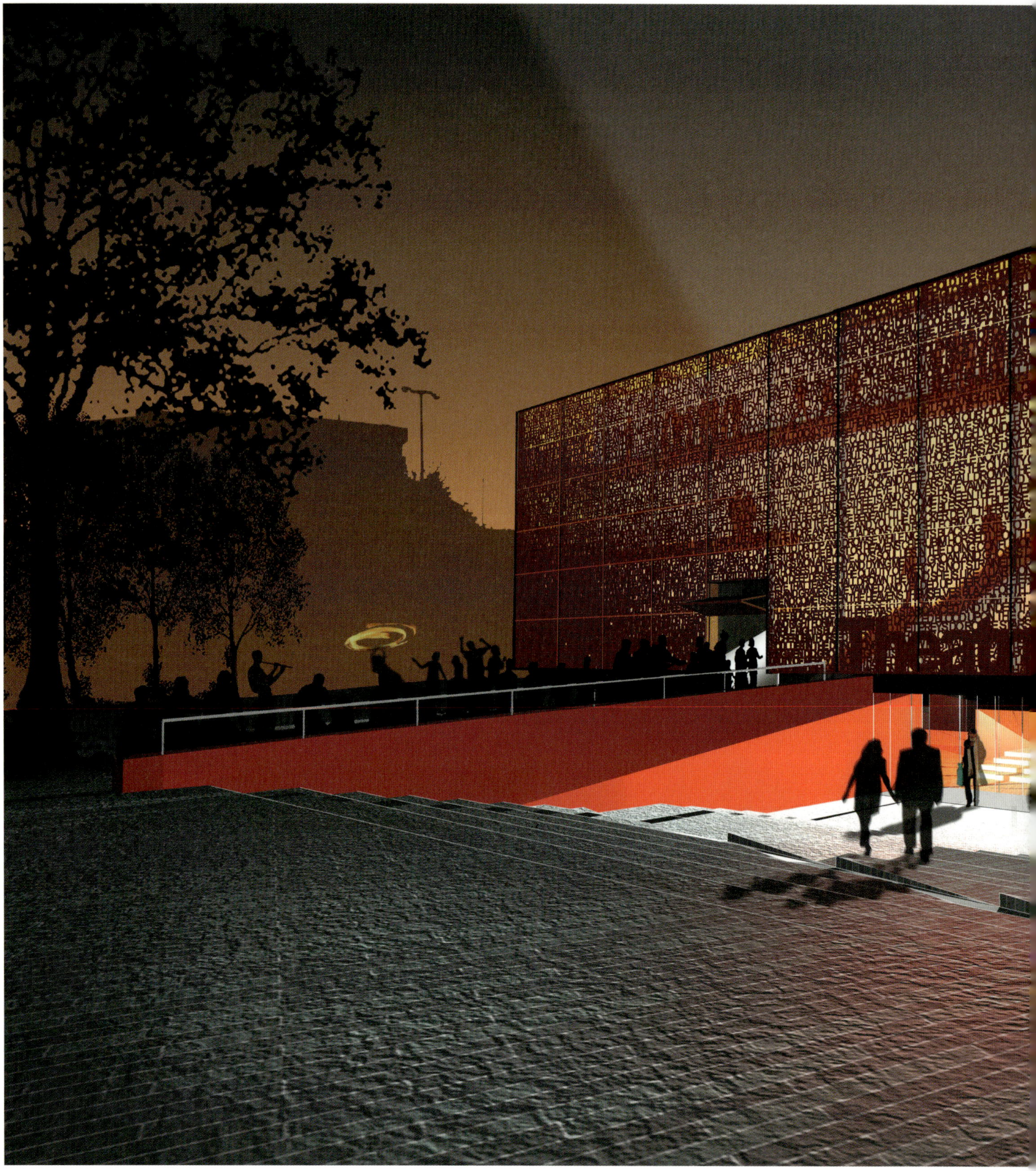

The proposed Gdansk Theatre: when seen at night the laser-cut pattern glows with text of varying weight composed of phrases from Shakespeare's plays. The text is ambiguous and progressively merges together bringing, into question the relationships between letters, words and patterns. As such, the facade is intentionally ambiguous in its meaning and open to multiple interpretations.

Surface Projection

ABOVE
The exterior of the Photography Building at Arts University Bournemouth refers to early cameras, taking the form of a black box.

The manner in which a building's surface both receives and emits light makes it a complex optical instrument, at one time the absorber and at others the transmitter of light. In this respect the elevation of a building is a complex visual instrument and parallels the optical device of the camera: the 'dark chamber' used to project an image of external reality onto a flat surface. The projection of external reality onto an elevation where surfaces receive patterns and textured projections is in turn projected into the interior during the day and outwards to the surroundings at night. The idea of projection is deeply rooted in architecture, and students learn various forms of graphic projection as a central tool of representation. Projection has other connotations of planning or forecasting future situations, and projection is an attribute not only of mathematical order but a phenomenon of time, as surfaces change their appearance throughout the course of the day. The history of photography and the use of the camera is that of the capturing of a moment in time, and equally in architecture this moment becomes what Goethe termed 'frozen music', with the freezing and focusing of projection made apparent through surface.[4]

Architecture is the masterly, correct and magnificent play of masses brought together in light.
— LE CORBUSIER

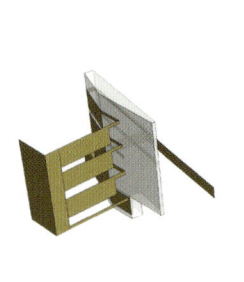

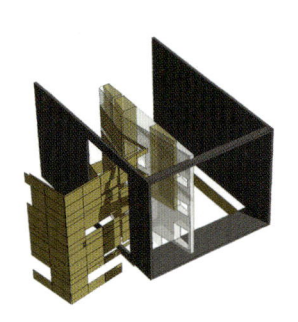

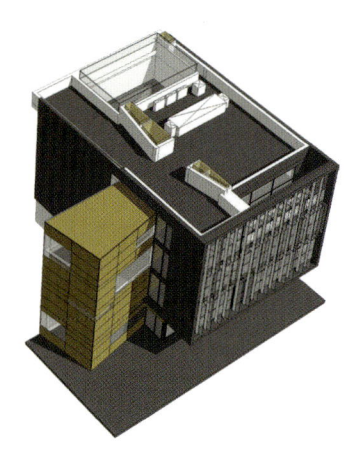

PHOTOGRAPHY BUILDING, ARTS UNIVERSITY BOURNEMOUTH

The new Photography Building extension infills a square site between wings of an existing 1980s building, where the technical darkroom and studio areas are located. The new four-storey building provides associated support spaces such as breakout, communal, social learning and general teaching spaces, lecture theatre and IT suites, as well as connecting to the existing building circulation routes at each floor level.

Conceptually, the design has been informed by photographic processes; the principal west-facing facade features an array of digitally printed glazed fins that act as an environmental filter to reflect, diffuse and moderate natural daylight into the building interior, utilising modern printing and imaging technology whilst referencing the early forms and glass plate negatives of photographic procedures.

The building's exterior refers to early cameras, taking the form of a black box with apertures forming the roof lights, windows and ventilation louvres. These also allow controlled natural light and air through the atrium and circulation spaces and provide low-energy environmental control.

ABOVE RIGHT
Initial concept model of the 'black box', with the penetrating staircase. This was changed to include the staircase within the overall box.

BUILDING STORIES | 124

RIGHT
Entrance to the Photography Building at Arts University Bournemouth.

BELOW LEFT
Glass fins.

BELOW RIGHT
Images of the repeated pattern at variable scales, used for testing purposes.

Surface and Depth

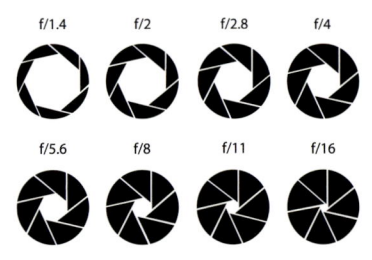

Surface is the absorber and reflector of light, and the opacity, translucency or transparency of surface fundamentally affects our perception of architecture. The surface depth of a building is revealed through the layers of transparency; gossamer veils that give an ambiguity to surface and afford buildings a sense of uncertain visual depth. The surface of a building in this way might be considered in terms of strata of reflection and refraction which affords a sense of ambiguity that exists between the two-dimensional surface and the three-dimensional depth.

The sun never knew how great it was until it hit the side of a building.
— LOUIS KAHN

The objective of surface in architecture is to reveal this magnificence, and for Kahn, in a philosophical sense, light was the giver of all presences and material was in essence spent light. The articulation of the visual depth of a surface through shadow plays an important role as buildings receive depth and form through the interplay of light and shade.

ABOVE
Camera f-stops and lens aperture.

RIGHT
Photograph of the Photography Building at Arts University Bournemouth's completed glass blades.

BUILDING STORIES | 126

RIGHT
The exterior of the Photography Building at Arts University Bournemouth refers to early cameras and apertures.

BELOW
Ken Russell at work, 1967, inspecting drying celluloid film strips.

PHOTOGRAPHY BUILDING, ARTS UNIVERSITY BOURNEMOUTH

The elevation of the Arts University Bournemouth Photography Building receives a series of glazed fins set perpendicular to the facade. These long and thin fins running the full height of the elevation and across the intermediate floor levels are intended to be reminiscent of the chemical process used for the developing of 35 mm film reels and the strip of framed shots hanging in the dark room to dry. The metaphor of photography extends to the fritted pattern on each fin and alludes to the changes in photographic processes. Here the elevation is pixelated according to a pattern taken from the advent of photography and the first Daguerreotype image invented by Louis-Jaques-Mandé Daguerre at the beginning of the nineteenth century. Each pixel is picked out in a circular dot whose pattern follows the f-numbers used to determine the size of the aperture of a camera. This opening size, which determines the amount of light admitted to the receiving plane of the camera, affects the focal depth of the image and is linked to the exposure time of each image. Thus the elevation alludes not only to optical mechanics but captures the idea of visual depth and exposure time both literally and metaphorically.

At a practical level the fins serve to mediate the luminous environment of the classrooms within, and the density of the pattern is arranged to respond to the internal environmental needs and orientation of the building to the passage of the sun. At night the fins are lit by the interior and, framed by the surrounding edge of the building, take on the form of a projection screen. The flickering lines of each fin evoke the magic lanterns that preceded the development of still photography, or the zoetrope, one of the pre-moving film animation devices that produce the illusion of motion by displaying a sequence of drawings or photographs set inside a rotating drum to show progressive phases of movement.

Surface Permeability

ABOVE
The eastern facade of the British Embassy in Yemen utilised a weathered steel veil to protect the building from the intense sun and also to shield views into the private quarters of the Ambassador.

BELOW LEFT
Exploded axonometric of the layered facade to the Perrodo pavilion.

BELOW RIGHT
Visualisation of the Perrodo pavilion showing a section through the facade.

The design of surface is frequently a question of permeability as the balance of openness and enclosure tells stories of the relationship between the inside private realm and the external public domain. The facade conceived in this manner finds parallels in Islamic and Indian architecture, where the *mashrabiya*, *shanasheel* or *jali* screen form a latticework of timber or stone, which provides ventilation in tropical and arid climates whilst affording privacy and security. These latticework screens traditionally use strong geometric patterns that follow sacred geometries and allude to the cosmological order. In using similar devices of permeability, the elevation treatment creates surfaces that, from a distance, have a sense of solidity yet, on closer examination, are subtly permeable. Often, with the delicacy of lacework these surfaces create an ambiguity so that the building is at once a clear geometric form in response to the surrounding context yet, at a smaller scale, creates a blurring between inside and outside. Rather than the symbolic patterns of Islamic art, these veils carefully balance horizontal and vertical lines with sections cut away or with the building pulled back from the screen, delaminating the building and the veil. The effect is one of an etched veneer inscribed to the elevation. It is a *yashmak*, the face veil of two pieces of fine muslin drawn across the face of some Islamic women. It is at once a gesture of modesty yet at the same time hints to an underlying beauty alluringly concealed.

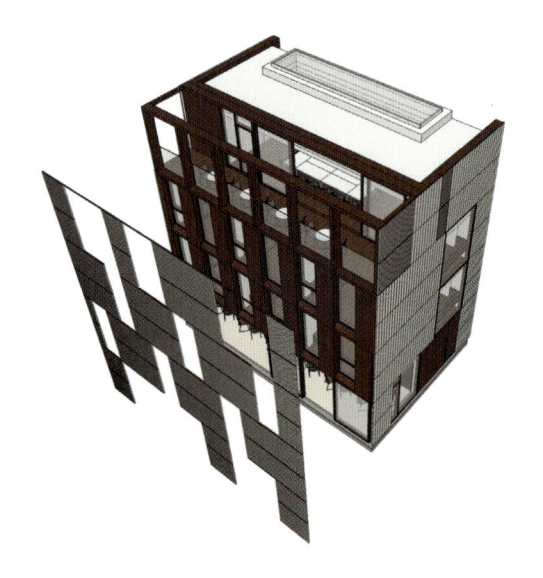

BUILDING STORIES | 128

ABOVE
Visualisation of the layering of the Perrodo pavilion's facade looking out onto the quad.

PERRODO PROJECT, ST PETER'S COLLEGE, OXFORD

The Perrodo Project is a new scheme to make St Peter's College a better place to study, teach and live by improving teaching and living accommodation, as well as external spaces. The arrangement in the new pavilion is intended to reflect the neighbouring Chavasse Building model with communal spaces on the ground floor, which open onto the re-landscaped quad, with more private study rooms above.

The proposed building draws its architectural language from the existing campus. Square-section ceramic rods are hung as a 'veil' or screen to the facade to help unify it and give coherence to different levels as well as providing shading and privacy to the windows behind. The ceramic has a natural finish, chosen to match the texture and tone of the stone detailing of neighbouring buildings.

The colour of the bronze cladding, echoing brickwork, is seen through this louvred facade when it passes across the solid elements.

The layering of the facade of the Perrodo pavilion has two functions: ceramic and bronze cladding combine to reflect the brick and stone hues of its immediate neighbours, but the spacing of the baguettes also provides a sensation of virtual movement. With a gentle nod to op art, the perception of the facade when moving within the building and around the quad changes as the facade opens and closes, giving the illusion of changing proportions of bronze and ceramic.

Theatre
Architecture and Theatre

ABOVE
The Gdansk Theatre was figured both literally as a distinct building type and metaphorically as an illustration of architecture as theatre in the city.

On the surface, architecture and theatre might be seen as polar opposites. Architecture is a spatial art experienced by the moving observer over time, whereas theatre is a time-based art of performance, perceived by a static observer fixed in space. However, from the theatricality of the Baroque city to the spectacle of the Situationists' events, the arts of architecture and theatre have much in common.

The view that architecture could be seen as analogous to theatre held little sway throughout the twentieth century. The perception of theatre as some kind of fakery meant that the term was held in broad disdain by those who prioritised the functionalist ideals of modernism. However such a literal interpretation denies the poetic analogies between architecture and theatre. This poetic sense calls for a metaphorical rather than literal relationship; it is important to be cautious when talking of architecture and theatre in any literal sense. In this metaphorical sense, the term theatre does not imply the design of theatres as a distinct building type in which plays and other performances are enacted, although there are examples of these in their work. Neither should architecture be reduced to the level of theatrical scenography, for although there are important overlaps such pejorative analogies are often used to disparage buildings for their reliance on surface impression, lack of substance and impermanence. In contrast, the idea of theatre can be symbolic rather than overtly theatrical and takes on a fundamentally poetic meaning.

> It was agreed that my endeavours should be directed to persons and characters supernatural, or at least romantic—yet so as to transfer from our inward nature a human interest and a semblance of truth sufficient to procure for these shadows of imagination that willing suspension of disbelief, for the moment, which constitutes poetic faith.[6]

The term 'suspension of disbelief' was first used in 1817 by the poet and aesthetic philosopher Samuel Taylor Coleridge.

OPPOSITE
The artwork on the St Alphege Building at University of Winchester forms the symbolic heart of the campus.

BUILDING STORIES | 130

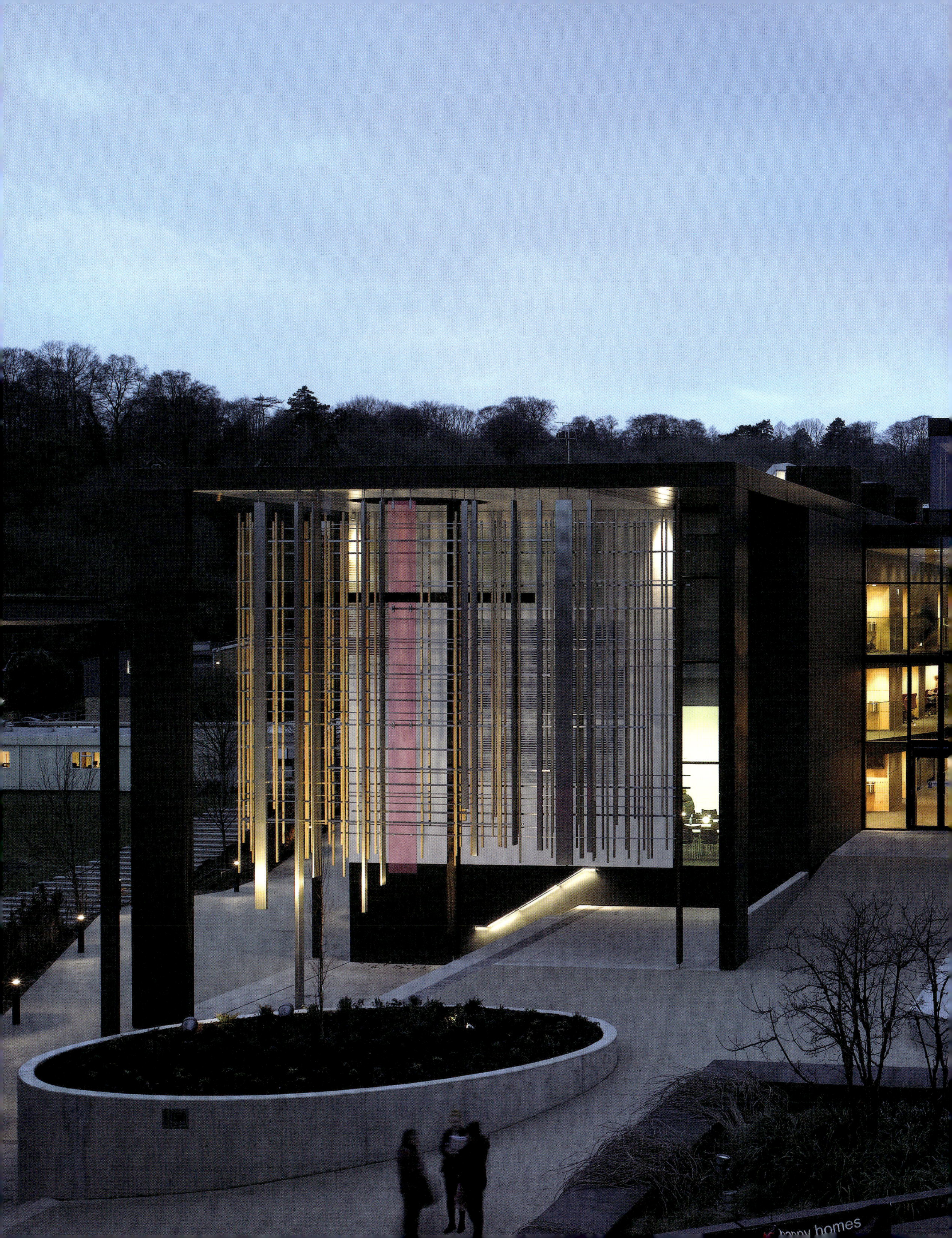

Wisdom in Theatre

ABOVE
Evangelistar von Speyer, dating from around 1220, was the liturgical book in the Catholic and Orthodox Churches. Created for the cathedral in Speyer, Germany, the book is now held in the Badische Landesbibliothek, Karlsruhe, Germany, and is famous for its gold illuminated miniatures. This image shows Christ framed in a vesica shape surrounded by the animal symbols of the four evangelists. The vesica piscis formed by the intersection of two circles is a symbol of the Christian faith, and this along with the vivid colours informs the design of the entrance portico of the St Alphege Building at the University of Winchester.

Theatre is fundamentally an act of artifice concerned with the illusion of reality. Whilst this world of illusion may be fantastical and wholly invented, to be seduced into accepting its fiction we must at a personal level be able to relate to that which is played out before us. In this, theatre relies on evoking elements of our own experience, and its success is contingent upon mankind's inherent ability to feel empathy, seeing in the spectacle a mirror of our own human condition. The role of the playwright or theatre director is one of constructing a world in which the sharing of emotional states can take place, and whilst this might be more direct and immediate in the context of the theatre the architect is fundamentally concerned with the way in which buildings make people feel. Whilst the theatre relies on illusion, visual trickery and deception that entices the observer into the fiction, architecture can rarely employ the same means without falling into a realm of pastiche. Rather, for the architect the device of allusion, which relies on subtle reference of indirect mention, affords the means of engaging the observer in the building narrative. Having empathy for the feeling of others and understanding the emotional effect that is achieved through art relies not only on the subject represented but the manner in which this representation takes place. The term 'mimesis' has its origins in ancient Greek and literally means 'to imitate'. However mimesis holds a crucial philosophical importance in aesthetics and is central to questions of representation both in art and architecture. For Plato and Aristotle mimesis was concerned with the representation of nature. In the case of Plato, faced with a world constantly subject to change and decay, the mimetic act was to look beyond the surface phenomena of fleeting reality to the perfection of mathematics, which he felt underpinned the world of appearance. Plato felt that this perfect world of timeless geometric shapes and forms provided the starting point for the artist or architect, who by representing rather than copying the visual appearance of the world was in fact representing the greater truth of timeless perfection.[7]

In opposition, Aristotle rejected these Platonic ideals in favour of artistic representation that embraced the processes of change. In his view, the role of the arts was to draw attention to some aspect of reality or experience, framing existence so that the observer might better empathise with that presented. Aristotle was cautious that such framing be seen as an aspect of artifice such that the observer retain sufficient distance to preserve it as ultimately nothing more than a construct. Indeed Aristotle's book *Poetics* is his treatise on the subject of mimesis and sets out the various ways in which imitation can be structured.

ST ALPHEGE BUILDING ARTWORK, UNIVERSITY OF WINCHESTER

The artwork for the St Alphege Building at the University of Winchester forms an integral part of the entrance portico. Each element of the filigree of steel, timber and coloured glass has a precise meaning that makes reference to the university's Christian foundations.

The entrance portico is governed by a precise geometry formed by a series of overlapping circles. The vesica piscis generated by the overlap is a symbol of Christian faith and is formed by the intersection of two circles with the same radius drawn in such a way that the centre of each lies on the perimeter of the other.

RIGHT
The entrance portico artwork for the St Alphege Building at University of Winchester is a backdrop to the students' gathering space below.

BELOW LEFT
The entrance portico is governed by a precise geometry, formed by a series of overlapping circles.

BELOW RIGHT
View looking out through the St Alphege artwork.

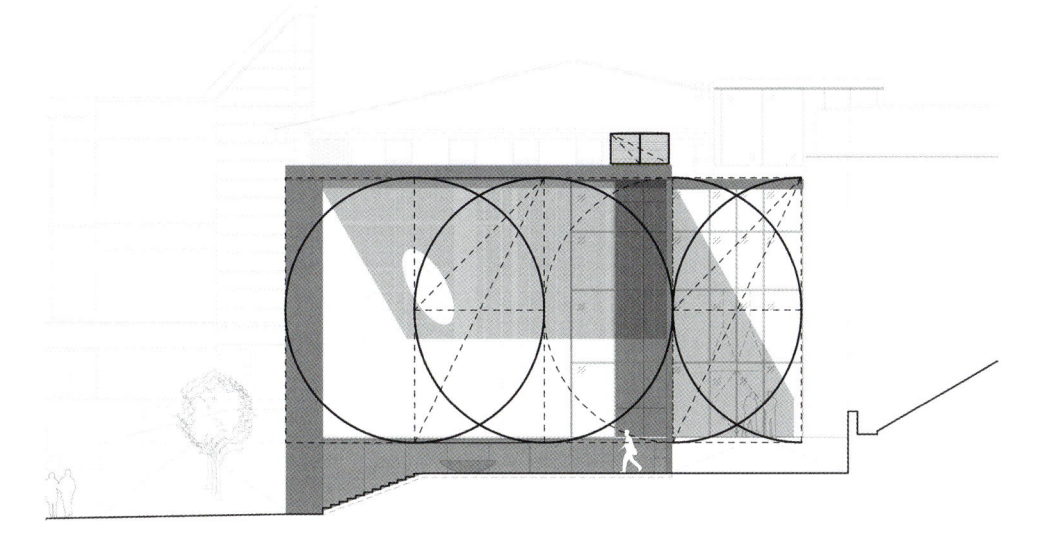

ST ALPHEGE ARTWORK

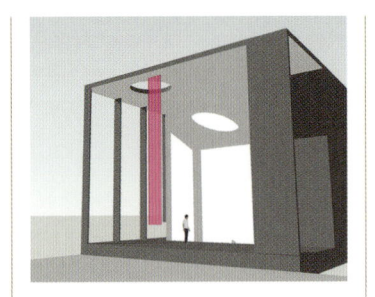

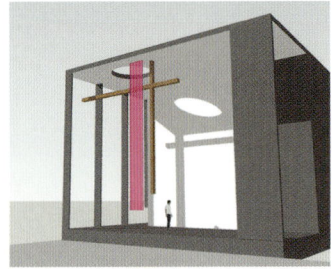

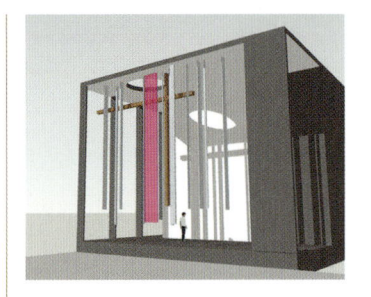

CHRIST

The rose-coloured glass panel represents Jesus and is located to relate directly to the oculus behind. The panel also includes an abstract curved line which echoes the vesica piscis as well as the curve of a pregnant woman's profile. The colour of the glass speaks of unconditional love within the Christian faith.

CROSS

The abstract cross, whilst referencing the crucifixion, also alludes to King Alfred after whom the University of Winchester's campus is named.

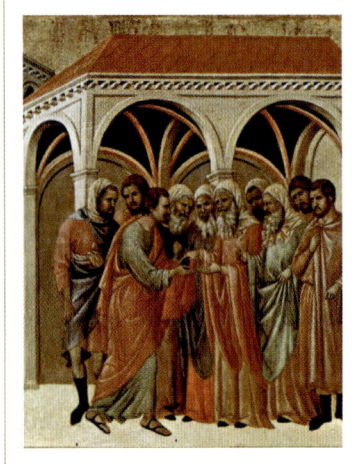

APOSTLES

The vertical stainless steel columns represent the 11 apostles. The material is meant to represent their untarnished characters. Their composition is influenced by the painting *The Last Supper* by Carl Heinrich Bloch.

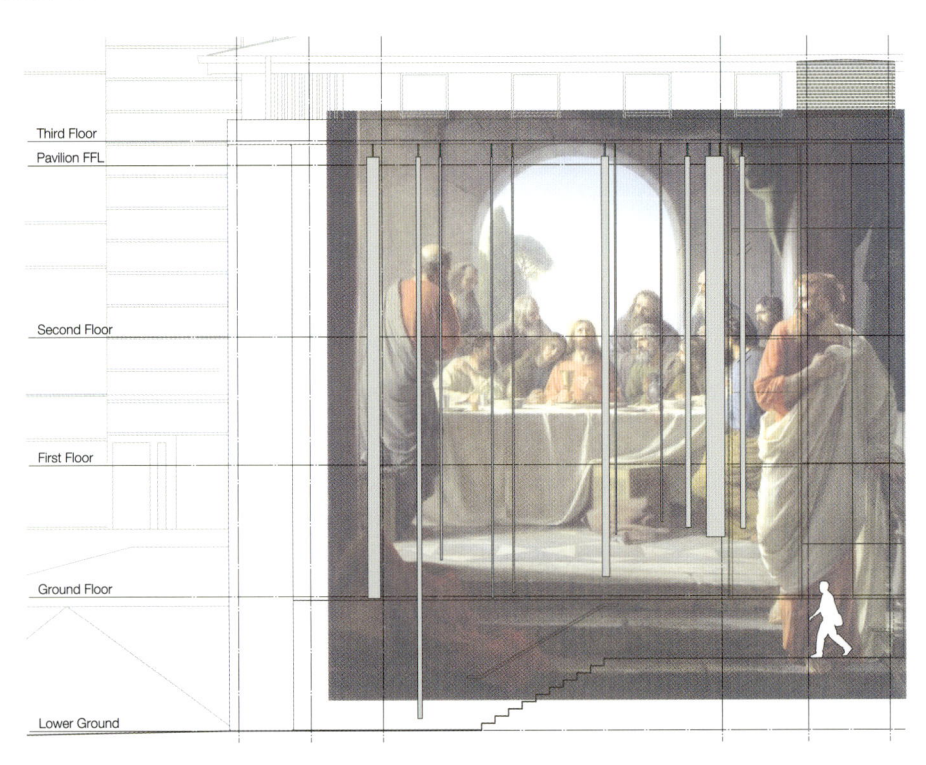

RIGHT
The Last Supper by Carl Heinrich Bloch with the composition of the 11 apostles overlaid.

BUILDING STORIES | 134

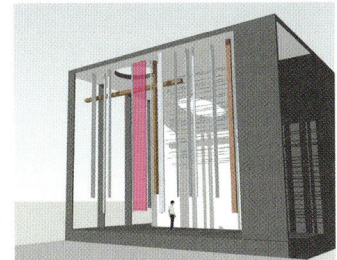

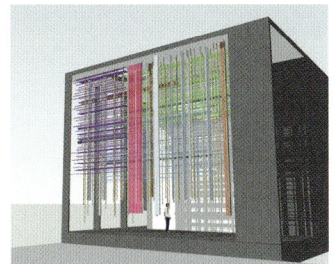

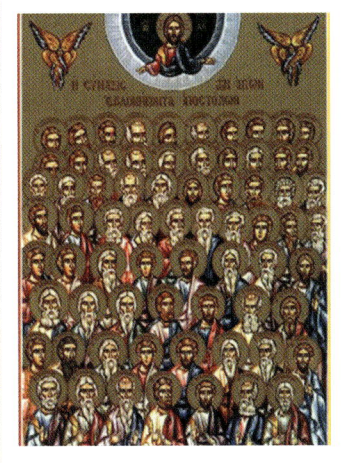

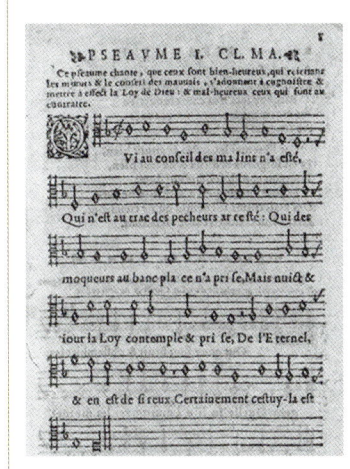

JUDAS

The single vertical column made from rusting steel represents Judas Iscariot and like the painting is placed to the very right of the sculpture.

30 PIECES OF SILVER

The overall structure of the piece is held together with 30 horizontal polished steel rods which represent the 30 pieces of silver that Judas was paid for his betrayal of Jesus.

DISCIPLES/STUDENTS

The multiple rough sawn vertical timber slats represent disciples as well as all the students of the university. Over time these pieces will weather and distort to reflect the natural passage of life.

PSALMS

The horizontal lines within the coloured glass panels represent musical notation and scripture and in particular Christian psalms. The colours are influenced by the illuminations within the Winchester Bible. The pattern within the lines is created by abstracting a typical human DNA strip.

RIGHT & FAR RIGHT
A typical human DNA profiling strip has been abstracted to create the horizontal lines on the six-coloured glass patterns.

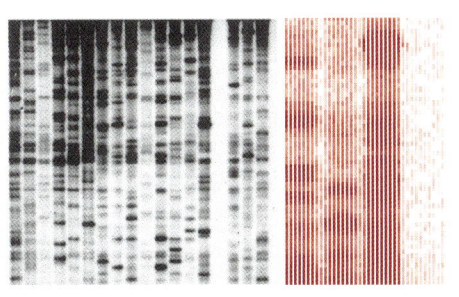

City as Theatre

ABOVE
The design for the new theatre is located on the site of the historic Gdansk Fencing School. The school was the place where itinerant English theatrical troupes first gave performances of Shakespeare's plays. One image of the old structure has been preserved in a drawing by Peter Willer from the late seventeenth century.

Giambattista Nolli's plan of Rome commissioned by Pope Benedict XIV is famous for its use of figure-ground representation, with built space blocked out and shaded in a dark poché, while open civic spaces or streets, piazzas and enclosed public spaces, such as the colonnades in St Peter's Square and the Pantheon, are left standing out in the residual white space of the plan. Around 100 years after the great Baroque urban replanning, Nolli's plan is a record of the Rome which prioritises the open spaces as rooms within the city and the venues in which the affairs of its citizens were played out.

Nolli's plan became a touchstone when towards the end of the twentieth century the Italian architect Aldo Rossi called for a return to the familiar urban models which had characterised the historic city fabric. In his seminal book *The Architecture of the City* of 1982, Rossi promoted an architectural rationalism which emphasised the importance of typology—what he saw as eternal architectural types or forms, such as the colonnade or city square, which persist across time and memory.[8] He drew on the painting of Giorgio de Chirico whose haunting metaphysical paintings sought to capture the timeless verities that constituted the urban environment. But most importantly, whilst modernism had framed design as a scientific, positivistic endeavour, Rossi reawakened architecture to its poetic possibilities as the bearer of human consciousness and memories.

> *The locus is a component of an individual artefact which, like permanence, is determined not just by space but also by time, by topography and form, and, most importantly, by its having been the site of a succession of both ancient and more recent events. For Rossi, the city is a theatre of human events. This theatre is no longer just a representation; it is a reality. It absorbs events and feelings, and every new event contains within it a memory of the past and a potential memory of the future.*
>
> — ARCHITETTURA DELLA CITTÀ, THE ARCHITECTURE OF THE CITY BY ALDO ROSSI, EXTRACT FROM THE INTRODUCTION BY PETER EISENMAN

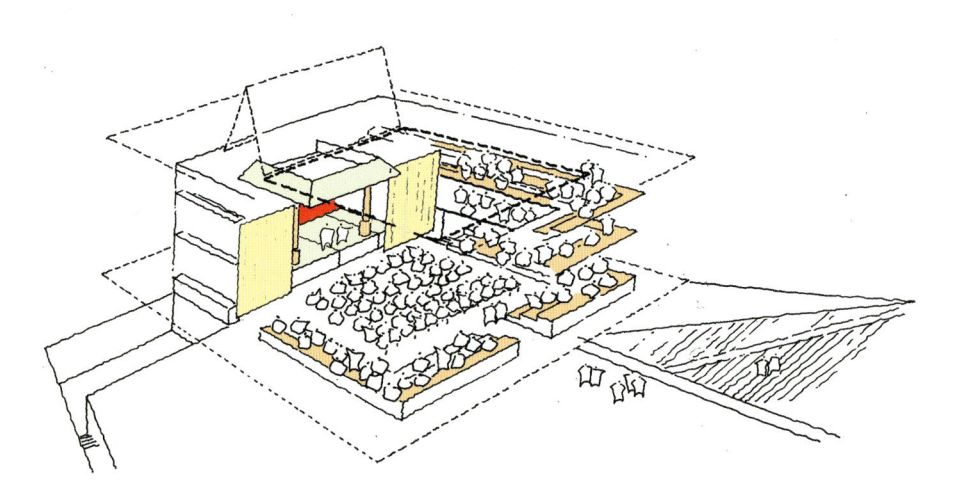

RIGHT
Perspective sketch illustrating the theatre layout to offer a proscenium performance.

ABOVE
Model showing the theatre with the roof raised, announcing that the theatre is open.

BELOW
Concept model highlighting the idea of placing a precious object within the city.

GDANSK THEATRE

The building provides a strong and clear narrative of our understanding of the history of Gdansk and the memory and importance to the city of the theatrum in particular. Using a contemporary architectural vocabulary, the building re-presents the essential symbolism of the original theatre to a twenty-first-century audience. Gdansk is the capital of Baltic amber production and the cubic volume of the theatre is seen as a box made from precious fossilised tree resin, delicately placed into the urban context. The building becomes a beacon and a monument to theatre and to the history of the city. Standing out against the everyday background buildings and grid of the urban fabric, this object follows Aldo Rossi's idea of a monument whose persistence and permanence in memory is the result of its ability to embody the collective consciousness of society.

THEATRE | 137

ABOVE
Visualisation of the River Hull Footbridge opening over the River Hull.

Architecture and Event

Architecture may be seen as analogous to theatre, but equally the city has been seen throughout history as a theatrical backdrop to the play that is human existence—the city as theatre. The idea of the *theatrum mundi*, meaning that the world is a stage, is captured in William Shakespeare's play of 1599, *As You Like It*, Act II, Scene VII:

> All the world's a stage,
> And all the men and women merely players;
> They have their exits and their entrances,
> And one man in his time plays many parts.[9]

This view that the city is in itself a theatre rose to prominence in the Baroque where the overt theatricality of architects such as Gian Lorenzo Bernini and Francesco Borromini drew directly on the growing popularity of opera and theatre, translating these on a grand scale into the city of Rome. The Piazza del Popolo and the Trevi Fountain, along with the many sinuous elevations of Baroque churches with their dramatic frescos and use of false perspective, were as much to entertain as they were to serve any direct functional requirement. The Piazza Navona, with Bernini's central Fountain of the Four Rivers set against the elaborate facade of Sant'Agnese in Agone by Borromini, was regularly flooded so that sea battles could be re-enacted. The Scala Regia, or Royal Staircase, in the Vatican, also by Bernini, enlisted the visual devices of the stage to distort the perspective of the Vatican entrance, exaggerating the barrel-vaulted colonnade. The Baroque was concerned with the spectacle of the event, and buildings animated the city as citizens played out their lives against the dramatic backdrop of sweeping curves. In this way architecture was transformed from static object to dynamic event.

RIVER HULL FOOTBRIDGE

River Hull Footbridge was a project for an opening bridge over the River Hull, linked to the proposed regeneration of the East Bank. The bridge raises and lowers to accommodate passing ships and in this movement creates a dynamic spectacle within the city which, along with its sweeping lines, evokes the theatrical qualities of the Baroque.

The project sees the bridge as an event within the city, the animated movement of the structure at once allowing ships to pass but also equally importantly providing a sense of theatre and performance that will form a vital part of the regeneration of the area. The design draws inspiration from Hull's unique condition as 'a city on the edge' and from the natural drama of the site. The development of the form was guided by the metaphor of the bridge as a 'found object', shaped by nature, like a piece of driftwood or a whale bone deposited by the sea in a foreign context. The bridge consists of two 'wings', one being the deck, the other the counterweight mast. Like the legs of a gymnast on the bar, these two wings are always perfectly balanced. As the deck rises the counterweight mast rises with it, ensuring the centre of gravity is always directly above the pier.

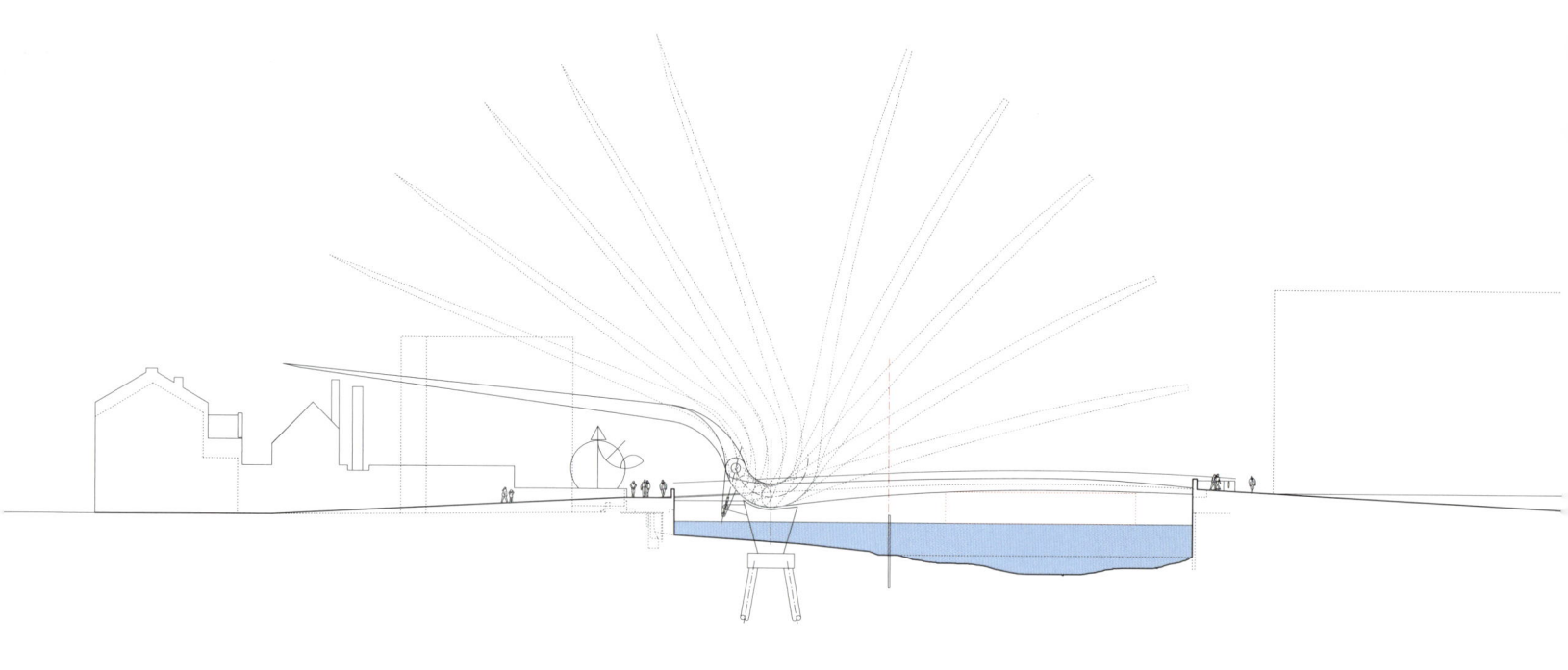

ABOVE
Elevation of River Hull Footbridge, showing the opening motion.

BELOW
Bernard Tschumi's Parc de la Villette follies.

BOTTOM
The legs of a gymnast perfectly balanced in equilibrium.

In the same way that Baroque architects had appropriated the city as a place of theatre and performance, in the mid part of the twentieth century the Situationist International movement sought to regain the city as a place of theatre. Their main protagonist was Guy Debord (1931–1994) who had seen the city as a site for radical, spontaneous events that would undermine what he perceived as the banality of consumer society.[10] Borrowing from the avant-garde art movements of the early twentieth century, particularly Dada and Surrealism, the Situationists sought to use the city as a field of artistic revolution. Through a series of spontaneous and often disruptive artistic events and gatherings through which they sought to destabilise the social order, they were the forerunners of street and graffiti art that emerged as a dominant countercultural movement. The architect Bernard Tschumi, building on the Situationists' project, was one of the first to observe that, whilst modernism had been fixated with the determined function of a building giving rise to its form, history was full of examples of buildings that had often accommodated radically different functions over the course of their existence.[11] He developed an idea that accepted this state of affairs from the outset and focussed on the events which shaped buildings and gave them new and often unpredictable meanings over time—*The Manhattan Transcripts*, 1981, where he posited that one might even need to commit a murder to fully appreciate architecture, said just as much.

Following along these lines, Tschumi developed the architectural ideas of crossprogramming (using spaces for unintended functions), transprogramming (combining two seemingly opposing functions) and disprogramming (allowing one function to subvert another), all of which cut to the heart of what had been the modernist functional imperative. Tschumi realised these ideas in his design for Parc de la Villette in Paris, begun in 1984. Here a Cartesian grid of nine red cubes seems to impose a universal order on the site, yet this order is subverted as different functions, winding routes and planes of activity clash with the putative order. Tschumi borrowed much of his thinking from film, and the sinuous paths that wind their way through the park can be seen as a series of chance encounters or frames of events cut and spliced together in the form of a surrealist filmic narrative.[12]

BUILDING STORIES | 140

ABOVE
Sketch of the view along the street illustrating how the bridge form encourages pedestrians to travel over the river.

BELOW
A simplified drawing of the mechanical movement of the bridge.

RIGHT
Stills taken from the moving film of the bridge opening.

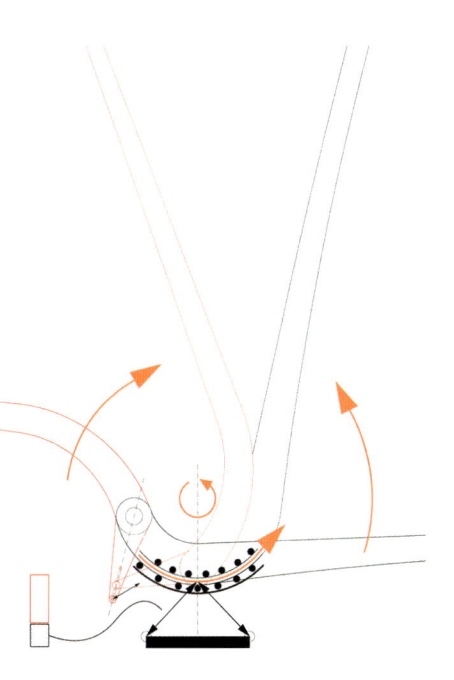

THEATRE | 141

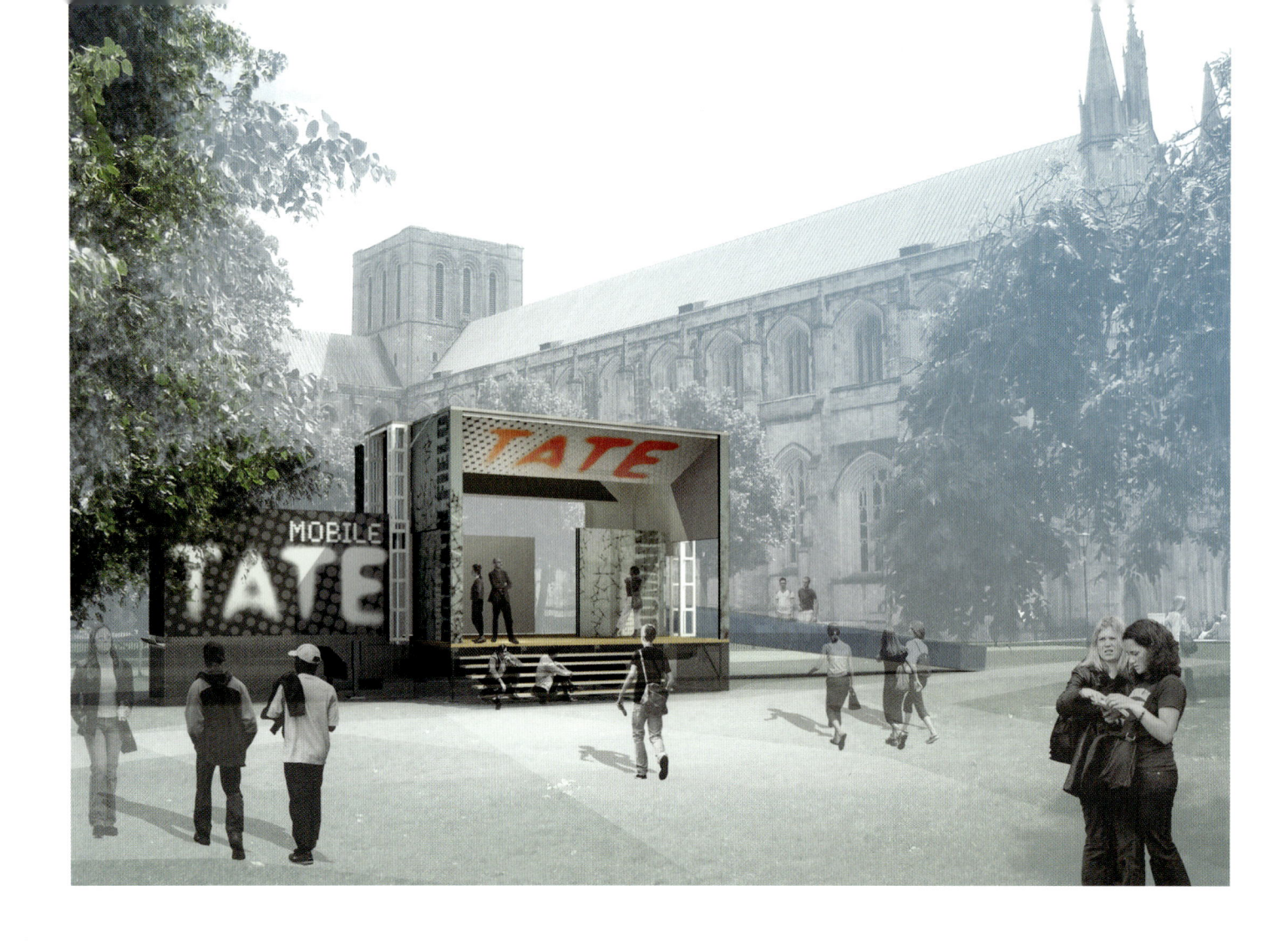

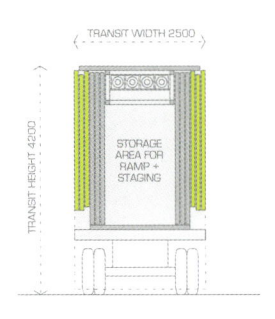

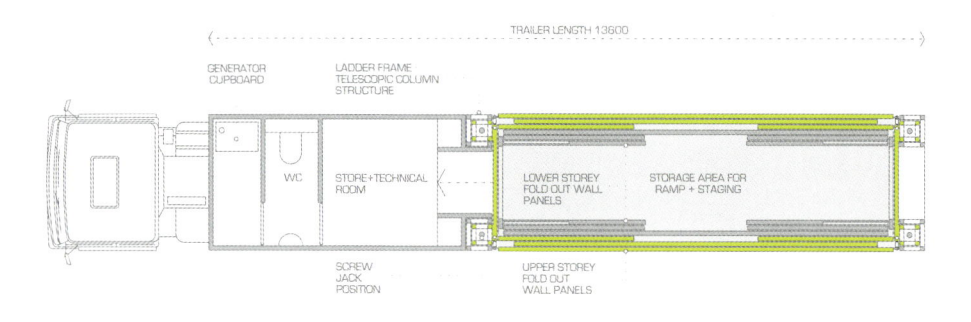

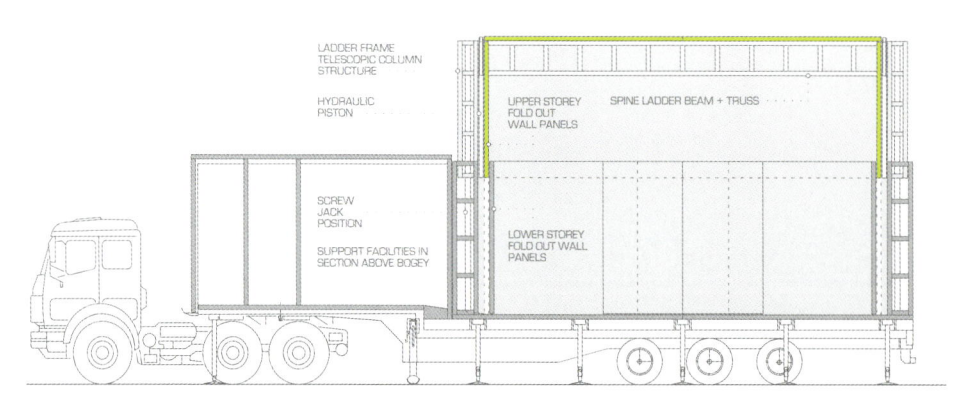

TOP
Visualisation of the Art Box project in use.

ABOVE & RIGHT
Technical drawings of how the mobile theatre is deconstructed to fit into an articulated lorry.

BUILDING STORIES | 142

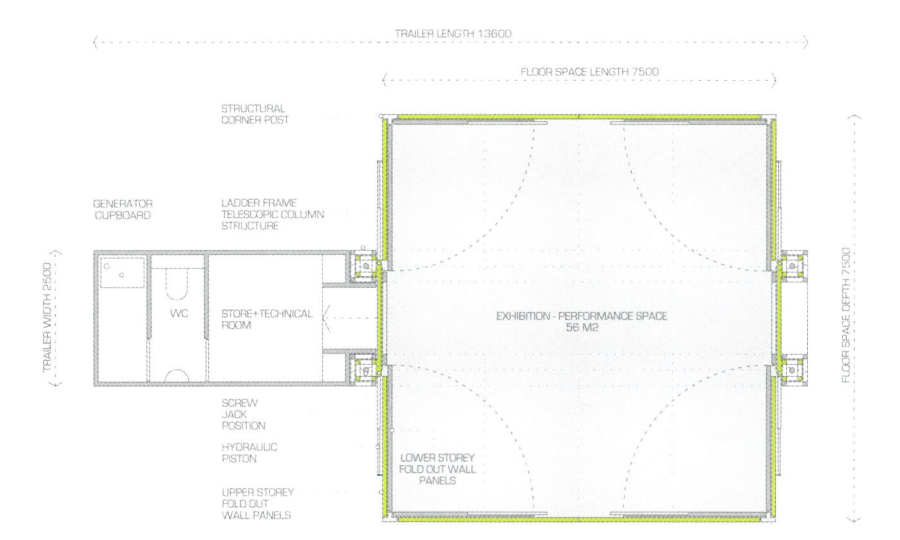

ABOVE & RIGHT
Technical drawings of the Art Box in use.

BELOW
Beat the Whites with the Red Wedge, 1919, by El Lissitzky is a poster depicting the Bolsheviks, represented by the red wedge, penetrating and defeating the White Army. Messages of political agitation and propaganda in these early Constructivist images were disseminated across Russia through mobile art venues on agitprop trains.

ART BOX MOBILE STAGE

The mobile Art Box is aimed at encouraging our enjoyment of the Visual and Performing Arts by involving a wider audience and aims to popularise what is sometimes seen as elite culture. Major galleries and theatre spaces in large cities struggle to influence and involve a wider audience in their work, especially in provincial and rural locations. The project provides for a transportable stage based on the module of a shipping container. The stage can be quickly erected and dismantled allowing for impromptu and spontaneous events to take place. The lightweight ephemeral nature along with its use of super-graphics is reminiscent of Venturi's concept of the decorated shed where the building acts primarily as a means of overt communication concerned with bringing art back to the people.

The Art Box project is reminiscent of the agit-train and agit-streetcars of the Russian Revolution Specially equipped for propaganda purposes by the Bolshevik government of Soviet Russia. Brightly painted and carrying on-board printing presses, printed political leaflets and pamphlets, library books and a mobile movie theatre, agit-trains travelled across Russia, Siberia and the Ukraine in an attempt to inculcate the values and program of the new revolutionary government to scattered and isolated communities.

Theatre and Flexibility

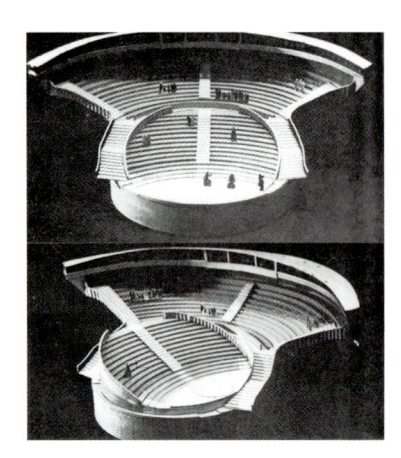

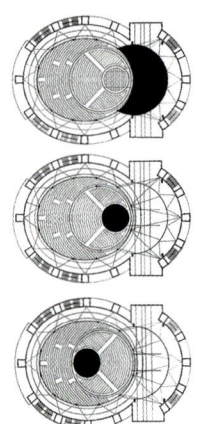

Where modernism had valued buildings that were 'either/or', postmodern architecture and later deconstructionism rejoiced in the possibilities of buildings that were 'both/and'. In many ways this was a rejection of architectural elitism and adopted a more populist and inclusive approach to design.

The possibility of inclusive buildings that could be used for a variety of purposes rather than one prescribed function brought into question the modernist dictum of form following function. The idea that a building might not only be able to accommodate a variety of functions across the course of its life, but also accommodate varied activity through the course of a week or day has gained traction over recent years. The pace of technological change has forced architects to think of buildings as resilient receptacles for as yet unspecified activities, requiring a built-in flexibility.

Modern theatre similarly broke the frame of the proscenium arch, developing new kinds of stage types to engage audiences in alternative ways of experiencing performance. The required flexibility of theatre as a building type was heralded by the unbuilt Total Theatre designed by Walter Gropius in 1926 for Erwin Piscator. Inspired by the Bauhaus idea to revolutionise theatre by including a more diverse range of theatrical elements with ballet, music, dance, song, spectacle and special effects working together, the performance pieces of Oskar Schlemmer and others required a new kind of space in which to enact their vision. The response of Gropius was to design one of the first flexible buildings where a series of rotating turntables could be raised and lowered effecting different stage configurations. Equally the seating configuration could be similarly altered to enable theatre in the round along with more linearly directional performances.

Whilst Gropius's design was for a unique building type, its ambition to create an architecture that was flexible and convertible is perhaps ever more relevant today as we build for a more uncertain future where the resilience of buildings to withstand change is ever more pressing.

ABOVE
Walter Gropius's Total Theatre, designed for Erwin Piscator, 1926.

OPPOSITE FAR RIGHT
The plan and sections of the Juniversity show the central teaching platform that can be transformed to accommodate various experimental classroom configurations. In section the building is flexible enough to change over time and in response to different locations and user needs.

JUNIVERSITY

Juniversity is a project that takes innovation from an outstanding school in a deprived area, in partnership with the University of Winchester, and links it to the Government's aspiration of more children achieving higher standards. The concept is of an 'experimental classroom', where teachers, inspectors and university colleagues all have the opportunity to experiment and innovate in a real school environment. The new self-contained learning space is connected to the university by a number of different technologies including video streaming and provides an environment to reimagine teaching and learning.

The teaching platform, a nine-square plan measuring 80 m² provides a blank canvas on which to create different learning environments and scenarios. Installations, enclosures, screens and fittings can be arranged on the platform surface to emulate traditional and experimental classroom layouts. Support spaces surround the teaching platform providing observation areas, storage zones, services and breakout areas. The space can be completely enclosed and introvert or expanded to engage with its context.

The ambition is to develop a prototype building that can be transferred to different locations where its envelope and section can be manipulated and tuned to its urban or rural settings. The fifth elevation, the roof, is imagined as its elevated footprint but also a safe haven for early years learning and play.

PLAN TYPES

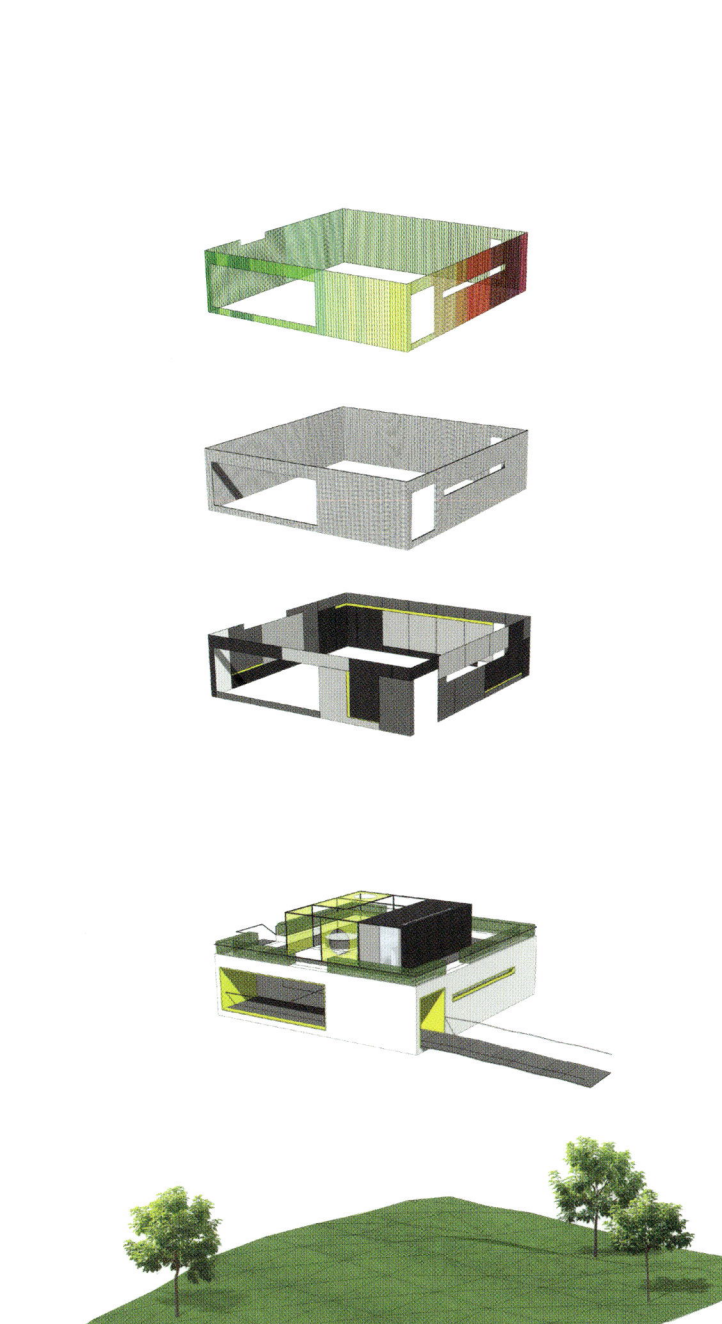

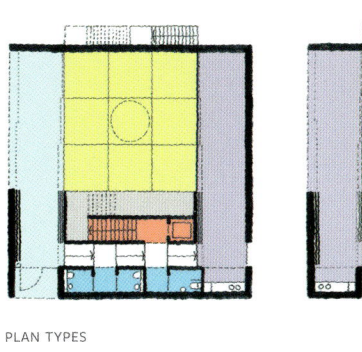

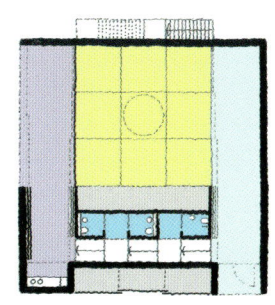

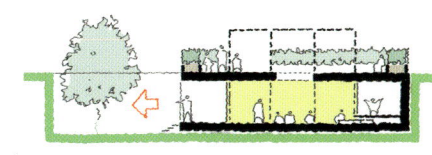

SECTION TYPE 01

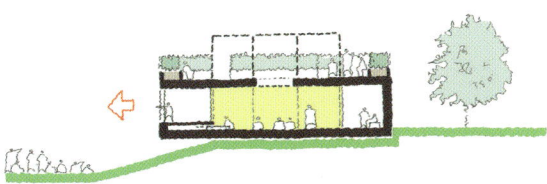

SECTION TYPE 02

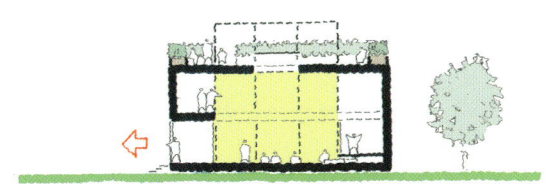

SECTION TYPE 03

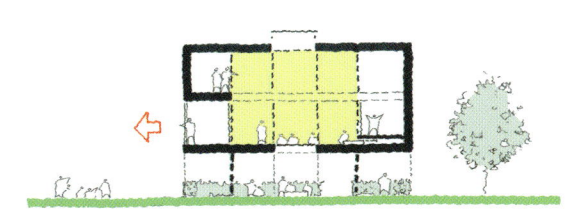

SECTION TYPE 04

ABOVE
The Juniversity is designed as a prototype whose external envelope can be varied in order that it can respond to the urban or rural location in which it is sited.

THEATRE | 145

The Symbolism of Theatre

For years architects had studied Giambattista Nolli's plan of Rome which represented the defined streets and squares of the eternal city. Teaching at Yale University, Robert Venturi, his wife Denise Scott Brown and their friend Steven Izenour led a student trip to study what might be considered the antithesis of Rome: Las Vegas, Nevada. What they found was a city built around the motor car, with vast parking lots and large neon signs designed to communicate at high speed rather than the more subtle symbols inherent in Nolli's compact urban density, which were designed with the pedestrian in mind.

They also found that the buildings took the form of what they described as 'decorated sheds'; generic buildings whose purpose was only communicated through applied signage. They contrasted these with 'ducks', a phrase drawn from a roadside duck-shaped building in eastern Long Island and used to classify buildings where form is used directly to symbolise internal function. They felt that many modernist buildings came under this latter category. Their findings were published in *Learning from Las Vegas: The Forgotten Symbolism of Architectural Form*, 1977, and awoke architects and urban designers to the vast unplanned suburban landscapes that the majority of people inhabited.[13]

Venturi drew on popular culture and challenged architectural elitism. He also heralded what is now termed postmodern architecture which, in the hands of lesser architects unversed in Venturi's comprehensive knowledge of classicism, was unable to play the complex and subtle games of allusion and metaphor, resulting too often in crude historical pastiche. Yet Venturi remains important because, in a period when the distance between the architectural elite and the public was becoming ever greater, he brought architecture back to the people and tried to make it relevant and understandable to all.

ABOVE
Learning from Las Vegas: The Forgotten Symbolism of Architectural Form by Robert Venturi, Denise Scott-Brown and Steven Izenour, 1977. The image shows a photograph of a Las Vegas roadside casino sign superimposed onto Nolli's plan of Rome.

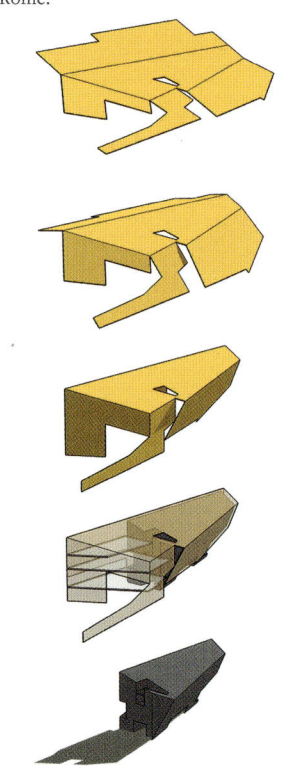

ABOVE
Concept drawings illustrating how the building is wrapped in 'embellage'.

CRICOTEKA, POLAND

The proposed design of the new museum for the Polish artist Tadeusz Kantor was influenced by Design Engine's understanding of four primary elements that featured within his work throughout his life.

SPACE: Kantor saw the dynamics of space as 'umbrella like' and was obsessed by 'the journey'. This has meant that whilst the building provides large and flexible exhibition spaces it is the way they link together that becomes equally important. The journey around Cricoteka is therefore a series of events offering unexpected perspectives.

EMBELLAGE: "the very activity of wrapping hides a very human need and desire to preserve, isolate and survive, as well as mystery and the taste of the unknown". Kantor's notion of 'embellage' informed Design Engine's thinking about the architectural language of the new building. The non-public spaces within the building, which are located at the west of the site (archives, stores, offices) have been conceived as a single 'body'—an apparently solid form, constructed as a concrete shell. Onto this 'body' is draped an outer 'wrapping' of timber cladding. In places this outer wrapping is tight against the body, hinting at the form beneath. In other areas it separates itself from the body, creating spaces 'in between'.

VILLAGE HOUSE: The stage for much of Kantor's work is the basic village dwelling, recalling his own upbringing in the village of Wielopole near Krakow. It is appropriate therefore that in responding to the urban context and to the architecture of the power station, Design Engine arrived at a building form that is in many ways an abstraction of the simple domestic model, with its familiar pitched roof and straightforward internal arrangement.

MATERIAL: Throughout his work Kantor professes an interest in 'reality of the lowest rank'—poor objects that through age and weathering recall their histories. For this building a palette of tough robust materials was envisioned, that would weather with dignity.

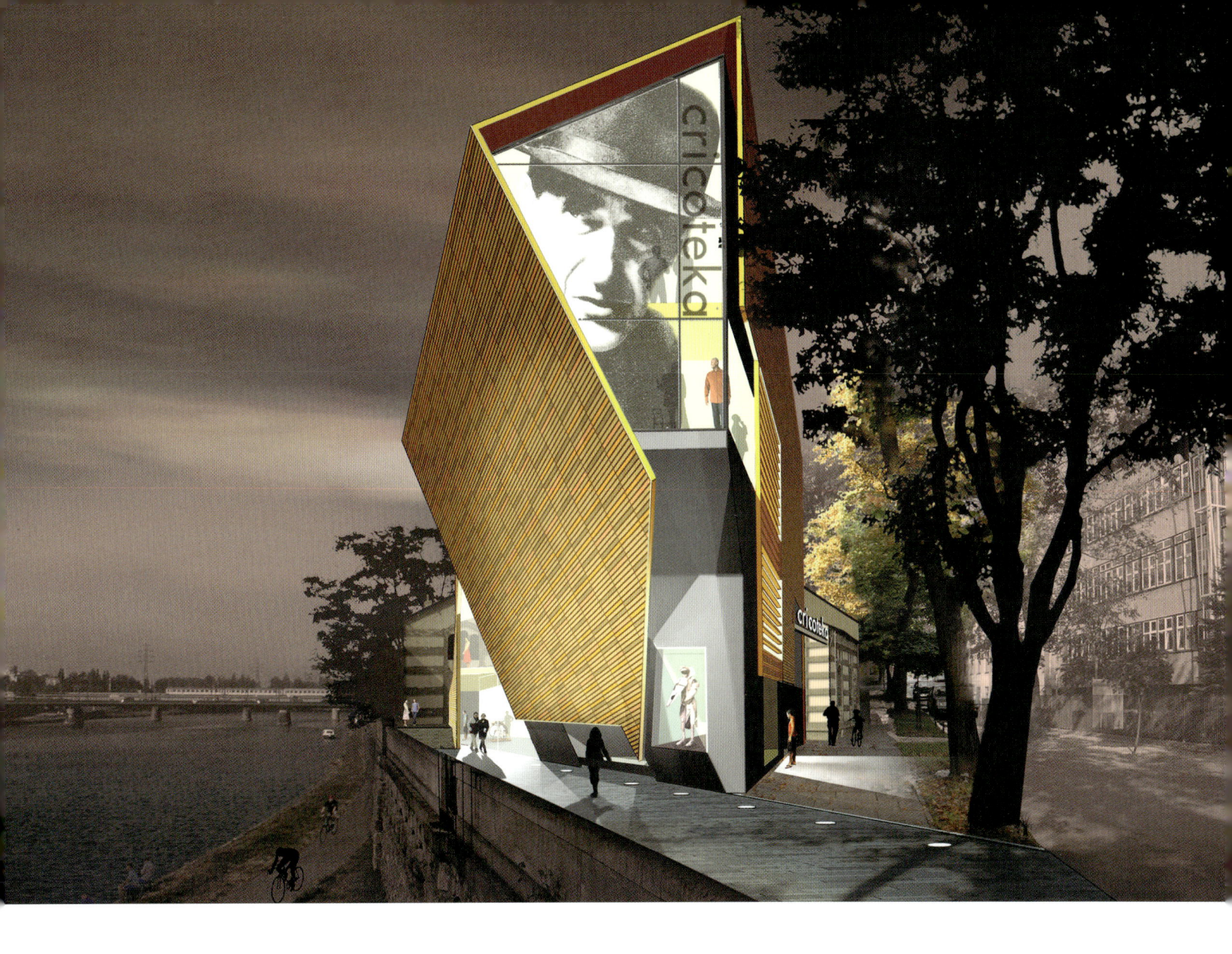

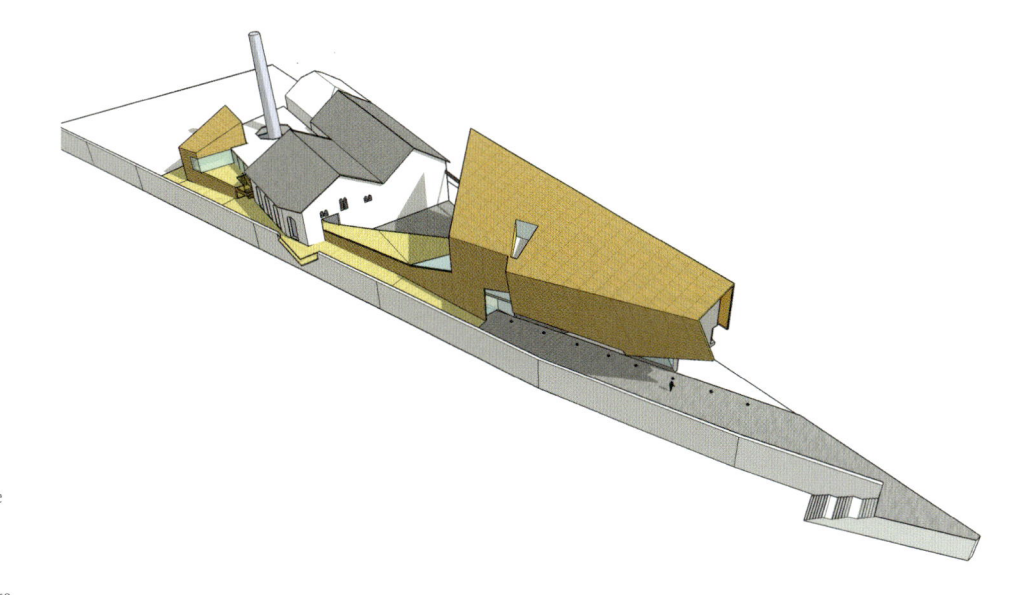

ABOVE
Visualisation of the new museum along the River Vistula.

RIGHT
Massing diagram of the new building and its relationship to the existing factory.

THEATRE | 147

ABOVE
Visualisation of the Cricoteka Museum,
Poland, from across the River Vistula.

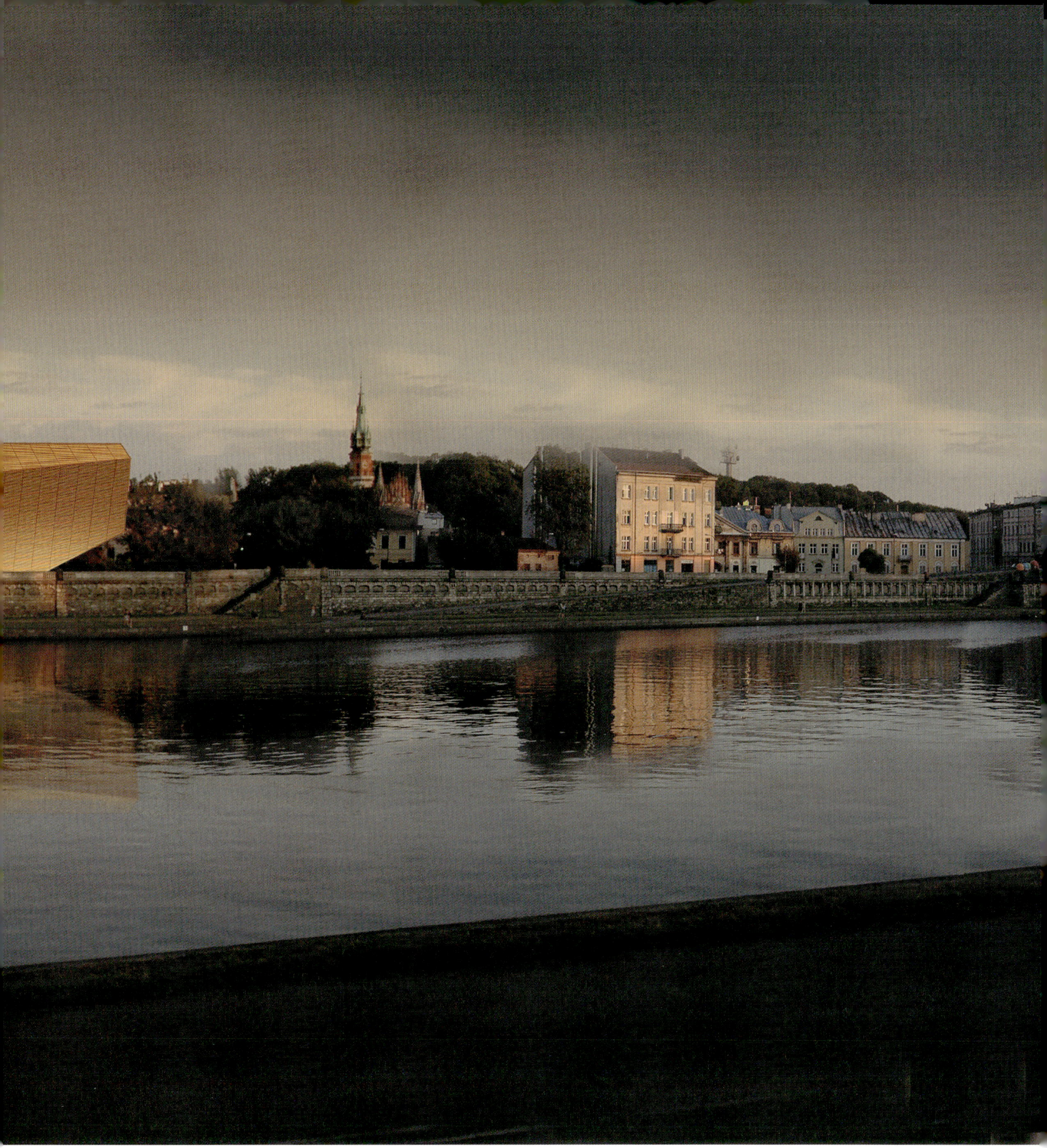

Composition
The Idea of Order

ABOVE
The Science and Mathematics Centre at Charterhouse School features three steeply pitched roofs, representing the six chemistry laboratories below, which creates a subtle but important architectural link to the original Hardwick campus with its Gothic revival towers and chimneys.

OPPOSITE TOP
The model shows how the Science and Mathematics Centre is composed. The repetition of three vertical elements follows Vitruvius in its strong sense of order, which relies on a rhythmic pattern of asymmetrical elements to achieve an overall compositional balance.

BOTTOM
The sketch shows how the new building will fit within the wider campus and provide balance to the northern approach to the school.

One of the essential properties of great architecture is the idea of order, an order that derives from a deep-rooted need in the human psyche to seek out patterns in the world around us. Whether this be in the structure of a leaf, the constellations of the heavens or through social ritual, we search for recurring patterns that in some way enable us to make sense of our experience and to find order and meaning in life. The history of architecture might be considered the history of the way in which mankind has found order in the world and reflected this through building.

Composition is the art of the placement and arrangement of elements and the way in which these arrangements combine to form a complete and harmonious whole. The relationship of the part to the whole was an underpinning concept in classical architecture. From the diameter of the column measured at the base, all parts of the building were derived as a multiple or fraction of this controlling module. The module was most evident in the height of the column as a multiple of its diameter, which gave each a particular ratio of height to width and identified the slenderness of different columns from which the architectural 'orders' of Doric, Ionic and Corinthian were derived. These proportional rules that govern classical buildings established a language or pattern that could be copied and repeated, the rules of which were first set out in the first century BCE by Marcus Vitruvius Pollio, or Vitruvius as he is commonly known. Vitruvius was an architect, engineer and scholar and his treatise *De Architectura*, published as *Ten Books of Architecture* and written in around 25 BCE, is the only text on architecture that has survived from the classical world to give us a first-hand description of the compositional ideas that governed the shaping of buildings at that time.[1] Vitruvius set out the fundamental principles of architecture in six categories: order, arrangement, eurhythmy, symmetry, propriety and economy. He went on to refine these contingencies: *utilitas*, meaning 'utility', *firmitas*, which broadly means 'durability' and *venustas*, which translates as 'beauty'. These were later translated by Henry Wotton in 1624 as "commodity, firmness and delight", and these three words have proved the touchstone for much of architectural design until the present day.

BUILDING STORIES | 150

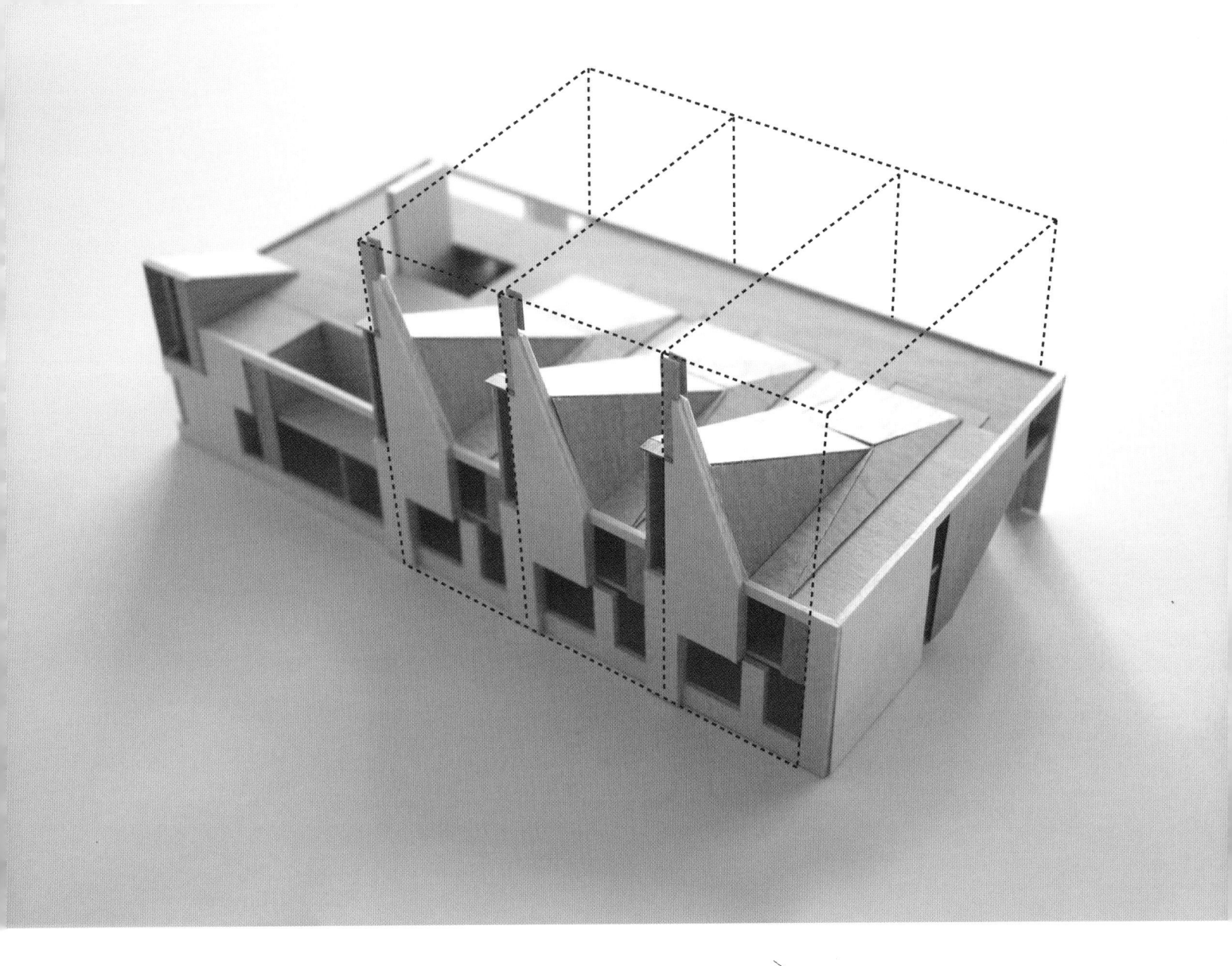

COMPOSITION | 151

The Language of Composition

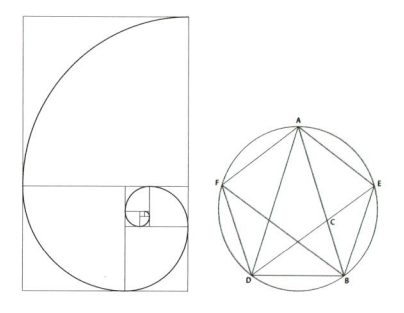

ABOVE
The composition of each of the three vertical elements is governed by the golden section spiral. Each radius is formed from a spiral of squares which follow the Fibonacci sequence: 1, 1, 2, 3, 5, 8 and so on. This spiral pattern mirrors the growth patterns found in nature as in for example the shell of the nautilus or the spiral patterns of a pine cone. The pattern was used extensively in Gothic buildings, where it provided a regulating system to form arches and buttresses.

BELOW
The drawing illustrates how the north elevation of the Science and Mathematics Centre at Charterhouse School incorporates the golden proportion spiral.

Composition is concerned with the ordering of the parts of a building and in establishing patterns related to the formal properties of number, geometry, proportion, hierarchy and orientation.[2]

The use of number gives buildings the idea of measure, not only in terms of size and scale but also in respect of appealing to a sense of ideal order found in mathematics. This is the language of order as seen in nature where growth patterns often accord to mathematical relationships and sequences, as is the case with the Fibonacci sequence, which governs the growth of seed heads and leaf distribution in plants. Number is closely related to geometry, a term which literally means the 'measure of the earth', and geometry in architecture is manifest not only in two-dimensional shape but also in three-dimensional volume. This volumetric geometry leads to the composition of shapes according to precise ratios and proportions such as the golden rectangle or double square often found in classical architecture. Hierarchy is concerned with the importance of one element relative to another, and this might be simply in terms of scale and comparative size, or the relative distribution of elements in a building. Lastly orientation relates composition to the particularities of location. The movement of the sun and the heavens along with the cardinal points give buildings orientation relative to their particular site. Internally a building's composition is concerned with orientation as each part can lead to, or indicate, other elements within the overall ensemble giving the building a legibility for the user, which serves as an important tool for navigation between spaces.

BUILDING STORIES | 152

RIGHT
North elevation of development model showing ventilation chimneys overlaid with golden rectangle.

FAR RIGHT
South elevation of development model showing colonnade overlaid with golden rectangle.

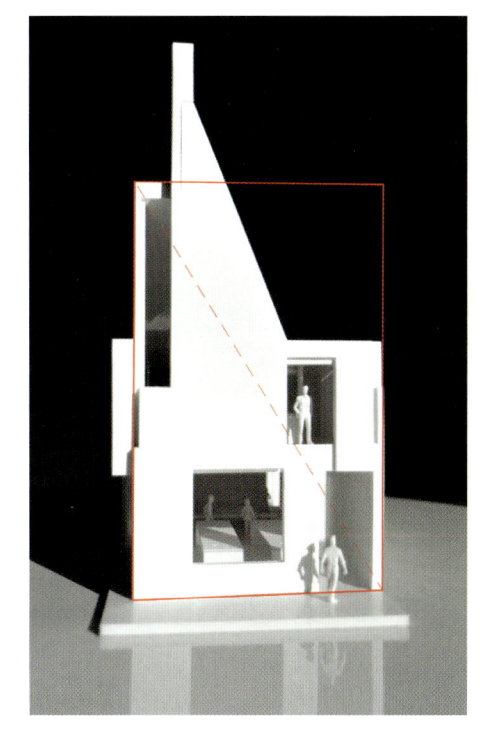

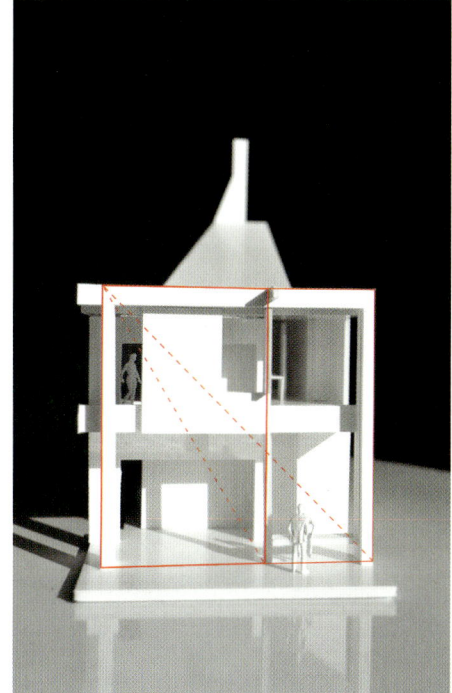

RIGHT
Context model of the Science and Mathematics Centre illustrating how each elevation responds to the surrounding existing buildings and spaces.

BELOW
Conceptual sketch showing how the chemistry classrooms are conceived as 'vessels'.

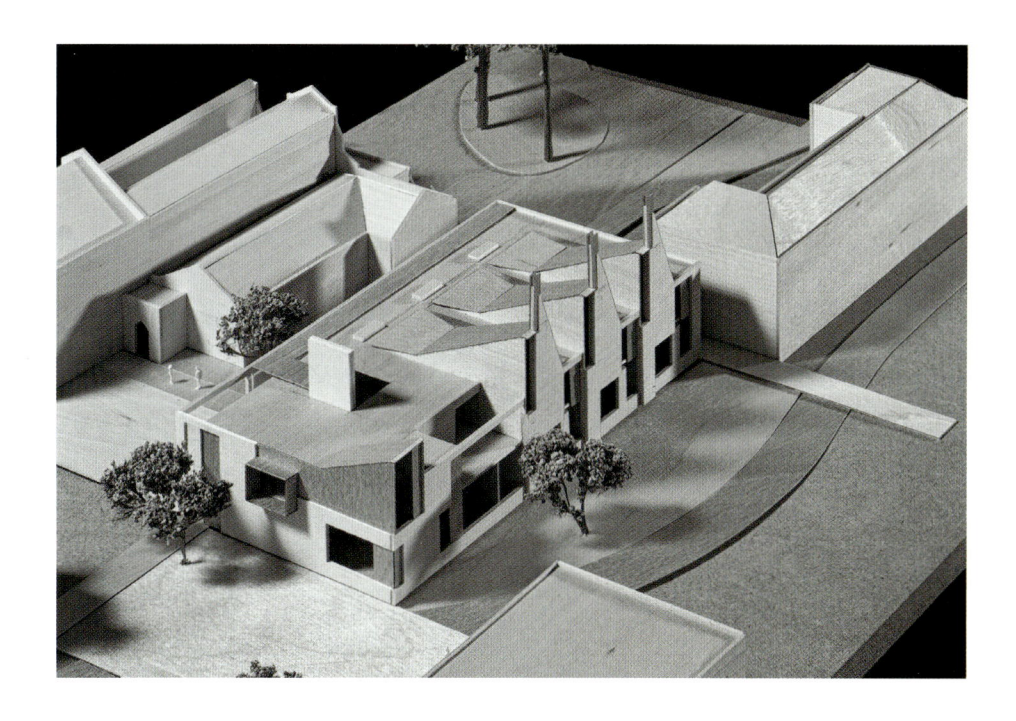

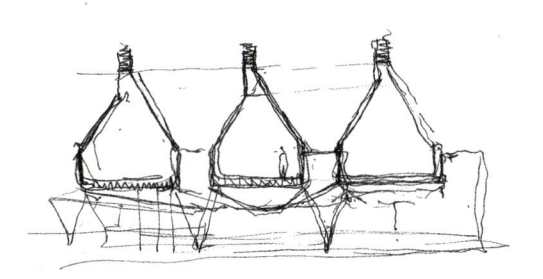

SCIENCE & MATHEMATICS CENTRE, CHARTERHOUSE SCHOOL

The repetition of similar elements is an important way in which order is represented in architecture. In the Charterhouse Science & Mathematics Centre the horizontal rhythm of the new building, when seen in the context of the adjacent structures, receives a counterpoint of three repeated vertical pitches. The new elevation continues the strong horizontal emphasis of the adjacent buildings, against which the vertical elements, slightly set forward, project.

The site lies towards the north-eastern edge of the campus. Characterised by the historic architecture and setting, the buildings here are predominately neo-Gothic and date back to the late nineteenth and early twentieth centuries. When seen in the surrounding context across open playing fields, the three elements provide a cadence or termination to the overall composition of the school buildings. The slender finials mirror the pinnacles of the school's spires and serve as an endpoint to the overall composition.

COMPOSITION | 153

Layered Facade

In the architectural order that is the result of the rules of composition, the facade becomes more complex and subtle as different layers of order are incorporated into the elevation. Whilst each layer obeys an internal logic, often driven by pragmatic requirements, the resulting over-layered interference of patterns presents a complex and richly nuanced facade open to multiple readings and interpretations.

The approach to designing the facade in this way often takes the form of pragmatic concerns for discrete requirements of the building skin developing their own logic. These concerns relate to aspect and view, along with the exposure of the elevation to environmental forces, most often expressed in the requirement to mediate solar gain. The requirement to draw attention to particular views, internal lighting necessities, the need for ventilation, along with the rhythm and order of adjacent buildings is balanced with aspects of the horizontal expression of floor and in particular where floor voids vent to atmosphere. Additionally, structural aspects of the material dimensions and its supporting framework offer further ordering logic. The superimposition of these differing needs affords fertile territory for the composition of facades, and the layered relief of these elements evokes the work of the twentieth-century painter and sculptor Ben Nicholson.

ABOVE
The abstract artist Ben Nicolson used a technique of low or bas-relief in his landscape and still-life compositions, achieving harmony and balance through the juxtaposition of coloured elements set at different levels upon the canvas.

ST ALPHEGE BUILDING

St Alphege Building: a new learning and teaching space for the University of Winchester. As part of the University's aspiration to drive higher standards of excellence for studying and the student experience, the building achieved excellent environmental performance from the outset. The facade has seen innovative technology and design used to harness and control passive environmental factors. The elevation comprises a series of louvres which are set in front of the glazed elevation. Each layer of louvres is arranged to achieve the required level of solar shading to the south-facing elevation whilst preserving views onto the landscape beyond. The overlap of the louvred panels results in an interference pattern, and the overall composition, governed by geometrical order, is adjusted to achieve a holistic visual rhythm and balance.

RIGHT & ABOVE
The drawings on the right illustrate a series of studies carried out for the south facade which utilise the same basic root 2 proportional system. The purpose of these diagrams is to illustrate that proportional systems can only act as a 'guiding hand' and are not in themselves capable of creating a definitive solution. The final decision of which version works best is left to the architect who has to balance the needs between the functional necessity of using brise-soleil and the quality of the experience of using the space as shown in the photographs above.

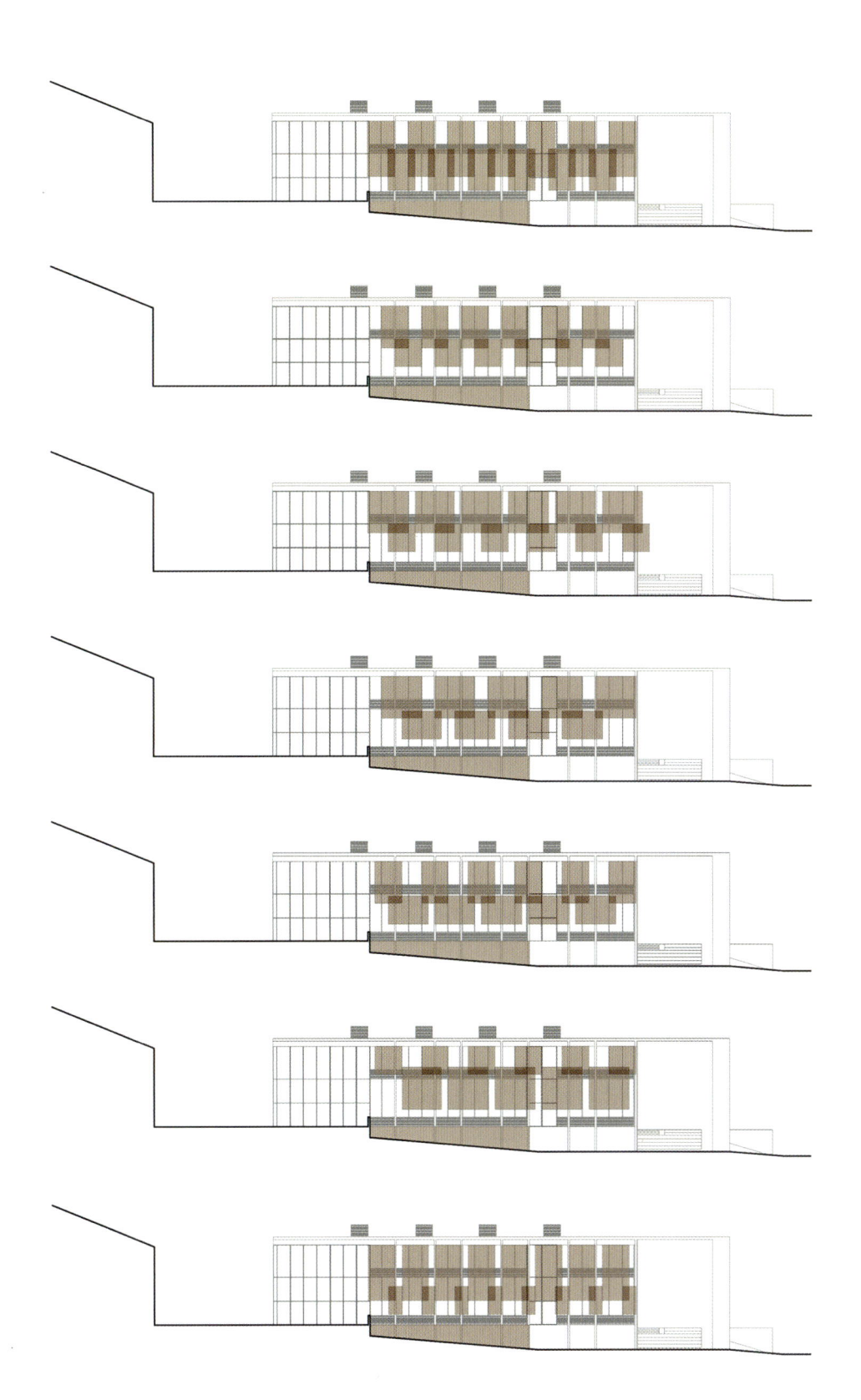

COMPOSITION | 155

Inflection and Juxtaposition

ABOVE
Maquette by Gerrit Rietveld and Vilmos Huszar for the Great Berlin Exhibition of 1923. Published in *L'Architecture Vivante*, 1924.

BELOW
Concept model showing juxtaposition of rear teaching building with rotunda (lecture theatre) and triangular roof (social learning/library).

OPPOSITE TOP
Concept sketches exploring spaces between the buildings and the relationship of the building to the main road.

OPPOSITE BOTTOM
Early massing drawing of new building in relation to the existing listed building.

Other than in the mind and the abstractions of platonic space, buildings rarely find themselves in context-free conditions. The particularities of site, the orientation to the sun and changing seasons, along with various and often competing functional requirements present in all cases a series of asymmetrical design parameters. To give order and balance to these frequently conflicting aspects is the role of the architect, and the use of an underlying rhythm or structure provides the skeleton around which these differing parameters are gathered and unified. However to force such parameters into a rigid structure is often to artificially constrain the potential of such diverse richness and allowing the expression of asymmetrical aspects of a design can bring variety and interest to architecture. To achieve this the compositional devices of inflection and juxtaposition are frequently employed. Inflection refers to changing an established order to emphasise certain aspects in response to site or functional expression, whilst juxtaposition is the compositional device of setting one element against the next in order to achieve emphasis through contrast. These architectural devices are analogous to musical composition where one finds that, whilst there is an underlying rhythm or beat, the lyrical and poetic qualities arise from the use of cadence and the emphasis of moments or melody along with the counterpoint of musical phrases which give the composition its narrative structure. Whilst the use of compositional order and structure are important in providing a framework of legibility, these are best understood as a framework against which events take place. It is against this framework that the asymmetrical irregularities which animate a building are accommodated and expressed to provide the narrative inflection and juxtaposition which is the life and story of the building.

WEST DOWNS CAMPUS, UNIVERSITY OF WINCHESTER

The project for the West Downs Campus for the University of Winchester provides a new gateway linking the university and the city. A linear block of classrooms and teaching facilities sets a background rhythm, against which a grand lecture theatre takes the form of a rotunda, whilst a pavilion under a triangular roof shelters the social learning and library spaces. The pavilion is irregular in plan and contrasts with the linear block acting as an inflection in the plan to highlight its relative importance.

The building responds to the sloping landscape with a terrace of stepped parterres radiating from the rotunda, setting the linear and radial planning in counterpoint. This response to the topography shows how the planning strategy inflects in response to the particularities of the site. The complex compositional balance is achieved through the careful juxtaposition of linear, radial and angular planning. Each volume expresses its unique function, whilst the overall composition in setting the three organisational arrangements against each other provides a visual tension whose balance, like an abstract painting, is achieved through the inflection of each relative to the others.

BUILDING STORIES | 156

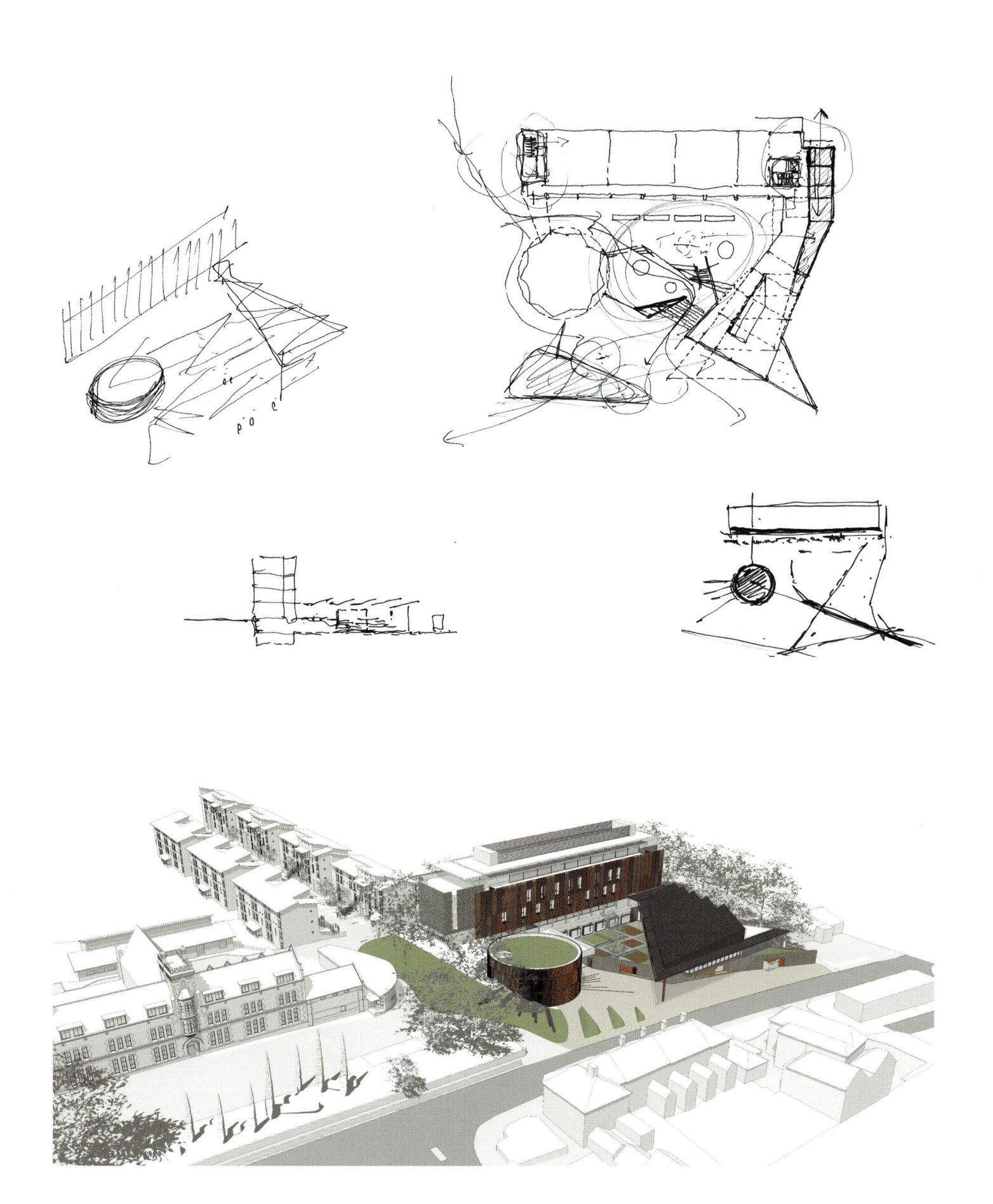

COMPOSITION | 157

Asymmetrical Balance

ABOVE
The Erechtheion Porch at the Parthenon in Athens.

BELOW
Initial sketch of the main entrance to West Downs Campus at University of Winchester.

Symmetry is too often taken to mean the bilateral or reflected symmetry of the butterfly, and mirrored symmetry underpinned much of the classical language of architecture with buildings reflected along a central axis. However this is a very crude understanding of symmetry as, in its original etymology, symmetry meant 'balance'. Whilst bilateral reflection does indeed achieve equilibrium, there are many other ways in which compositional balance can be attained.[3]

The use of the mechanical reflection of bilateral symmetry can result in static, inanimate buildings and, although much of classical architecture is often seen in these terms, the architects of classical antiquity saw matters of balance as a far more complex affair. The sculptures that adorn the pediment elevation of the Parthenon comprise an asymmetrical narrative, whilst the Erechtheion's porch of caryatids make the building wholly asymmetrical in plan. These examples of classical irregularity have parallels in the human body whose skeletal structure is bilaterally symmetrical about the vertical central axis but whose armature serves to accommodate the various unsymmetrical internal organs and in whose detail, for example the human face, asymmetrical inflection gives rise to unique character and identity.

Asymmetrical composition is employed not only in elevation but also in plan, and through this to section and three dimensions. The asymmetrical balance to be found in modernist painting at the advent of the twentieth century, particularly in the Bauhaus and the De Stijl movements, have formed a basis for much of modern architecture.[4] For these pioneers of asymmetrical composition, clearly defined blocks and strong colour were the tools of composition and the masters of this abstract sense of balance were Theo van Doesburg, Piet Mondrian and the architect Gerrit Rietveld.

For these artistic innovators the process of abstraction was, whilst brilliant, ultimately reductive to a world of primary colours with white, black and grey. This visual language has been much aped, and today the radical ideas that emerged 100 years ago now seem rather hackneyed in their endless thematic repetition. Their goal of a vision in which the scales would fall from the eyes of man to reveal the underlying beauty of the order of the universe has become little more than an applied style.

BUILDING STORIES | 158

01

02

03
04
05

06

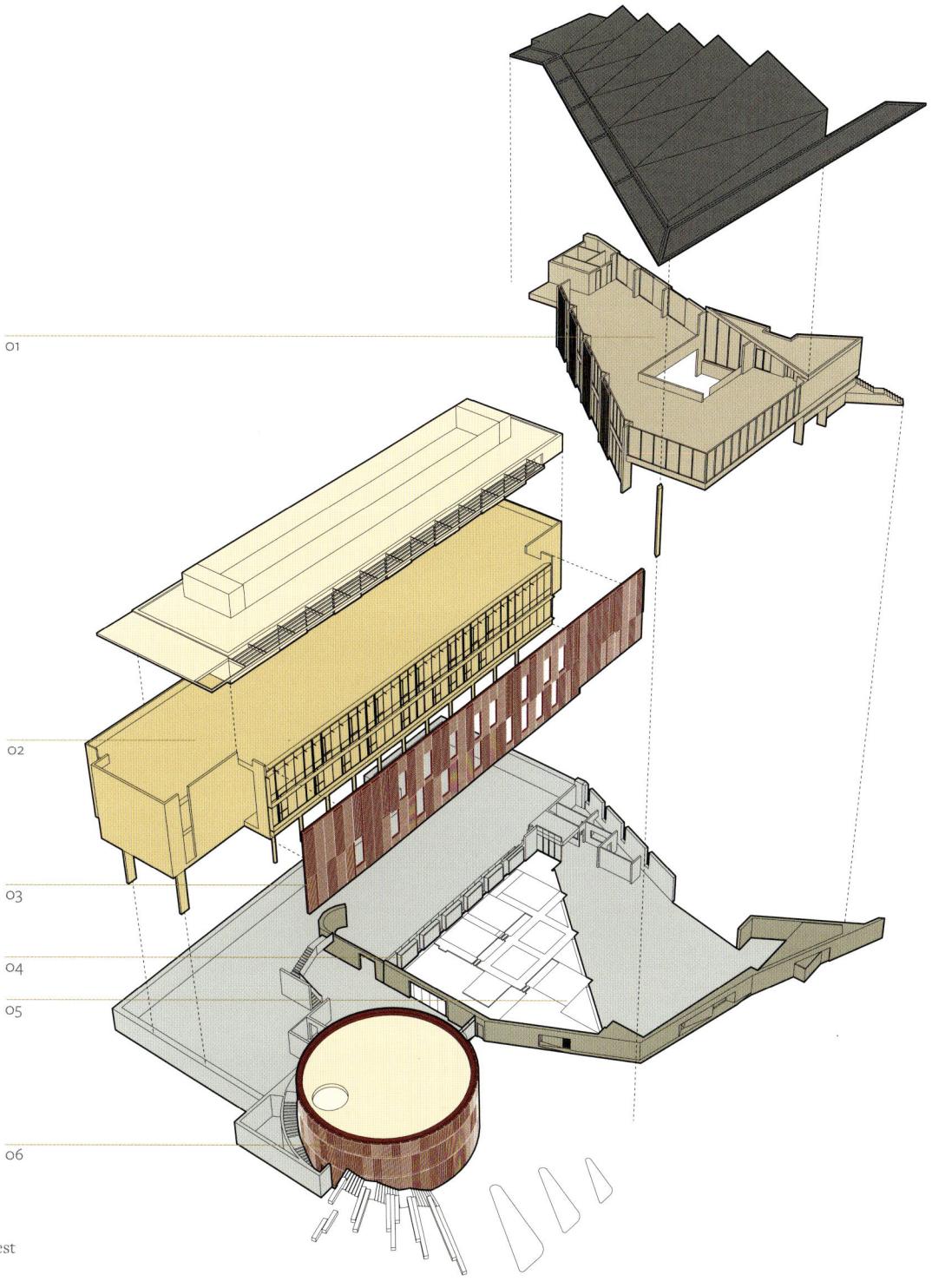

ABOVE
Exploded axonometric drawing of West Downs Campus development.

WEST DOWNS CAMPUS, UNIVERSITY OF WINCHESTER

The compositional arrangement of the triangular entrance pavilion with oversailing roof has strong directional emphasis when seen in perspective. The solidity and visual stability of the rotunda contrasts with the dynamic emphasis of the open entrance canopy framing the sky. The horizontal banding of the rotunda is set against the vertical glazing fins of the entrance building, and in juxtaposing these two contrasting visual forms a dialectic interplay is established between different elements of the overall composition.

01. The Learning Hall contains the library and social learning spaces. The roof has a relationship with the university's 'University Centre' building on the King Alfred campus.
02. 'Teaching Building' forming the main teaching accommodation.
03. The ground floor is dug into the existing site to create a level access to the building and the campus from Romsey Road.
04. A protective wall leads the pedestrian into the main entrance of the building, creating an enclosed 'secret' garden.
05. Secret garden.
06. Auditorium 'Drum'. This is the heart of learning in the building and will provide seating for 250 people, both for the university as well as the local community and city.

COMPOSITION | 159

Interlocking Composition

ABOVE
Eduardo Chillida's Poet's House I, 1980.

Composition is the art of placement, and architectural elements can be seen as a series of interlocking parts which when combined form an integrated whole. This is the sense of placement that derives its art from the making of puzzles, and in many respects architecture might be considered the completion of a very complex puzzle, where both the design of the parts and the vision of how all of these will ultimately interlock is the role of the architect. This idea of interlocking space is found in the sculpture of Eduardo Chillida, the Spanish artist who began his studies as an architect but turned to sculpture. Chillida was known for his wood, iron and steel sculptures, in whose interlocking parts and strong sense of material and spatiality the practice have found inspiration. For Chillida the dialectic between empty and occupied space has strong architectural parallels. The interlocking of solid and void is a powerful metaphysical expression as the space of absence, the missing elements of the spatial puzzle is the realm filled in or completed by the imagination. The wish for completeness, but its inherent absence, is a parallel of the human mind's quest for the absolute and the patterns of completeness imagined yet never found in the imperfect lived world of experience.

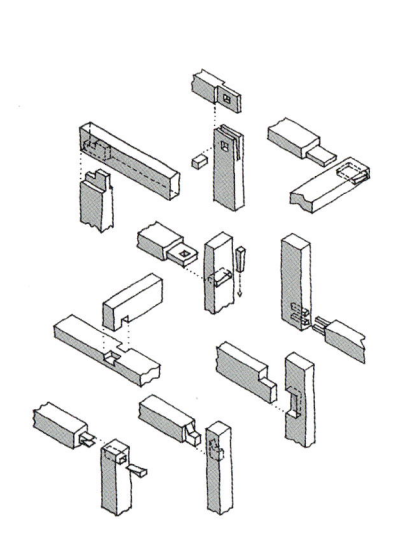

ABOVE
Timber construction details.

ABOVE RIGHT
Wooden concept model used in the development of the John Henry Brookes Building at Oxford Brookes University.

JOHN HENRY BROOKES BUILDING, OXFORD BROOKES UNIVERSITY

The influence of the interlocking forms is most powerfully exemplified in the design of the John Henry Brookes Building, where a series of 'pegs' are inserted into 'boxes', like the mechanical challenge of interlinked pieces of Chinese and Japanese wooden puzzles. This idea flowed from the university's desire to create a more inclusive and integrated campus. The pegs both reached out to touch other buildings on the campus whilst also reaching into the heart. Against the material solidity of the peg, the box is simultaneously a solid mass into which something is inserted, yet also a void that acts as a container whose spatial definition exists only in light of that which it receives. The fragile interplay of solid and void, material and absence, definition and ambiguity are played out in the building.

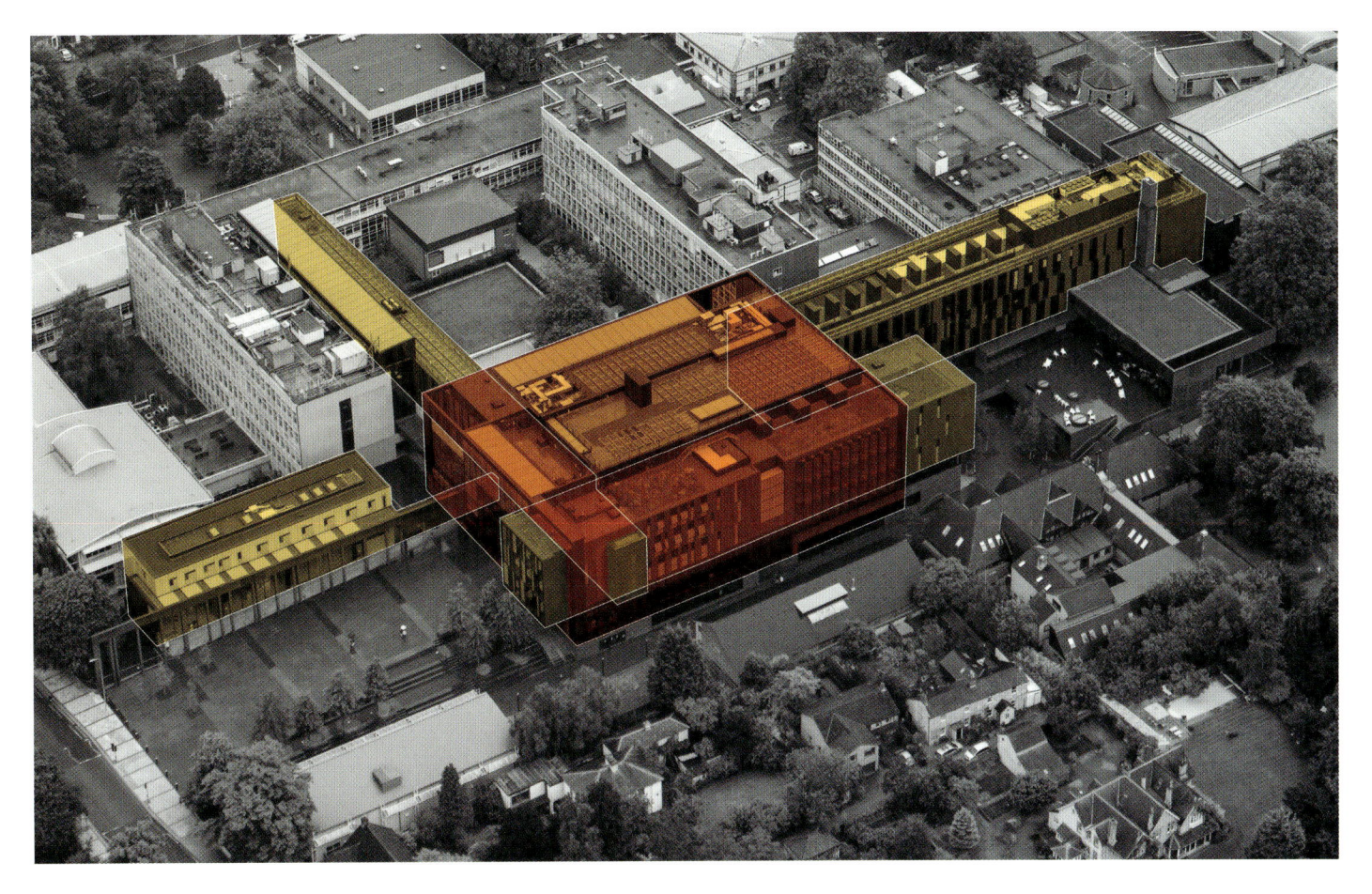

ABOVE
Aerial view of the John Henry Brookes Building at Oxford Brookes University.

BELOW & OPPOSITE
Concept models and sketches illustrating the idea of the scheme seen as a series of pegs inserted into a box.

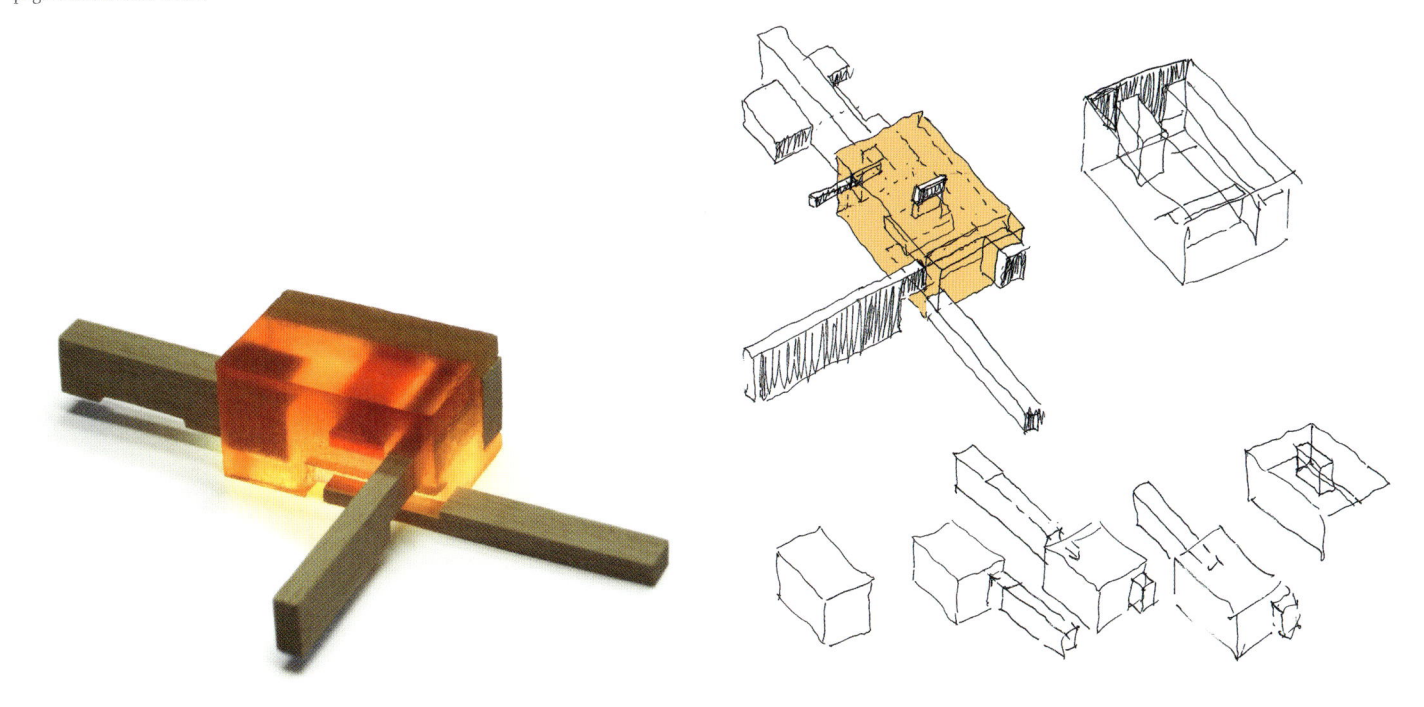

COMPOSITION | 161

RIGHT
South western view of the library peg which interpenetrates the eroded central box. The pooled teaching peg is set behind and links the central box to the food hall.

COMPOSITION | 163

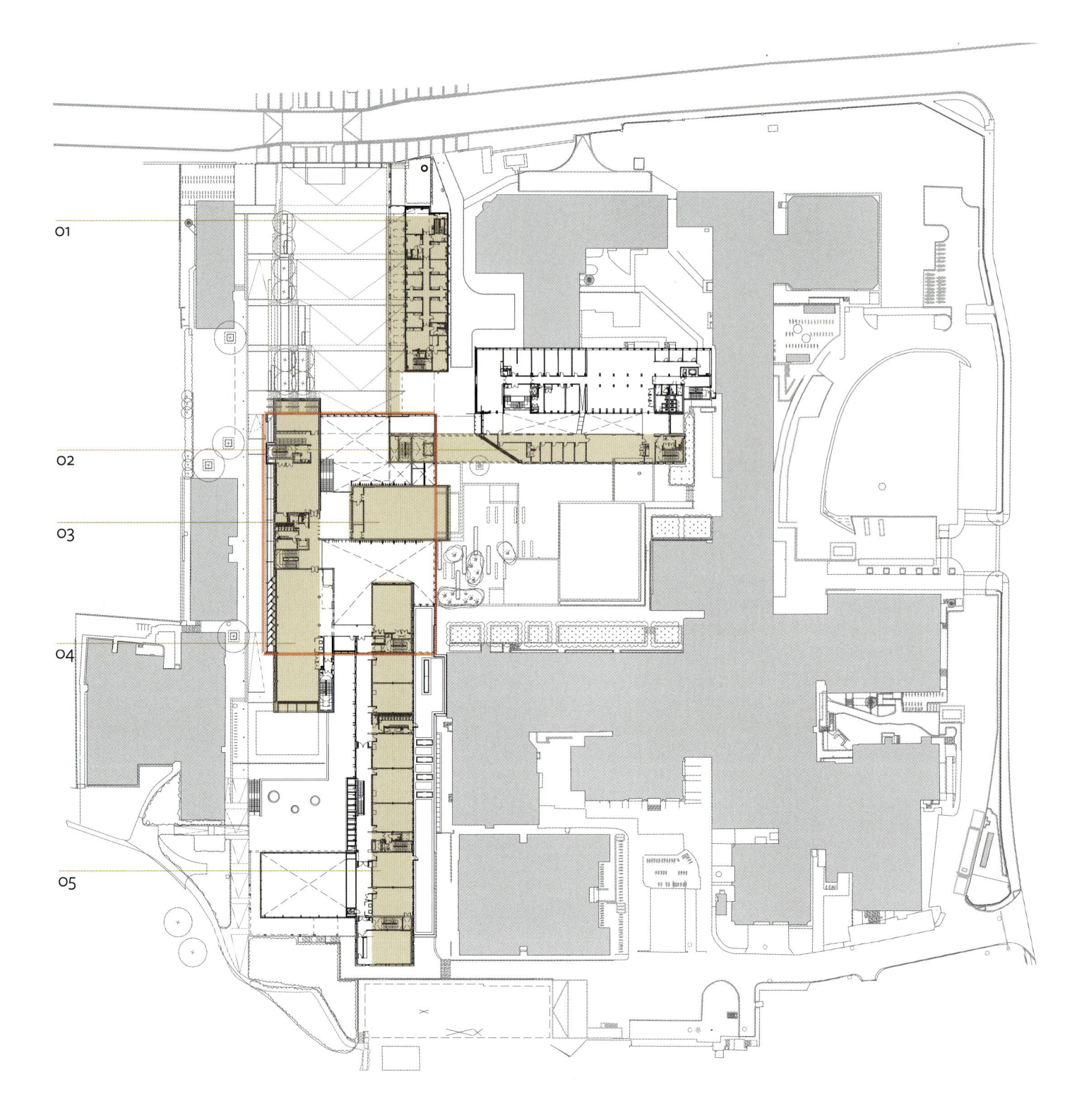

ABOVE
Ground floor plan of the John Henry Brookes Building.

01. Colonnade peg
02. Abercrombie peg
03. Lecture Theatre peg
04. Library peg
05. Food hall and pooled teaching peg
06. Red Box indicates the central box and the heart of the campus

Solid and Void

Chillida's work represents the architecture of pure space and pure object to be found in the artist's sculptures, however the pattern of interlocking in two dimensions also has strong architectural parallels.

Chillida's paper overlays of contrasting black and white strips might be seen as abstract compositions of modernist planning that mirror Rowe and Koetter's famous contrasting example of the city of object and the city of void set out in their book *Collage City*, 1978.[5] The example of the city plan as a series of placed objects is represented by Le Corbusier's St Dié-des-Vosges, a tabula rasa onto which objects are positioned. They contrasted this with the plan of Parma, the city of void where space was eroded or carved out from the solid. For Rowe and Koetter the figure and ground map was a powerful tool of comparison and drew on Nolli's famous depiction of Rome, where public streets and piazzas were left white, as too were the interior public spaces of the inner world of the city, whilst the buildings were set in solid black outline and fill. The inversion of such figures and ground mappings reveals that the solid poché or blacked-out spaces only make sense when read in association with the white void space. For Chillida this dialectic of interdependency is the very material of spatial composition, as the manipulation of void is considered in equal measure to the creation of its solid counterpart. Chillida's woven paper lattices of black and white are remarkable, not only as they make reference to this dialectic interplay of solid and void but in that they show nothing else, and so draw attention to this most vital of architectural compositional concerns.

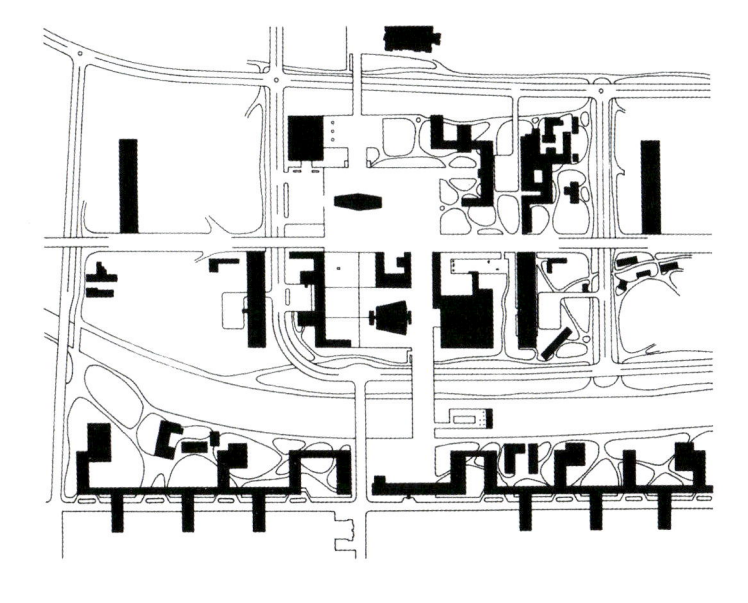

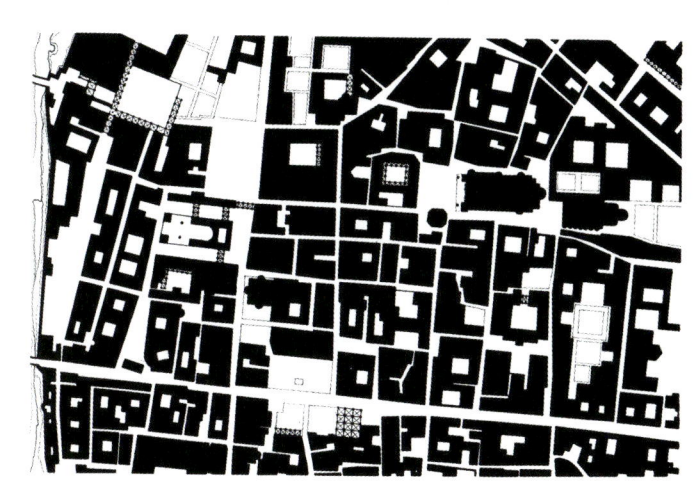

ABOVE
Eduardo Chillida, *Gravitación*, 1997.

BELOW
Collage City by Colin Rowe and Fred Koetter contrasts the city plan of Le Corbusier's St Dié-des-Vosges with that of the plan of historic Parma. The former shows a tabula rasa onto which objects are placed, whilst the latter space is carved out from solid.

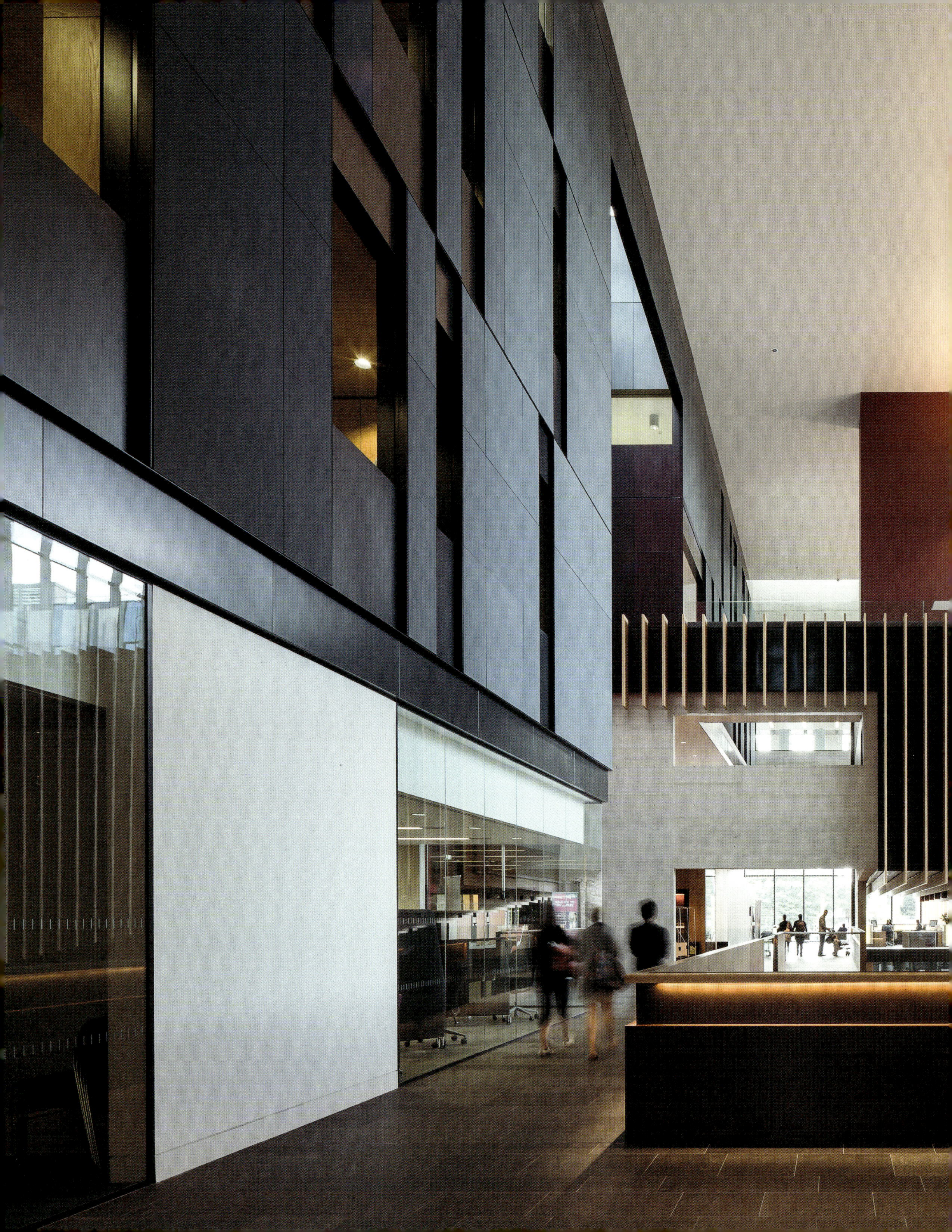

LEFT
The John Henry Brookes Building atrium is conceived as the receiving box into which a series of pegs are inserted. The peg of the lecture theatre, shrouded by a series of vertical timber fins, evokes the pieces of a Chinese puzzle, penetrating the volume of the atrium to form part of an interlocking compositional arrangement.

Colour
Colour in Architecture

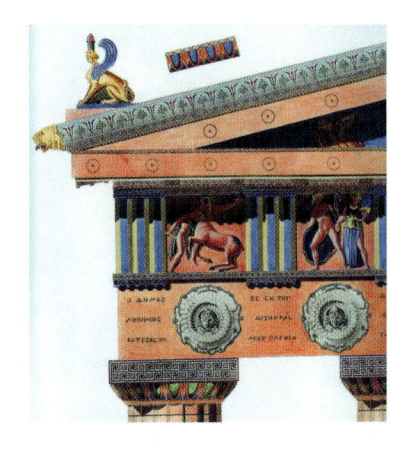

ABOVE
The drawing by Benoit Loviot of part of the Parthenon entablature (Paris, École Nationale Supérieure des Beaux Arts, 1879–1881) shows the building restored in the lavish colours that it is thought once adorned the now white marble.

Architecture is all too often a sombre affair, and much of modern architecture today eschews the use of colour as if anything other than black, white and shades of grey are in some way morally corrupting. However, architecture was once anything but monochrome and delighted in the use of colour.

Today we perhaps think of classical architecture exemplified by the Parthenon or Erechtheion standing as stark white marble objects set on an elevated plateau, pristine artefacts removed from the rest of the world with a backdrop of the endless horizon of the sky. They radiate the lofty serenity and calm order of an aesthetic and timeless architectural ideal placed above the ever-changing, messy, quotidian affairs of man. Yet this is in all respects a very modern view of these great monuments; they were in fact at the very heart of ancient civic life and were adorned in the colours that represented that vitality. Archaeological research has revealed that these buildings known for their exquisitely crafted detail were originally painted in what today we would see as some garishly vivid colours and were as visually lively and chromatically diverse as the great melting pot of humanity that was Athens in the golden age of Pericles.

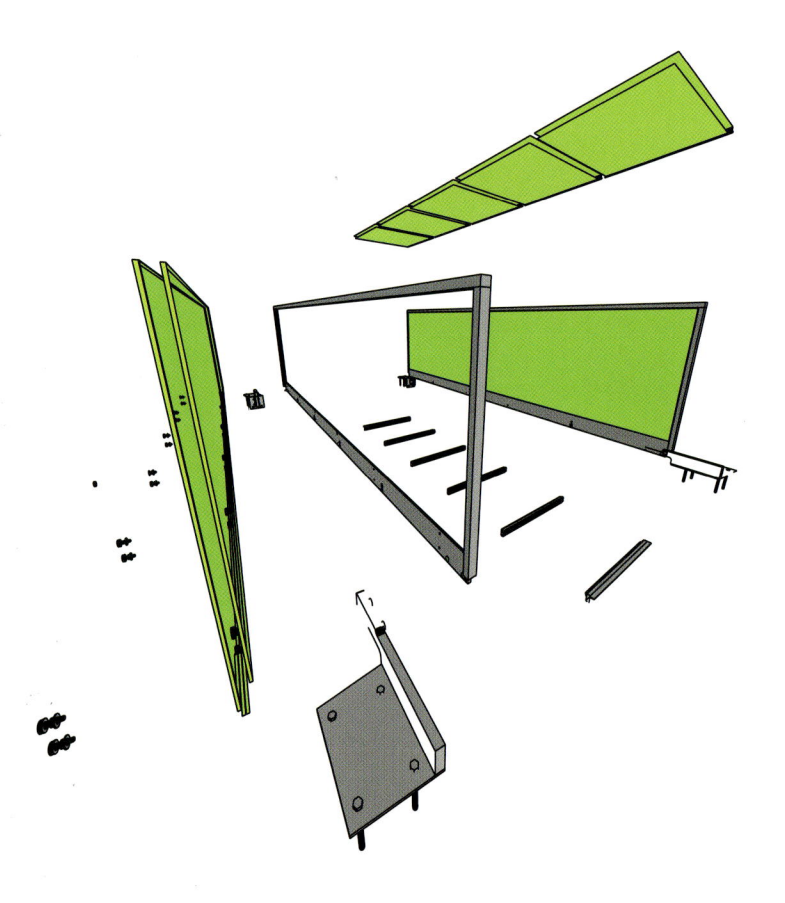

RIGHT
The bridge in the Abercrombie Building is shown in exploded perspective to capture the dynamism and visual movement evoking the early Constructivist and Suprematist drawings of the Russian revolutionary artists and architects.

BUILDING STORIES | 168

In the Abercrombie Building at Oxford Brookes University, coloured glass bridges span the atrium and place colour at the heart of the campus. As the great Gothic cathedrals used stained glass to illuminate a kaleidoscopic vision of heaven, so the atrium of the university becomes a modern day cathedral of learning.

01

Green of the Abercrombie Building exterior.

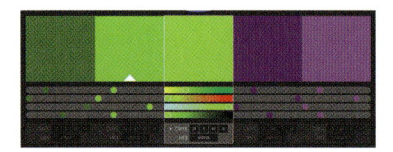

ABOVE

The use of a colour rule to create themes using analogous, complementary or compound colours ensures a distinctiveness for each colour choice throughout the building whilst maintaining a chromatic consistency.

The colour of the water-based paints of antiquity easily faded or were washed away over time, such that what the pioneers of the Renaissance found and copied were the sun-bleached vestiges of what had once been a polychromatic cascade of colourful brightness. In copying these artefacts, the Renaissance focused more on mathematical order, proportion and architectural detail. This concern with the Platonic ideals of architecture was reflected in the mathematical and newly emerging mechanical world view that brought the machines of Leonardo da Vinci and perspective space of Brunelleschi.[1] In seeking to speak of a rational eternal order that underpinned the world around him, Renaissance man, in architecture at least, largely abandoned the empirical world of human emotion, and all of the luminous vitality and feeling that colour brought to life.

BUILDING STORIES | 170

The Colour of Illumination

ABOVE
The Sainte-Chapelle is the royal chapel in the courtyard of the Palais de la Cité in Paris. Begun around 1238, the building is the embodiment of Gothic architecture with vast expanses of stained glass depicting biblical narratives and affording an emotional insight into the heavenly realm.

Colour was of central importance in the Gothic world. Much of life throughout the Dark Ages was as visually gloomy as it was intellectually lacklustre. Against this background grew an enhanced value for objects of colourful decoration which shone as visual and intellectual beacons in a grey world. Objects of religious veneration show how medieval man saw colour as a conduit to a perfect world existence that stood in stark contrast to his all too miserable way of life. The illuminated manuscripts of the Lindisfarne Gospels or the Book of Kells show the use of vividly colourful florid patterns that were intended as a window on paradise. Exquisite detail and brightness gave an insight into the heavenly realm, and the sacred texts shone like guiding lights of colour in what was otherwise a rather insipid visual domain. Visualisations of the gospel narratives for the illiterate masses were intended not only to be didactically instructive but also to serve as a physical realisation of St Augustine's theology that the dull mind bound up in the earthly world of human affairs could receive the grace of God through what he termed "divine illumination". This revelation is manifest in the otherworldly character of spaces like the nave of Chartres Cathedral or the kaleidoscopic spectacle of Saint-Chapelle in Paris, where shafts of multi-coloured sunlight play across the interior of the space in a way that cannot fail to move the onlooker in their promise of miracles and the life hereafter, as the spiritually uplifting possibilities of colour in architecture shines forth.

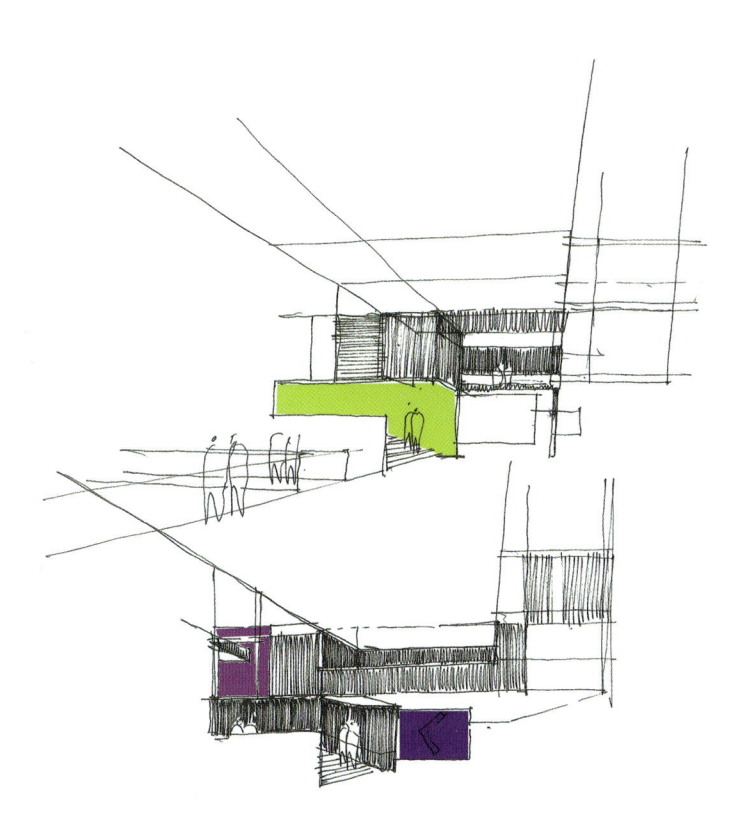

RIGHT
Perspective sketches of the Abercrombie Building at Oxford Brookes University show the inclusion of colour at the early design stages to highlight certain elements in the spatial progression through the building. The use of recessive and dominant colours help to lead the observer through the spaces, and the sequence of colours follows the movement through the building.

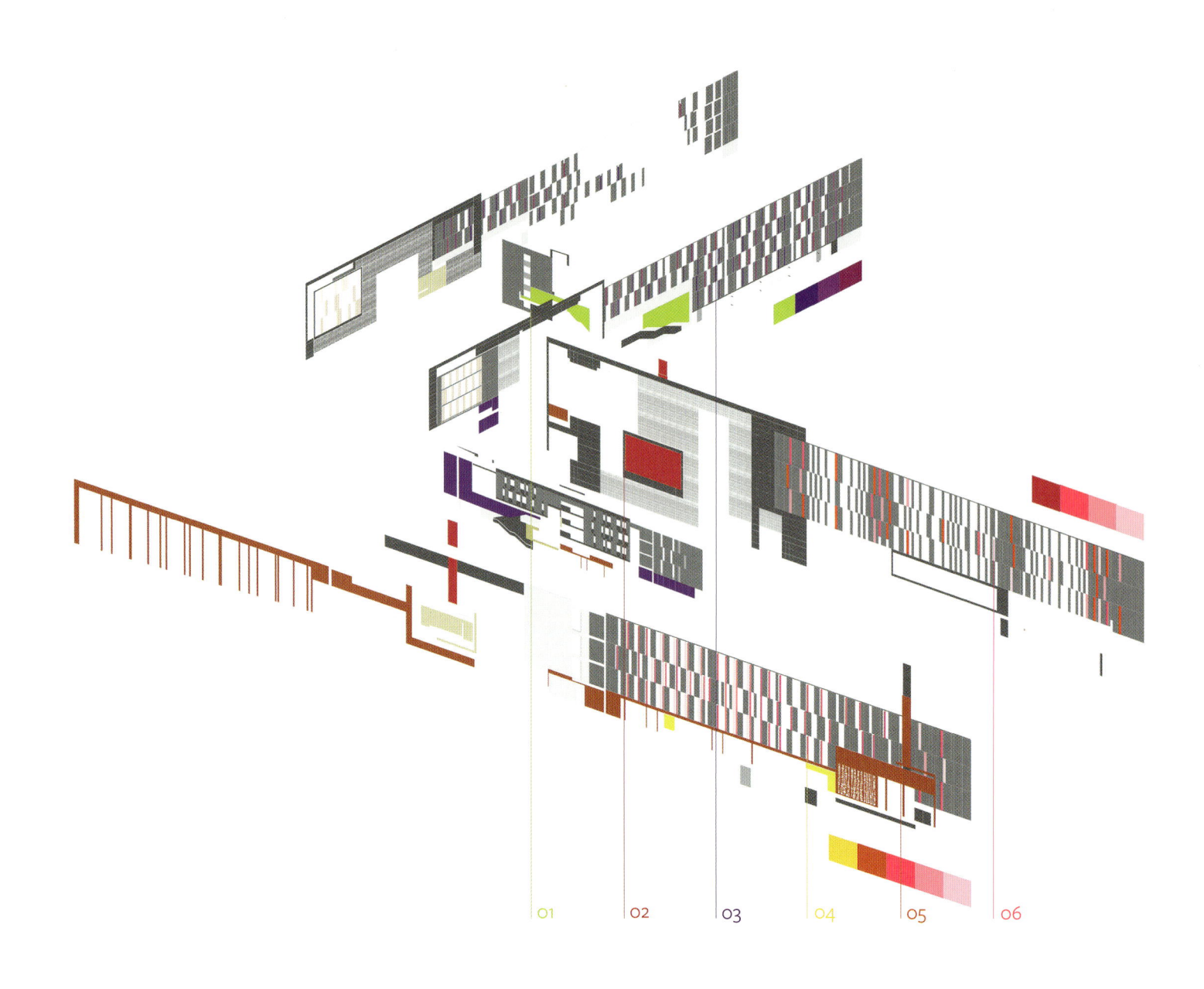

OXFORD BROOKES UNIVERSITY CAMPUS

BELOW
CMYK colour references for the 11 colours used throughout the John Henry Brookes and Abercrombie Buildings.

The choice of colour in the stained glass of the Gothic cathedral was symbolic, used to represent aspects of biblical narratives. For the Oxford Brookes campus, Design Engine secularise this symbolism, with each element of the building receiving a colour derived from the changing colours of the oak leaf, the emblem of the university. This gradation of colours moves from the verdant green of spring growth through to the rich autumnal reds and browns signifying the changing colours of the tree across the year. Subsequently, the use of colour, along with the Corten Ribbon, aids in the wayfinding of the building: a change in colour conveys to the visitor that they are moving through to a different area.

BUILDING STORIES | 172

03
Abercrombie
Building interior.

02
Courtyard at the end of
the main lecture space.

04
Interior view of the
circulation route
connecting the forum
to the food hall.

05
Leaf reference image
which helped determine
the colour strategy.

COLOUR | 173

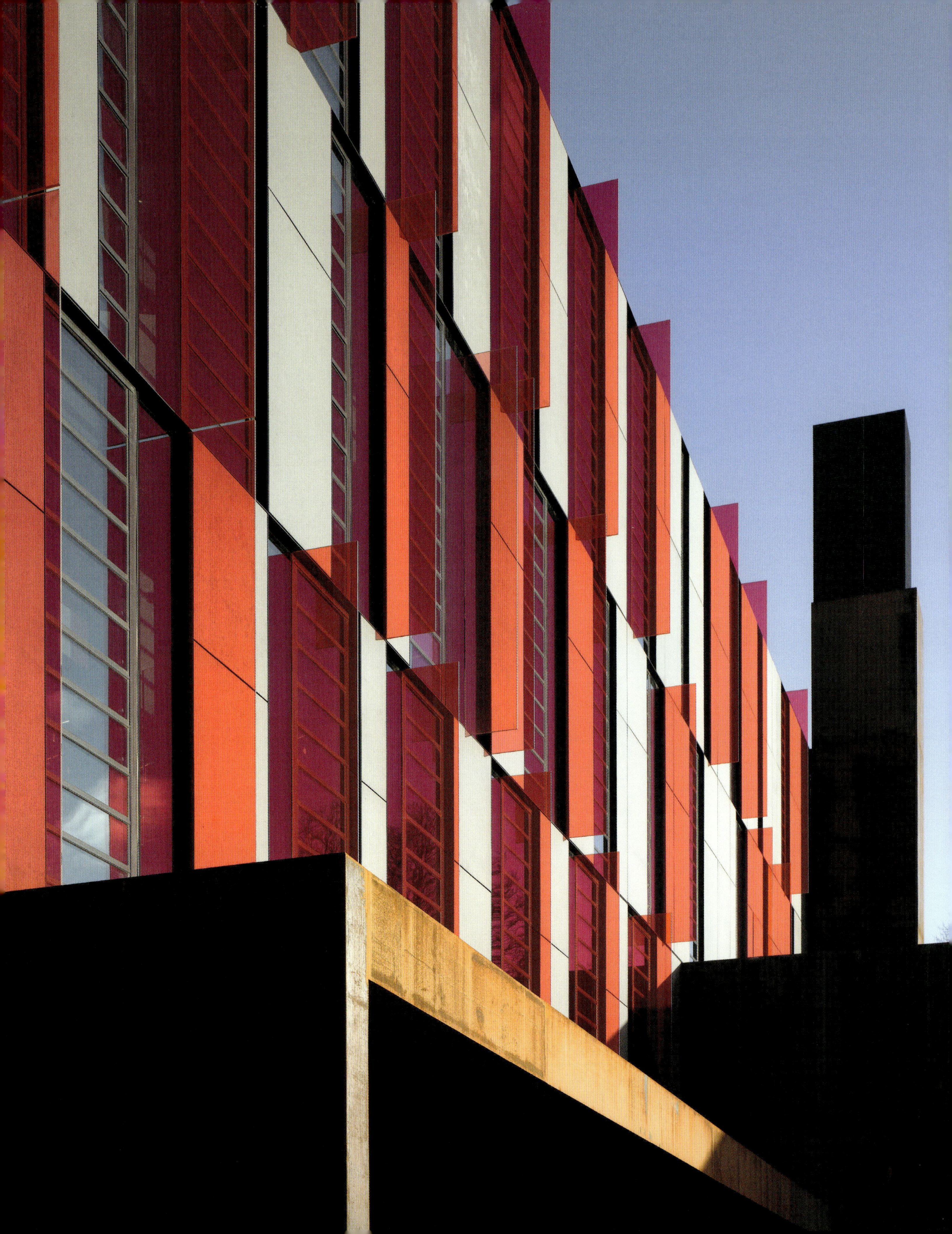

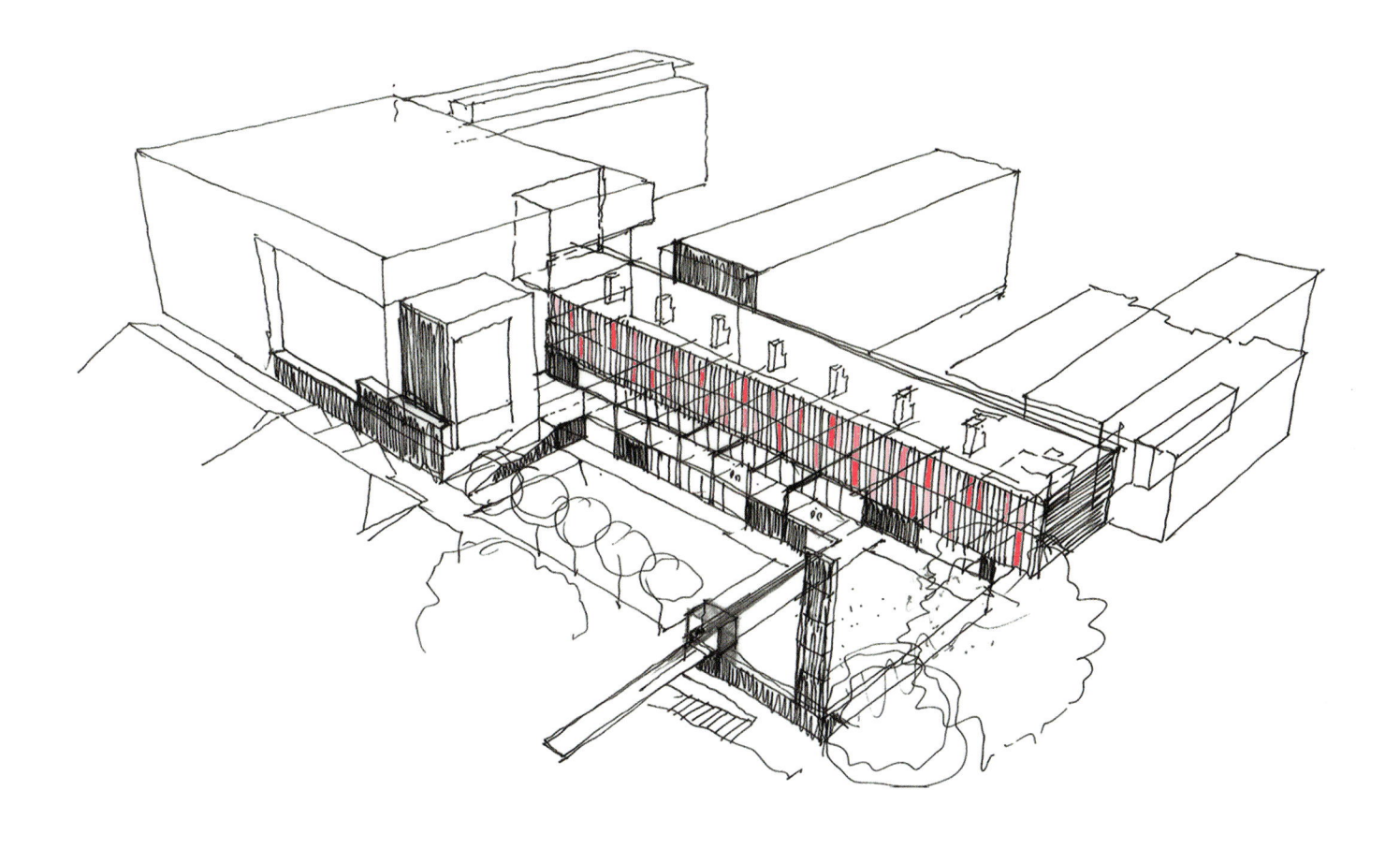

06

OPPOSITE
Teaching Building at Oxford Brookes University. The pink glass fins provide protection from the western sun whilst creating the building's unique identity.

ABOVE
Sketch of the Teaching Building highlighting the reference colour of the fins.

RIGHT
Interior view of circulation to the first-floor Teaching Building.

Colour in Heart and Mind

ABOVE
Le Corbusier's High Court Building, Chandigarh, India.

BELOW
Visualisation of Design Engine's Baptist Church, Lyndhurst.

The battle of the Protestant Reformation and the Catholic Counter-Reformation of the sixteenth century was a fight for the hearts and minds of men played out in colour. Calvin and Luther had objected to the opulent excesses of Catholicism writ large in the building of St Peter's in Rome.[2] They felt such overindulgences of the papacy and their extravagant architects had diverted the gospels away from man's responsibilities to his fellow man and that power had been placed in the hands of the few who had little more than their own self-aggrandisement in mind. In so doing, Protestantism forged the link between visual austerity and moral rectitude. This ethically aesthetic stance has persisted in various forms throughout architectural history thereafter, and colour has often been seen as a morally dubious aspect of architecture—a view that came to the fore in the Modern movement, where buildings were again seen as purveyors of social ethics.

Visa entrance to the new British Embassy Building, Sana'a, Yemen.

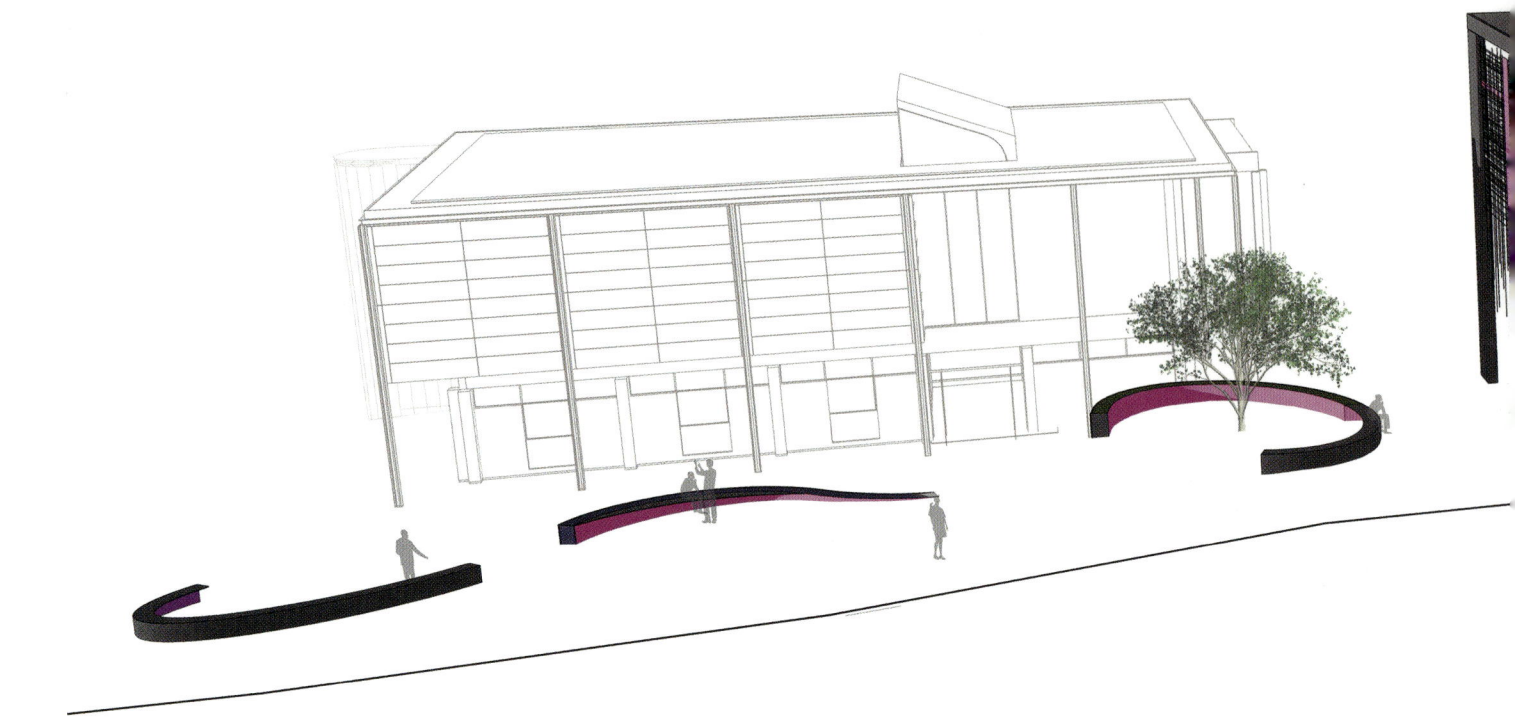

BUILDING STORIES | 178

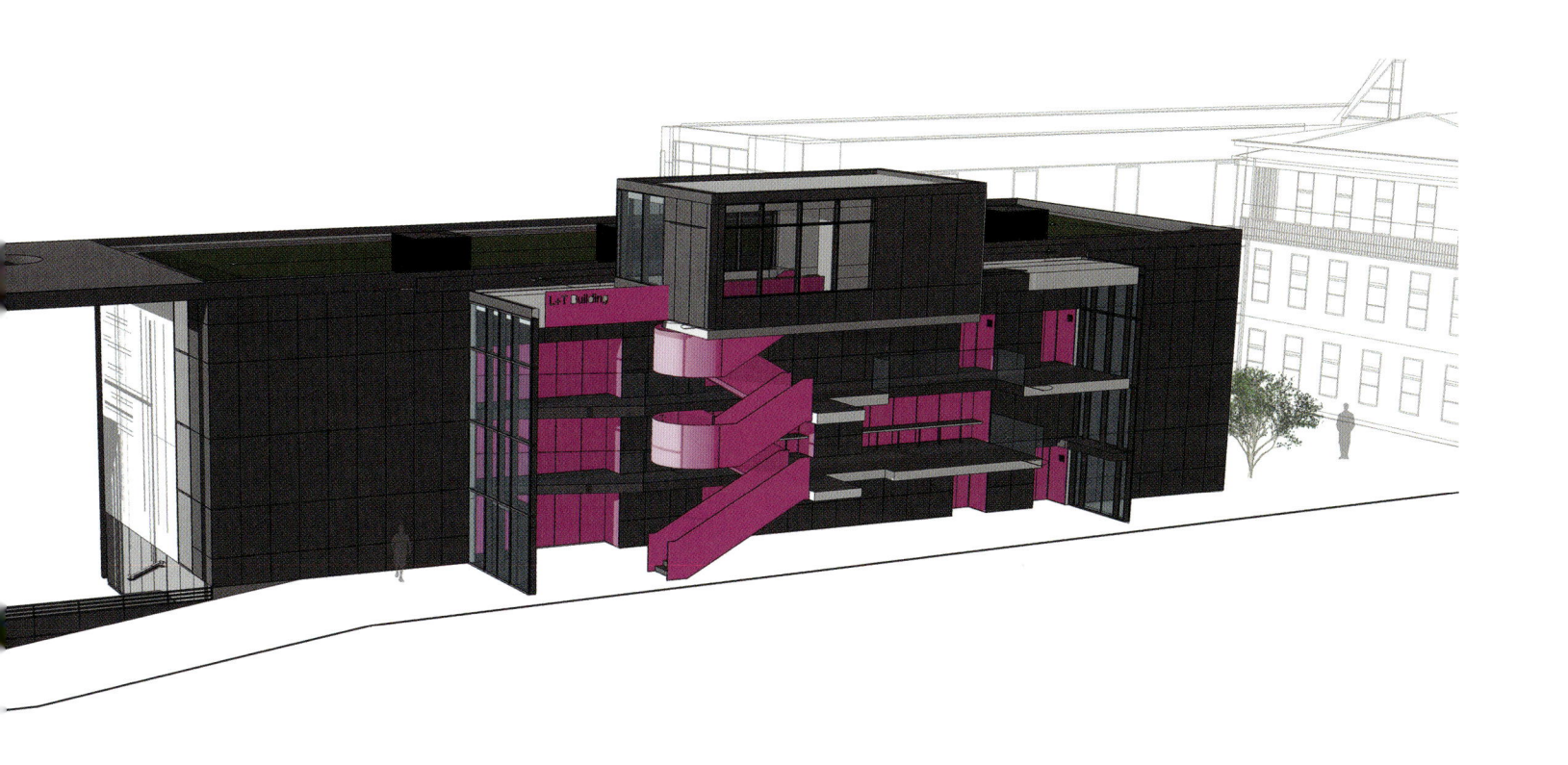

ST ALPHEGE BUILDING, UNIVERSITY OF WINCHESTER

The St Alphege Building provides a range of learning and teaching spaces that serve the campus. Occupying a site at the lower part of the estate, the building is entered both at the lower level from a public square via a portico and also from high level further up the slope of the site. To unite these two points of entry, a sweeping staircase doubles back on itself through a three-storey atrium. The staircase becomes the moment of theatre and movement in what is otherwise a highly pragmatic series of spatial requirements. Each half-landing looks down into the atrium void and provides a moment of pause as one moves up through the building.

The section through the St Alphege Building is taken in parallel with the contours of the site showing the relationship of the staircase to the public piazza beyond. Placed within the triple-height atrium the staircase links the high-level entrance at the top of the staircase with the lower-level public square. The staircase not only serves the functional requirement of linking the various levels of teaching rooms, but also animates the atrium and the open space beyond through its striking colour and the movement of people that bring the spaces to life.

TOP
Section and perspective of St Alphege Building atrium.

LEFT
Main staircase in St Alphege Building at University of Winchester.

Le Corbusier: The Concept of Colour

ABOVE
Le Corbusier's main door at Ronchamp Chapel Notre Dame du Haut.

BELOW
Le Corbusier's colour keyboard system.

Le Corbusier's early villas are synonymous with the white-walled modernism of the International Style, and from afar can evoke the pristine monochrome solemnity of the Parthenon. However Le Corbusier was a master of colour and set out a logically structured system for colour design in the magazine *l'Esprit Nouveau* in 1921.[3] Here he outlines a series of colour concepts which relied on three key principles. Firstly he defines the concept of 'constructive' natural pigments used to create pleasing atmospheres and to alter the perception of space. Secondly he describes 'dynamic' synthetic pigments which are used to create highly contrasting effects of heightened emotion. Finally he identifies 'transitional' transparent, synthetic pigments which alter surfaces without affecting the perception of volume.

Le Corbusier produced a series of colour palettes for the Swiss wallpaper manufacturer Salubra—first in 1931, comprising 43 colour shades, and later in 1959, adding 20 extra stronger colours. Arranged as a series of 'keyboards', Le Corbusier's colour system is structured in such a way that, with the help of slide bars, a single shade or a combination of two or three shades can be detached against two background tones such that they make for a harmonious combination.

In application, Le Corbusier used his colour system to create warmth, light and atmosphere and, carefully employed, used light and dark colours to control the perceived depth of space. He was also concerned with the psychological effect of colour to elicit particular mood effects, and colour was also employed to denote function. For Le Corbusier, the choice of colour was not an arbitrary matter of personal preference but rather a system with a limited choice of colours which are seen as working as a system with other specifically chosen colours to create a particular effect on space, function and the human psyche.

> *These Keyboards of Colour aim at stimulating personal selection, by placing the task of choosing on a sound systematic basis. In my opinion they offer a method of approach which is accurate and effective, one which makes it possible to plan, in the modern home, colour harmonies which are definitely architectural and yet suited to the natural taste and needs of the individual.*
> — LE CORBUSIER

BUILDING STORIES | 180

ABOVE
Entrance portico to Student Services Building at Arts University Bournemouth.

STUDENT SERVICES BUILDING, ARTS UNIVERSITY BOURNEMOUTH

The Arts University Bournemouth campus comprises a series of buildings that are designed to bring the campus together, and the use of colour provides a clear identity for each building, unified across the campus through the use of a keyboard of colours. The Student Services Building defines a new approach and entrance to the campus. Here a strong yellow colour takes the form of a folded plane that wraps the underside of a porte cochère to create a grand scale at the point of arrival. The plane of yellow wraps around the entrance penetrating the brick skin and leading into the building. With the canopy spanning the roadway, the folded coloured plane winds its way to the top of an existing chimney tower to announce the point of entrance from afar. The use of this simple colour set against the muted brickwork of the new building brings a sense of highlight and drama to announce one's arrival at the university.

Luis Barragán: The Colour of the Mind

ABOVE
Luis Barragán, la Cuadra San Cristobal Mexico City.

BELOW
Computer visualisation of the new facade to the Design Workshops & Studios at Arts University Bournemouth.

The great master in the use of bold colour to surprise and evoke strong emotion was the Mexican architect Luis Barragán. For him colour took on a metaphysical importance, and his buildings bring to mind the Surrealist paintings of De Chirico and Magritte with large expanses of vivid colour set against the azure of the sky. His work was mainly the private houses of wealthy clients in and around Mexico City where the azure sky, brilliant sunlight and deep shadows made for a strangely abstract context in which to place his vibrant contrasting colour combinations. At his famous riding stables for the Egerstrom Residence, known as 'San Cristobal', Barragán combined water in the form of reflecting pools and cascades, where the fluid surface texture takes the form of another plane of material precisely framed at the edges, juxtaposed with lavender purple walls or channelled through monoliths of burnt umber. At a time when colour was eschewed in modern architecture, Barragán captured both regional identity and the Hispanic fascination with vivid colour in brilliant sunlight and took the painted surface out beyond the traditional boundaries of architecture, famously denying any distinction between architecture, landscape and gardening. This merging of interior and exterior spatial definition through planar surfaces give his buildings and landscapes an ambiguity of scale and a strangely surreal and timeless feeling. The intensity of the experience is both unsettling but also uniquely sublime and serene, as through the affective emotional experience of this architecture of colour and atmosphere Barragán sought to create a refuge not only of the body but more importantly of the mind.

Architecture is an art when one consciously or unconsciously creates aesthetic emotion in the atmosphere and when this environment produces well-being.
— LUIS BARRAGÁN

TOP
Photograph of renovated Design Workshops & Studios at Arts University Bournemouth capturing the Student Services Building.

BELOW
The old elevation of the building, which was previously the Halls of Residence.

DESIGN WORKSHOPS & STUDIOS, ARTS UNIVERSITY BOURNEMOUTH

The Design Workshops & Studios at Arts University Bournemouth is the transformation of the two former on-campus halls of residence into modern studio and teaching spaces. The buildings are capped by a series of sawtooth north-facing roof lights atop a raised roof podium providing even natural daylighting to new drawing studios for model-making, illustration and fashion design students. Clad in telemagenta pink, they point to a concept of feature surfaces and planes that highlight new interventions into the existing fabric.

The transformation of the building is completed with a perforated aluminium veil over the existing building at first and second floor. A pattern of two sized circular apertures is formed into a randomised arrangement that extends across the upper facades. Working within the grids of both the former window arrangements and the new steel structure, the 50 per cent overall-free area patterns allows continued venting whilst regulating excessive solar gain.

RIGHT
Renovated Design Workshops & Studios at Arts University Bournemouth.

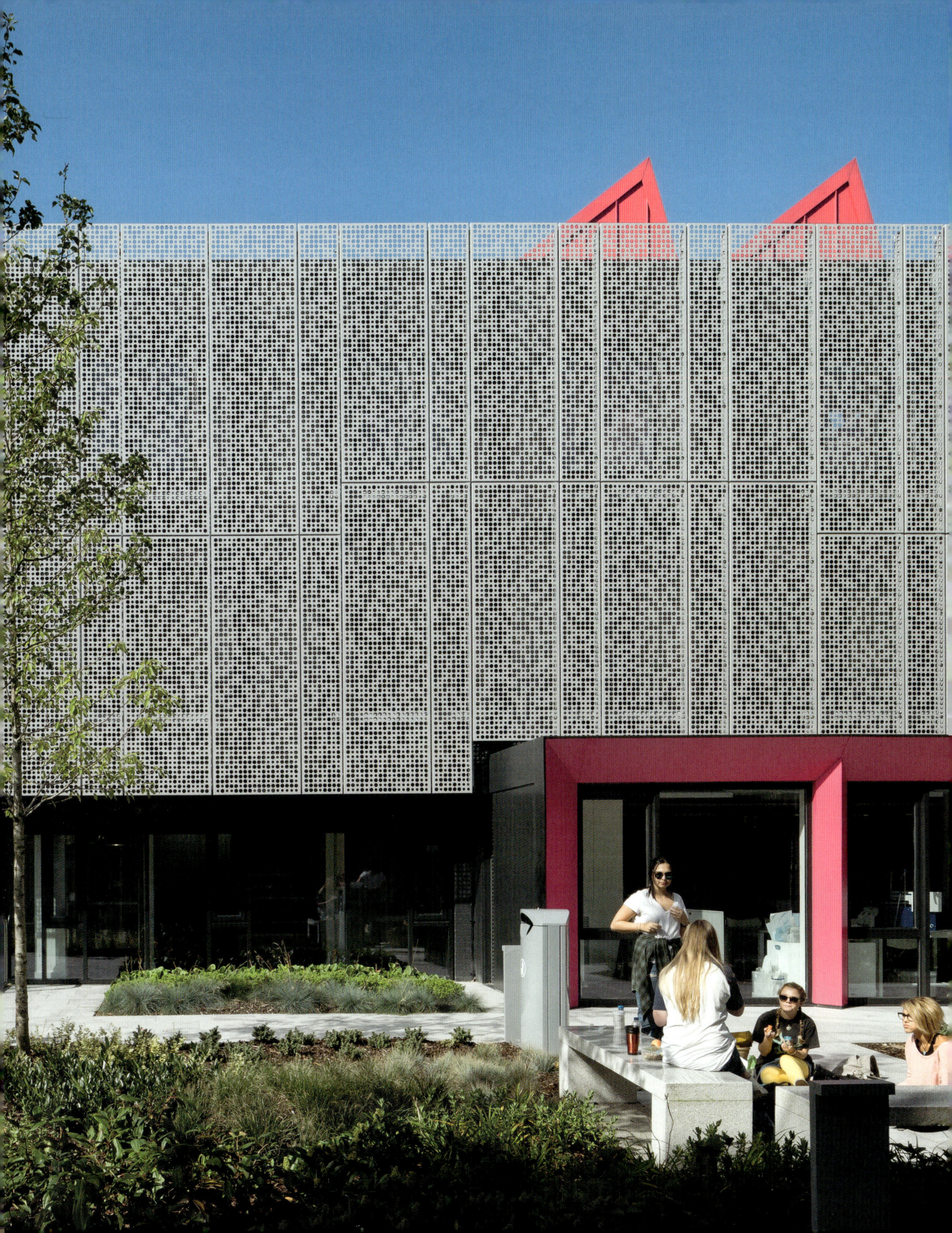

Endnotes

PLACE
1. Hitchcock, Henry-Russell, and Philip Johnson, *The International Style*, New York: WW Norton, 1997.
2. See Heidegger, Martin, *Being and Time*, Oxford: Blackwell, 1967; and Husserl, Edmund, *Logical Investigations*, London and New York: Routledge, 2015.
3. Norberg-Schulz, Christian, *Genius Loci: Towards a Phenomenology of Architecture*, New York: Rizzoli, 1980, p 8.
4. Norberg-Schulz, Christian, *Meaning and Place and Other Essays*, London: Academy Edition, 1984, p 8.
5. Rykwert, Joseph, *On Adam's House in Paradise: The Idea of the Primitive Hut in Architectural History*, Cambridge, MA: MIT Press, 1997.
6. Bachelard, Gaston, *The Poetics of Space*, Marie Jolas trans, New York: Penguin, 2014.
7. Gehl, Jan, *Life Between Buildings: Using Public Space*, Washington, DC: Island Press, 2011.
8. Alberti, Leon Battista, "Of the Compartition, and of the Origin of Building", *The Ten Books on Architecture*, Cosimo Bartoli and Giacomo Leoni trans, vol 1, New York: Dover Publications, 1987.
9. Heidegger, Martin, "Building Dwelling Thinking", *Poetry, Language, Thought*, Albert Hofstadter trans, New York: Harper Perennial Modern Classics, 2013, pp 143–159.
10. See Pearce, Martin and Richard Jobson, *Bridge Builders*, Chichester: Wiley, 2002.
11. Howard, Ebenezer, *Garden Cities of Tomorrow*, Builth Wells, Powys: Attic Books, 1985.

PEOPLE
1. Lévi-Strauss, Claude, *Myth and Meaning*, London and New York: Routledge, 2016, p 4.
2. Sennett, Richard, *Flesh and Stone: The Body and the City in Western Civilization*, London: Penguin, 2002, p 326
3. See Bauman, Zygmunt, *Liquid Modernity*, Cambridge: Polity, 2015.
4. See Mitchell, William J, *City of Bits: Space, Place, and the Infobahn*, Cambridge, MA: MIT Press, 2010; and Mitchell, William J, *e-topia*, Cambridge, MA: MIT Press, 1999.
5. Baudrillard, Jean, *The Ecstasy of Communication*, Los Angeles: Semiotext(e), 2012, p 30.
6. Jencks, Charles, *The Language of Post-Modern Architecture*, New York: Rizzoli, 1991.

CRAFT
1. Ruskin, John, and Russell Sturgis, *The Seven Lamps of Architecture*, New York: D Appleton, 1901.
2. Ruskin, John, *The Stones of Venice*, New York: Cosimo Classics, 2007.
3. Morris, William, *News from Nowhere*, James Redmond ed, London and New York: Routledge, 2012.
4. See Sennett, Richard, *The Craftsman*, London: Penguin, 2009.

SEQUENCE
1. Cullen, Gordon, *The Concise Townscape*, Abingdon: Architectural Press, 2015.
2. Burke, Edmund, *On Taste; On the Sublime and Beautiful; Reflections on the French Revolution; A Letter to a Noble Lord; with introduction, notes and illustrations*, New York: PF Collier & Son, 1909.
3. See Aristotle, *Poetics*, David Gorman and Michelle Zerba eds, James Hutton trans, New York: WW Norton, 2016.
4. Samuel, Flora, *Le Corbusier and the Architectural Promenade*, Basel: Birkhäuser, 2010.

WISDOM
1. Marinetti, Filippo, "The Foundation and Manifesto of Futurism", *100 Artists' Manifestos: From the Futurists to the Stuckists*, Alex Danchev ed, London: Penguin, 2011, p 6.
2. Frampton, Kenneth, "Towards a Critical Regionalism: Six Points for an Architecture of Resistance", *Postmodern Culture*, Hal Foster ed, London; Pluto Press, pp 60–70.
3. Frampton, "Towards a Critical Regionalism", pp 22–23.
4. Rudofsky, Bernard, *Architecture Without Architects: A Short Introduction to Non-Pedigreed Architecture*, New York: Museum of Modern Art, 1964, p 1.

SURFACE
1. Le Corbusier, *Towards a New Architecture*, New York: Brewer, Warren & Putnam, 2014.
2. Semper, Gottfried, *The Four Elements of Architecture and Other Writings*, Harry F Mallgrave and Wolfgang Herrmann trans, Cambridge: Cambridge University Press, 1989.
3. Saussure, Ferdinand de, *Course in General Linguistics*, Charles Bally, Charles Sechehaye and Albert Riedlinger eds, Wade Baskin trans, London: Fontana, 1974.
4. Goethe, Johann Wolfgang von, *Conversations with Goethe in the Last Years of His Life*, Johann Peter Eckermann, and Margaret Fuller eds, Margaret Fuller trans, Boston: Hilliard, Gray, & Company, 1839, p 282.
5. Debord, Guy, and Ken Knabb, *The Society of the Spectacle*, Berkeley, CA: Bureau of Public Secrets, 2014.
6. Coleridge, Samuel Taylor, and John T Shawcross, *Biographia Literaria*, London: Electric Book, 2001.
7. Plato, *Timaeus*, Peter Kalkavage ed and trans, Indianapolis: Focus, 2016.
8. Rossi, Aldo, *The Architecture of the City*, Cambridge, MA: MIT Press, 2007.
9. Shakespeare, William, *As You like It*, New York: Pocket Books, 1997, p 83.
10. Debord, *The Society of the Spectacle*.
11. Tschumi, Bernard, *Architectural Manifestos*, London: Architectural Association, 1979.
12. Tschumi, Bernard, Jacques Derrida, Anthony Vidler, and Alvin Boyarsky, *Bernard Tschumi: La Casa Vide, La Villette, 1985*, London: Architectural Association, 1986.
13. Venturi, Robert, Denise Scott Brown, and Steven Izenour, *Learning from Las Vegas: The Forgotten Symbolism of Architectural Form*, Cambridge, MA: MIT Press, 2000.

COMPOSITION
1. Pollio, Vitruvius, *The Ten Books on Architecture*, MH Morgan trans, New Delhi: Kaveri Books, 2016.
2. See Lawlor, Robert, *Sacred Geometry: Philosophy and Practice*, London: Thames & Hudson, 2007.
3. See Tzonis, Alexander, and Liane Lefaivre, *Classical Architecture: The Poetics of Order*, Cambridge, MA: MIT Press, 1999.
4. See van Doesburg, Theo, "Towards a Plastic Architecture", *De Stijl*, Hans LC Jaffé trans, New York: HN Abrams, 1971. "The new architecture has eliminated both monotonous repetition and the stiff equality of two halves.... There is no repetition in time, no street front, no standardization.... In place of symmetry the new architecture offers a balanced relationship of unequal parts; that is to say, of parts that differ from each other by virtue of their functional characteristics as regards position, size, proportion and situation. The equality of these parts rests upon the balance of their dissimilarity, not upon their similarity. Furthermore, the new architecture has rendered front, back, right, left, top, and bottom, factors of equal value."
5. Rowe, Colin, and Fred Koetter. *Collage City*, Cambridge, MA: MIT Press, 1978.

COLOUR
1. See Wittkower, Rudolf, *Architectural Principles in the Age of Humanism*, Chichester: Academy Editions, 1998.
2. See Cameron, Euan, *The European Reformation*, Oxford: Oxford University Press, 2012.
3. See Eliel, Carol S, *L' Esprit Nouveau: Purism in Paris, 1918–1925*, Los Angeles: Los Angeles County Museum of Art, 2001.

Credits

All images copyright Design Engine unless otherwise stated

IMAGE CREDITS

12 (BOTTOM LEFT) Traditional Islamic carpet, *Creative Commons Attribution 3.0 License;* **16 (TOP LEFT)** Hilltop town, Urbino, Italy, *©Dario – stock.adobe.com.* **28** Levi-Strauss people, *©Andy Eick, Creative Commons Attribution 2.0 License;* **36** London Metropolitan University, *©Mapbox, ©OpenStreetMap;* **37** Athens agora, *©Tomisti, Creative Commons Attribution-Share Alike 4.0 License;* **39 (BOTTOM LEFT)** Campanile, Siena, *©pyty – stock.adobe.com;* **44 (TOP)** 18th/19th century libraries, *https://flickr.com/commons/usage/;* **44 (MIDDLE)** 20th century libraries, *Creative Commons Attribution-Share Alike 3.0 Germany license;* **48** Byker Wall, *©Andrew Curtis, Creative Commons Attribution Share-Alike Generic License 2.0.* **50** Seven Lamps of Architecture, John Ruskin, *public domain;* **54 (TOP LEFT)** Deutsche Werkbund exhibition, *Peter Behrens, source Plakatkontor.de, public domain;* **60 (TOP LEFT)** 12th century reliquary, *source: "Catalogue of stolen and missing cultural achievements", Warsaw 1988, Editor: Wojciech Jaskulski, Piotr Ogrodzki, public domain;* **65 (BOTTOM)** University Centre, *©University of Winchester.* **68 (TOP LEFT)** Gordon Cullen sketch, *RIBApix;* **82 (TOP)** Procession, *©Gary Bridgman for St.Mary's, Creative Commons Attribution Share-Alike 3.0 unported license;* **84 (TOP)** Acropolis, *©Lambros Kazan– stock.adobe.com.* **92 (TOP LEFT)** Jørn Utzon's Bagsvoerd Church, *©seier+seier Creative Commons Attribution 2.0 License;* **94 (TOP)** Mojacar, *©Ziegler175 Creative Commons Attribution Share-Alike 4.0 International License;* **102 (BOTTOM)** Mesopotamian qanats, *©Hadi Karimi Creative Commons Attribution 3.0 unported License;* **106 (TOP)** Giorgio Grassi, Restoration of the Sagunto Theatre, Valencia, Spain, *©Pakmor– stock.adobe.com;* **111 (TOP)** Castelvecchio Museum, Scarpa, *©Paolo Monti, Creative Commons Attribution Share-Alike 4.0 International License.* **115 (TOP)** Eames "Powers of 10", *Eames Office LLC, eamesoffice.com;* **118** Woven wooden strips, *©mejn – stock.adobe.com;* **120 (TOP)** Gdansk shipyard, *©Mike Peel www.mikepeel.net, Creative Commons Attribution Share-Alike 4.0 International License;* **120 (MIDDLE)** Last Judgement, Hans Memling, *source National Museum, Gdansk, public domain;* **124 (TOP)** Early camera, *19th century Dictionary Illustration, author unknown, public domain;* **127 (BOTTOM)** Ken Russell at work, *Getty Images.* **132** Vesica Piscis, *Evangelistar von Speyer, c1220, Manuscript in the Badische Landesbibliotek, Karlsruhe, Germany, public domain;* **134 (BOTTOM)** The Last Supper by Carl Heinrich Bloch, *late 19th century, source www.carlbloch.org/The-Last-Supper.jpg, public domain;* **134 (COL 2, BOTTOM)** Christ, *Anthony van Dyck, source FAEvU48wSGOX6g at Google Cultural Institute, public domain;* **134 (COL 3, BOTTOM)** St Alfred's statue, *©BobW66, Creative Commons Attribution Share-Alike 3.0 unported license;* **134 (COL 4, BOTTOM)** Apostles, *Maesta of Duccio, 1308, ©Zenodot Verlagsgesellschaft mbH, GNU Free Documentation License;* **135 (COLS 1 & 2, BOTTOM)** Judas, *©Vassil, Creative Commons CC0 1.0 Universal Public Domain Dedication license;* **135 (COL 3, BOTTOM)** 70 Disciples/students, *author unknown, public domain;* **135 (COL 4, BOTTOM)** Psalms, *Psaumes de David, 1562, Marot & Beze, public domain;* **135 (BOTTOM RIGHT)** DNA strips, *author unknown, public domain;* **136 (TOP)** Gdansk Fencing School, *scanned from Gazeta Wyborcza, Warsaw, Poland, September 12-13, 2009, public domain;* **140 (MIDDLE)** Parc de La Villette, *Guilhem Vellut from Paris, France - Folie @ Parc de La Villette @ Paris, CC BY 2.0* **140 (BOTTOM)** Gymnast *©Friday– stock.adobe.com;* **143 (BOTTOM)** Agit-prop train, *public domain;* **144 (TOP)** Walter Gropius, *Louis Held, c.1919, public domain;* **146 (TOP)** Las Vegas: The Forgotten Symbolism of Architectural Form, *VSBA.* **154 (TOP)** Ben Nicolson, *©Angela Verren Taunt. All rights reserved, DACS 2017;* **156 (TOP)** Dr Hartog's consulting room, Gerritt Rietveld, *public domain;* **158 (TOP)** Erechtheion Porch, *public domain;* **160 (TOP)** Eduardo Chillida, *Eduardo Chillida, La Casa del poeta I (Poet´s House I), 1980. Copyright Eduardo Chillida Archives, photographer Jesús Uriarte; ©Zabalaga-Leku, DACS, London 2017;* **165 (TOP)** Eduardo Chillida, *Eduardo Chillida, Gravitación (Gravitation), 1997. Copyright Eduardo Chillida Archives; ©Zabalaga-Leku, DACS, London 2017;* **165 (BOTTOM)** Collage City by Rowe/Koetter, *MIT Press;* **168 (TOP)** Parthenon entablature, Gottfried Semper, *public domain;* **171 (TOP)** Sainte-Chapelle, *©Maximillian Puhane, Creative Commons Attribution 3.0 unported License;* **173 (BOTTOM LEFT)** Autumn leaves, *public domain;* **176 (TOP)** High Court Building, Chandigarh, India, *Léopold Lambert for The Funambulist, 2009, ©FLC/ ADAGP, Paris and DACS, London 2017;* **180 (TOP)** Notre-Dame-Du-Haut, Le Corbusier, *Shutterstock, ©ADAGP, Paris and DACS, London 2017;* **180 (BOTTOM)** Le Corbusier colour keyboard, *Swann Galleries, ©FLC/ ADAGP, Paris and DACS, London 2017;* **182 (TOP)** La Cuadra, San Cristobel, Luis Barragán, *Sarunas Burdulis.*

PHOTOGRAPHER'S CREDITS

Peter Blundy 59, 61, 62–63; **Rob Boltman** 42 (bottom), 169; **Keith Collie** 09, 10 (left), 17–18 (top), 20, 65 (top), 66–67, 94 (bottom), 95 (bottom), 96–97, 98, 99 (bottom); **Julia Conway** 78, 121, 137, 153, 154 (bottom); **Peter Cook** 14–15, 55, 56–57, 128, 177; **Tim Crocker** 116–117, 162–163, 173 (top left); **Paul Freeman** 88–89, 90, 92 (bottom right); **Richard Jobson** 22, 51, 52 (right), 53–54 (bottom), back cover; **Nick Kane** front cover, 21, 52 (left), 69, 70, 101, 104, 107, 108–109, 119, 125 (top), 131, 133, 134 (col 1), 135 (bottom left), 155, 166–167, 170, 173 (top right & bottom right), 174, 175 (right), 178 (bottom); **Jim Stephenson** 23 (top), 24–25, 43 (top), 125 (bottom left), 126, 127 (top), 181, 183 (top), 184–185; **Edmund Sumner** 29, 33 (top), 34–35; **Paul Tait courtesy of Oxford Brookes University** 42 (top), 43 (bottom), 44 (bottom), 46–47, 114.

Project Timeline
A selection from the last 16 years

COMFORT STATION
2001–2002 Leighton Buzzard, Comfort station and public car park, South Bedfordshire District Council

GREATFIELD STABLES
2001–2004 Bucklers Hard, Private residence & client

PARKHILL HOTEL (LIMEWOOD)
2001–2005 Lyndhurst, Hotel & leisure, Private client

RAMBOLL HEADQUARTERS
2001–2005, PP 88–93 Netley Marsh, Office headquarters, Ramboll (Gifford)

PARCHMENT STREET
2001–2005 Winchester, Affordable housing, Winchester Housing Group

HILL CLOSE GARDENS
2002–2005 Warwick, Visitor centre, Hill Close Gardens

ROSEVILLE HOUSING
2002–2006, PP 8–11 Guernsey, Affordable housing, Guernsey Housing Association

HARDWICK HALL PARK
2002, PP 74–77 Durham, Visitor centre competition, Durham County Council

JOHN STRIPE LECTURE THEATRE
2003–2005 Winchester, University lecture theatre, University of Winchester

STEGBUNT
2003 Zürich, Switzerland, Housing international competition, Belvedere

BURO HAPPOLD HQ
2003–2005 London, Commercial workspace interiors, Buro Happold

BRITISH EMBASSY, SANA'A
2003–2006, PP 12–15, 54–57, 100–103, 177 Yemen, Embassy building, Foreign & Commonwealth Office

LES BEAUCAMPS HIGH SCHOOL
2003–2013, PP 28–35 Guernsey, Secondary school, States of Guernsey Education

BURO HAPPOLD
2004–2006 Leeds, Commercial workspace interiors, Buro Happold

UNIVERSITY CENTRE
2004–2007, PP 16–20, 64–67 Winchester, HE student centre, University of Winchester

GDANSK THEATRE
2005, PP 120–123, 130, 136–137 Gdansk, Poland, competition, Theatrum Gedanense Foundation

RIVER HULL FOOTBRIDGE
2005, PP 138–141 Hull, Competition, Hull Citybuild

WARLEY RESERVOIR
2005–2007 Essex, Commercial development, Broadfield Properties

BURO HAPPOLD HQ
2005–2008 Bath, Commercial workspace interiors

MONOCHROME RETAIL
2005 London, Retail store design, Monochrome Ltd

INEOS HQ
2005–2007 Lyndhurst, Commercial office, Ineos Capital

GUILDHALL MASTERPLAN
2005–2006 Winchester, Urban masterplan, Winchester City Council

ART BOX MOBILE STAGE
2005, PP 142–143 Ireland, Competition, Cork City Council

JOHN KEBLE SCHOOL
2006–2008 Hursley, Primary school extension, John Keble CE School governors

TESTWOOD PARK MASTERPLAN
2006–2007 Southampton, Business park masterplan, UBS/Frobisher

PIG IN THE WALL RESTAURANT
2006 Southampton, Conversion and extension of listed building and interior, Private client

CRICOTEKA
2006, PP 146–148 Krakow, Poland, Competition, Cricoteka, Krakow

PETER SYMONDS COLLEGE
2006–2007 Winchester, FE Campus masterplan, Peter Symonds College

OXFORD EXAMINATION SCHOOLS
2006–2008, PP 110–111 Oxford, Retrofit of listed buildings, University of Oxford

UNIVERSITY OF WINCHESTER
2007–2008 Winchester, HE Campus masterplan, University of Winchester

OXFORD BROOKES UNIVERSITY
2007 Oxford, HE Headington, Wheatley and Harcourt Hill Campus masterplans, Oxford Brookes University

ABERCROMBIE BUILDING
2007–2012, PP 169–173 Oxford, Refurbished & extended HE building, Oxford Brookes University

JOHN HENRY BROOKES BUILDING
2007–2014, PP 42–43, 46–47, 68–73, 112–119, 160–167, 172–175 Oxford, New teaching & learning building, Oxford Brookes University

JOHN PAYNE BUILDING
2007–2009 Oxford, New HE accommodation, Oxford Brookes University

WILLIAM STREET QUARTER/LINTONS
2007–2008 London, Residential development, London Borough of Barking

LSE STUDENT CENTRE FEASIBILITY
2008 London, HE feasibility study (Saw Swee Hock), London School of Economics

SPORTS BUILDING RECEPTION
2008 Southampton, HE interiors, University of Southampton

VICE-CHANCELLOR'S RECEPTION
2008–2011 Southampton, HE interiors, University of Southampton

YEW TREE FARM
2008 Southampton, B1 work units, Barker-Mill Estate

PERFORMING ARTS STUDIOS
2008–2009, PP 94–99 Winchester, HE building, University of Winchester

QUAINTON STUD
2008–2011 Aylesbury, Private residence & client

SCIENCE & MATHEMATICS CENTRE
2009–CURRENT, PP 150–153 Godalming, Independent school teaching facility, Charterhouse School

REDBRIDGE LANE HOUSING
2009, PP 26–27 Southampton, Residential development, Barker-Mill Estates

BRADBURY PLACE
2009–2015 Andover, Accessible housing, Enham Trust

SUSU CAFE
2009 Southampton, HE Student Union cafe interior fit-out, University of Southampton

FRIARSGATE SURGERY
2009 Winchester, Interior fit-out, Friarsgate Practice

WOODCOTE FARM
2009 Upham, Private residence & client

WESSEX ACADEMY
2009–2010 Winchester, Interior fit-out, Hampshire County Council

LSE OLD BUILDING RECEPTION
2009–2011 London, HE retrofit, London School of Economics

REDHAYES M5 BRIDGE
2009–2011 Exeter, Infrastructure, Devon County Council

CLOCKTOWER COURT
2009–2013, PP 104–109 Abingdon, New teaching & social centre, Radley College

CHARTERHOUSE DINING HALL
2010–2011 Godalming, Extension to listed dining rooms, Charterhouse School

QUEEN'S SPORTS CENTRE
2010–2012 Godalming, Sports centre extension and new pavilion, Charterhouse School

ST ALPHEGE BUILDING
2010–2012, PP 21, 51–53, 131–135, 154–155, 178–179 Winchester, HE building, University of Winchester

JUNIVERSITY
2010, PP 144–145 Basingstoke, Experimental training classroom, University of Winchester

CORNWALL ECO-TOWN
2010–2011 Cornwall, Residential development, Eco-Bos Development Ltd

LA CRIQUE GUESTHOUSE
2010–2011 Lake Geneva, Private residence & client

INEOS HAWKSLEASE
2010–2012 Lyndhurst, Commercial workspace extension, Ineos Capital

SOUTHAMPTON AIRPORT AIRSIDE PIER
2010–2012 Southampton, Infrastructure, Southampton International Airport Ltd

SLEEPER'S HILL
2010–2014 Winchester, Private residence & client

BASIL STREET PRIVATE APARTMENT
2011 London, Private residence & client

LYNDHURST BAPTIST CHURCH
2011–2012, P 176 Lyndhurst, New church building, Lyndhurst Baptist Church

ARTS UNIVERSITY BOURNEMOUTH
2012–CURRENT Poole, HE Campus masterplan, Arts University Bournemouth

AUB PHOTOGRAPHY BUILDING
2012–2015, PP 124–127 Poole, HE building extension, Arts University Bournemouth

AUB STUDENT SERVICES BUILDING
2012–2015, P 181 Poole, HE building, Arts University Bournemouth

LIGHTHOUSE
2012–2016 Poole, Theatre and arts centre retrofit, Lighthouse, Poole's Centre for the Arts

NAB HOUSE
2012–CURRENT Chichester, Private residence & client

LISTENING POD
2013, PP 44–45 Mobile, Competition, BBC/British Library

UOW SMT SUITE
2013–2016 Winchester, HE interior fit-out, University of Winchester

CHRISTCHURCH BRIDGE
2013–2015, PP 22–25 Reading, Infrastructure, Reading Borough Council

LA MARE DE CARTERET
2013–CURRENT Guernsey, New co-located primary & secondary school, States of Guernsey Education

HERDSMAN'S COTTAGE
2013–CURRENT Upham, Private residence & client

ABBOTS BARTON
2013–2016 Winchester, Affordable housing, Winchester City Council

JESSELTON QUAY
2013 Kota Kinabalu, Malaysia, International competition, SBC Corp/Sunia Capital Holdings

CENTRE FOR LEARNING
2014–CURRENT, PP 78–81 Cold Ash, New library, teaching and social building, Downe House School

AUB DESIGN STUDIOS & WORKSHOPS
2014–2016, PP 182–185 Poole, HE retrofit, Arts University Bournemouth

BURO HAPPOLD HQ
2014–2016 London, Commercial workspace interior fit-out, Buro Happold

FLETCHERITES
2014–2015 Godalming, Independent school boarding House, Charterhouse School

REYNOLDSTON
2014–CURRENT Gower Peninsula, South Wales, Private resident & client

CHAPEL YARD
2014, PP 82–87 Oxford, Competition, New College, University of Oxford

CEDAR PARK
2014–CURRENT, PP 48–49 Enham Alamein, Mixed-use regeneration, Enham Trust

CHESIL STREET EXTRA-CARE
2014–2016 Winchester, Extra-care residential homes, Winchester City Council

GUILDFORD PLAZA
2014–2016 Guildford, Residential, Pegasus Life

WINTON CHAPEL
2014–2016, PP 58–63 Winchester, Chapel retrofit/extension, University of Winchester

LYNDHURST PARK
2014–CURRENT Lyndhurst, Residential, Pegasus Life

MARTIAL ROSE LIBRARY
2015–CURRENT Winchester, HE Retrofit/extension, University of Winchester

PRINCE'S MEAD SCHOOL
2015–CURRENT Winchester, New teaching, dining & drama facilities, Prince's Mead School

PERRODO PROJECT
2015–CURRENT, PP 128–129 Oxford, New HE pavilion building & conversion of listed buildings, St Peter's College

SOUTHERN CAMPUS MASTERPLAN
2015–CURRENT Winchester, Independent school campus redevelopment, Winchester College

WEST DOWNS ONE
2015–CURRENT, PP 156–159 Winchester, Landmark HE teaching building, University of Winchester

FELDON VALLEY GOLF
2015–CURRENT Lower Brailes, Golf & hotel development, Private client

HOLLOWAY ROAD MASTERPLAN
2015–CURRENT, PP 36–41 London, HE Campus masterplan/redevelopment, London Metropolitan University

NEW MILTON CREMATORIUM
2016–CURRENT New Forest, Crematorium development, New Forest Crematorium Company

TWYFORD SCHOOL
2016–CURRENT Twyford, Preparatory school campus masterplan, Twyford School Governors

RES BEAUFORT COURT
2016–CURRENT Kings Langley, Commercial workspace interior fit-out, Renewable Energy Systems Ltd

EMERSONS GREEN FOOTBRIDGE
2016–CURRENT Bristol, Infrastructure, South Gloucestershire Council

NEW DESIGN TECHNOLOGY BUILDING
2016–CURRENT Stowe, Independent school teaching building, Stowe School

J BLOCK
2016–CURRENT Social learning, London Met University

BERKHAMSTED SCHOOL MASTERPLAN
2017–CURRENT Berkhamsted, Independent school, Berkhamsted School

Acknowledgements
Staff past & present

We have been joined on this journey by a team of highly talented and dedicated people. These personalities have helped shape the practice that Design Engine has become and we thank them all.

PRESENT STAFF
James Altham, Adam Barlow, Anna Beer, Raquel Blasco Fraile, Peter Blundy, Kamila Ciszewska, Peter Collins, Elliott Dennis, James Fewtrell, David Gausden, Rodney Graham, Alison Jackson, Rob Jackson, James Jacques, Richard James, Richard Jobson, Jennifer Kwok, Alberto Lopez, Marco Marriage, Amanda Moore, Oliver Moore, Laia Mulet, Nicola Perrett, Jessica Reid, John Ridgett, Paul Ridgley, Sean Roberts, Richard Rose-Casemore, Anna Ross, James Salman, Sally Snow, Katie Stokes, James Thomas, Tamsin Thomas, Jessica Tubb, Christina Varvouni-Giatrakou, Matthew Vowels, Alex Wallis, Phil Webb.

PAST STAFF
Sean Bailey, James Barnfield, Kathryn Bonham, Tim Bradley, Philip Breese, Richard Burgess, Philippa Cameron, Rebecca Campbell, Paul Cashin, Oliver Choyce, Sam Crick, Oli Cunningham, Adrian Czuraj, Matthew Davies, Catherine Dunlop, Russ Edwards, Keith Evans, Beatriz Fernandez Torres, James Ferrero, Peter Foulk, Alastair Fraser, Laura Fryer, Dominic Gaunt, Colin Graham, Duncan Greenaway, Jenny Hampson, Frank Harding, Rebecca Howard, Abi Hudson, Sam Johnston, Stephen Kavanagh, Alex Keeler, Elle Keyser, Nicola Kitson, Adam Knibb, Katharina Konig, Beatrix Kovacs, Simon Lamprell, Nina Langner, Adam Lansdown-Bridge, Joanna Lawson, Zoey Le Brocq, Dan Lewandowski, Paul Lovegrove, Richard Mather, Lindsay Meyer, Guan Ming Wong, Rebecca Muirhead, Simon Mundy, Gemma Murphy, Chris Newberry, Tim O'Rourke, Kasia Owkzarec, Jamie Pearson, Katherine Pegrum, Arran Pexton, Tracey Pitt, Hugh Richardson, Lauren Ruffell, Rebecca Ryder, Jake Sadler-Forster, Khalid Saleh, Alison Sampson, Alise Silina, Natalie Skeete, Sophie Tuffin, Irina Vancea, Charlie Walker, Stephanie Wynn, Abigail Yeates.

© 2017 Artifice books on architecture, London, UK; © 2017 Design Engine Architects Ltd. Winchester, UK and © 2017 Martin Pearce. All rights reserved.

Artifice books on architecture
308 Essex Road, London, N1 3AX
United Kingdom

t: +44 (0)20 7713 5097
e: sales@artificebooksonline.com
www.artificebooksonline.com

Authored by Martin Pearce
Designed by Katie Stokes at Design Engine Architects
Edited by Phoebe Colley

Design Engine Architects
The Studios, Coker Close, Winchester, SO22 5FF
United Kingdom

t: +44 (0)1962 890111
e: mail@designengine.co.uk
www.designengine.co.uk

All opinions expressed within this publication are those of the authors and not necessarily of the publisher.

British Library in Cataloguing Data
A CIP record for this book is available from the British Library

ISBN 978-1-908967-85-5

No part of this publication may be reproduced, stored in a retrieval system, or transmitted, in any form or by any means, electronic, mechanical, photocopying, recording, or otherwise, without prior permission of the publisher.

Every effort has been made to trace the copyright holders, but if any have been inadvertently overlooked the necessary arrangements will be made at the first opportunity.

Artifice books on architecture, London, UK, is an environmentally responsible company. *Building Stories: Design Engine Architects* is printed on sustainably sourced paper.

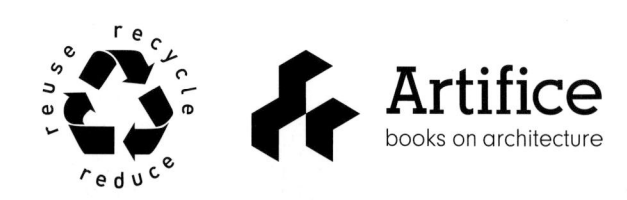